# Shadow on a Tightrope

# Shadow on a Tightrope

## Writings by Women on Fat Oppression

Edited by Lisa Schoenfielder and Barb Wieser
Foreword by Vivian Mayer

spinsters | *aunt lute*

SAN FRANCISCO

Spinsters/Aunt Lute Book Company
P.O. Box 410687
San Francisco, CA 94141

First printed by Aunt Lute Book Company, Iowa City, Iowa, 1983

Text Design and Typesetting: Annie Graham & Company
Cover Design: Pam Wilson Design Studio
Cover Art: Lisa Schoenfielder

Printed in the U.S.A.

Library of Congress Catalog Card Number: 88-060189

ISBN: 0-918040-03-5

The title *Shadow on a Tightrope* comes from the poem "whoever i am i'm a fat woman" by Sharon Bas Hannah.

*To the struggle of fat women*
*to hold on to their dreams.*

# Table of Contents

---

\* From "Fat in a Blue Tu-Tu," by Kate Allen
\*\* The title of an article by Kelly in *Common Lives / Lesbian Lives*, Number 1, Fall 1981.

# *Foreword*

## Vivian F. Mayer

In the spring of 1972 I used to spend a lot of time with a friend named Naomi, whom I'd met at the newly formed Los Angeles Women's Liberation Center. Naomi was a tall, fat, gray-haired spinster with a sharp wit and sharp tongue. I saw her as a real brick wall of a woman for her ability to stand firm without flinching. She had been in the army and they made a mistake when they let her go.

One morning, however, she knocked on my door in tears. She had gone to a doctor to get help to lose weight. She had asked for diet pills. The doctor, a young man, had ridiculed her, called her childish, and refused to prescribe them. Now, without getting into whether or not a woman should take diet pills, the issue that amazed me was: what power on earth could possibly have made Naomi cry?

Actually, I knew the answer, being, myself, fat. If you, reading this, are fat, you certainly know, too, what made such a tough woman cry. The pain of fat women is no secret. Recently some popular books have dwelt on it at length, adding perhaps to the puzzlement as to why they stay fat. However, the pain is rarely expressed unequivocally, in our own words. One of the remarkable things about this book which you are about to read is that, in it, fat women talk about their pain unequivocally. Without covering it up with excuses such as "they mean well, they're only trying to get me to lose weight." Strong women have no use for excuses.

The strength of fat women is not so well known. But as you read this book you'll come to know it. And if you're fat, in case you haven't yet seen the strength in yourself, I promise you, you will.

The essays in *Shadow on a Tightrope* represent the first ten years of the feminist fat liberation movement. The earliest essays were part of a literature package developed by the Fat Underground, which formed in Los Angeles late in 1973 (and was active until some time after 1977). The most recent are by fat women who are just coming to relate to the movement personally.

The feminist fat liberation movement is not the only alternative to weight loss groups. There are a number of fat people's clubs around the world, providing social outlets and services for fat people. One in the USA, the National Association to Aid Fat Americans (NAAFA), pre-dates feminist fat liberation by a few years, and was involved in the movement's early development. Fat liberation activists have flowed in and out of NAAFA over the years, and the process continues today. NAAFA itself is becoming more clearly aligned with fat activism. However, so far, feminist fat liberation is the only fat voice that offers a cogent and radical analysis of fat oppression, and that suggests ways to end the oppression that are linked with other human liberation struggles.

This introduction presents the "origins and first developments" of the fat women's liberation movement. It is not a definitive history and is not a chronology. It is a personal view, and mentions only those events which I personally participated in. It is written from memory rather than from research. My main reasons for writing it are to acknowledge events and individuals who would otherwise be forgotten; to initiate an analysis of fat liberation as a developing movement; and to stimulate other fat liberation workers to write down the events as they saw them, to correct my omissions and mistakes, and to carry our self-understanding further.

The fat women's liberation movement in Los Angeles grew out of the blending of two sources, radical feminism and radical therapy. In summer of 1971 a group of women met at the Los Angeles Women's Liberation Center to develop a feminist radical therapy service for local women. Judy Freespirit and I were among this group. Inspired by the work of the Berkeley Radical Psychiatry Center in Berkeley, California, we arranged for a member of the BRPC to come to Los Angeles to train us.

Radical therapy is fiercely critical of mainstream psychotherapy. Such therapy is seen as an instrument of social control that upholds oppressive conditions (sexism, class privilege, the ideals of competitiveness by which the majority have to lose, etc.) by convincing the victims that the problems lie within themselves. The proposed "cure" is, in fact, to adjust to oppressive conditions. Echoing the feminist slogan "the personal is political," radical therapy seeks to relate ordinary "personal" problems such as shyness or anxiety to broad political injustices. Several excellent books and journals explain how this is done. The goal is to teach people how to support and encourage one another, and how to work together to change oppressive situations. Groups taking collective power translate into individuals feeling good about themselves.

The relevance of radical therapy to fat people's oppression should have been obvious from the start. Fat people, women especially, are looked upon with contempt and deprived of both civil rights and courtesies. Their unhappiness is blamed on their appetites. Their allegedly "abnormal" appetites are often blamed on "deeper problems" in personality or sexuality. In the fifteen years I spent trying to lose weight, my parents paid psychotherapists tens of thousands of dollars to unravel the personality kinks that, so we all thought, kept me from staying on diets long enough to get thin. When, after years of dieting, I started to alternate between starving and binging, again the psychotherapists were called upon. The relevance of radical therapy to fat liberation should have been obvious.

Back in 1972, however, fat oppression had not yet been recognized as a problem. "Overweight" was mentioned only briefly by our radical therapy trainer. She said that fat is caused by overeating in response to oppression. I recall feeling foolish and hurt when these words were said. It was the only time I ever felt hurt by a radical therapy discussion. In Berkeley Radical Psychiatry groups at that time, fat people were encouraged to solve their problems by "radical" means — fasting, for example. Having no other information with which to debate the issue, I did the next best thing and ignored it.

It was around that time that Naomi came to me crying because a man half her age had ridiculed her for wanting diet pills. Something stirred in me. Since joining women's liberation I was feeling so good, so strong. I hadn't binged for over a year, but I hadn't tried to lose weight for over a year either. Maybe now was the time to get serious and finally take off weight? For Naomi's sake, and also for mine, I decided to find out once and for all how, truly and forever, to get thin.

The Hollywood Public Library had a better than average collection of diet books. It also had a copy of *Fat Power,* by Llewellyn Louderback. Amused by the title, I checked it out, along with several diet books. But I never got to read the diet books, because I started reading *Fat Power* first—and it proved to be a stunner! The author, a fat man, challenged every notion that there is anything wrong with being fat. He did this through information from the fields of law, medicine, history, psychology, popular culture, and so on. He pointed out the cruelty with which fat people are treated. The text was a monument of facts. Yet (as I learned later from the author), the publisher had undermined the book's credibility by refusing to print the references. Louderback's analysis of why the oppression exists was sketchy; and suffering due to eating problems—a major issue in my life—was dismissed as a minor statistic. Yet the book's impact on me was tremendous.

Soon afterwards I presented a new idea, fat liberation, to the women of the radical therapy collective. The main points were as follows:

1   Biology, not eating habits, is the main cause of fat.
2   Health problems of fat people are not inherently due to fat, but are the result of stress, self-hatred, and chronic dieting.
3   Weight loss efforts damage health, almost never "succeed" except temporarily, and should not be used.
4   Food binges are a natural response to chronic dieting.
5   The role of a radical therapist is to help fat women feel good about themselves as fat women and stop trying to lose weight. To accomplish this, radical therapists should learn and teach accurate information about fat women's health and nutrition. They should provide emotional support for women on binges to continue eating and stop feeling guilty!

At that time, to assert that binges should be encouraged rather than suppressed was an act of blind faith, because no one had any idea how it would turn out. Would a binging woman just keep on binging forever, gaining hundreds of pounds and finally dying in agony? Since then, experience has shown that when women stop trying to lose weight, their "eating problems" tend to go away, and weight eventually stabilizes. Women connected with fat liberation were the first guinea pigs for this experiment in self-healing. I have sometimes wondered whether we would have dared to take such risks with our bodies now as we did then. The early 1970s were such a time of risking and glorious iconoclasm!

Soon, Judy Freespirit and I began to organize fat liberation in Los Angeles. A chapter of NAAFA was forming at the same time, so we joined it and became officers. This was in 1972. NAAFA activities were mainly social. During this first year our main development was through talking — clarifying ideas and relationships and building a new self-image.

When NAAFA refused to go as far as we wanted to go in confronting the health professions, we broke from NAAFA and formed the Fat Underground. The Fat Liberation Manifesto was written at that time. Lynn Mabel-Lois joined us and brought her experience as a medical librarian. Thus we were able to begin the medical scholarship upon which the movement's critique of health politics is based. We remained a small group, including one man, for about a year. During this time the feminist nature of our group crystallized.

At the same time the radical therapists, now known as the Los Angeles Radical Feminist Therapy Collective, began a problem-solving group for fat women. Simone Wallace suggested it, and she and I facilitated it together. Eventually most members of the group became active in fat liberation. These include Sharon Bas Hannah, Gudrun Fonfa, Merry Demarest, Linda Torn, and Reanne Fagan-Pinkston.

The death of singer "Mama" Cass Elliot in the summer of 1974 catalyzed the growing fat feminist community to speak out. Her death, following yet another diet, and the sniggering reaction of the press ("She choked to death on a ham sandwich.") presented a pattern of martyrdom and villification which we'd become intolerably sensitized to. The annual Women's Equality Day celebration came a few weeks later. Before a thousand women gathered in a Los Angeles park, members and fat friends of the Fat Underground and Fat Women's Problem-Solving Group marched onto the speakers' platform wearing black armbands and carrying candles. Lynn Mabel-Lois made a speech denouncing the medical profession as murderers of fat women. We had finally taken the irreversible, inevitable public step.

Over the next few years the growth of fat women's consciousness was strongly influenced by the flourishing lesbian feminist movement. By the mid-1970s, lesbian feminism was the dominant creative force in radical women's liberation. Such a huge amount has been written and talked about lesbian feminism — and it is still very much a living force — that I won't even attempt to define it. I'll only say, for the benefit of those unfamiliar with the movement, that it is far, far more than "gay women's liberation." Lesbian feminism goes beyond opposing sexism to affirming the community of women — a feminism based on the strongest and the most intimate bonds of love between women. A great flux of women entered the women's movement in the mid-1970s. Many of them left relationships with men and sought primary companionship, including sexual love, with other women. Fat women sought the same. The companionship of other women offered fat women a social environment in which — often for the first time in their lives — they could be loved for their intelligence and personalities, and their "ugliness" according to conventional standards could be overlooked. Indeed, those conventional standards were attacked as oppressive to women. In theory, then, lesbian feminism offered a haven wherein a fat woman could affirm her beleaguered sense of womanhood and could almost forget that she was fat.

The expectation was satisfied up to a point. That point came when fat women sought lovers among other women. Then the "support" of slim lesbian feminists often revealed itself to be liberalism that easily turned into rejection. Laurie Ann Lepoff's article, "Fat Politics," in this anthology, although addressing a different geographical community, describes the same problem. The struggle itself helped to sort out issues of fat politics versus generalized sexism, and was enormously important in developing fat women's consciousness.

Meanwhile, the core group of the Fat Underground, consisting initially of Lynn Mabel-Lois, Reanne Fagan-Pinkston, Gudrun Fonfa, and myself, continued writing, public workshops, and media efforts. Representing fat women, we joined coalitions to work on other feminist problems, and the bonds of politics and friendship grew stronger.

Among the highlights of this period were the following: weekly drop-in rap groups for fat women at the Women's Liberation Center; a demonstration against NBC for airing, on local TV news, a month-long misinformative series designed to provoke Southern Californians into losing tons of collective fat (1975); and another speech by Lynn Mabel-Lois at a city-wide march and rally protesting crimes against women, linking the starvation and surgical treatments imposed on fat women to world-wide patterns of violence based on sexism (1975).

In summer of 1976, several political struggles which had been internal in the Los Angeles radical feminist community, concerning "political correctness" and elitism, burst into the open. Because of the interlinking of our personal and political lives, a great many women in the community were literally "blown away." I was among those who fled out of state. Those I went with thought that we could continue fat liberation work in our new locale, but under the stresses of interpersonal problems the situation fell apart. The Fat Underground continued for another year, but its influence upon local feminism was greatly diminished.

Work on *Shadow on a Tightrope* began in Los Angeles during the last months before the storm. Sharon Bas Hannah and I undertook to produce an anthology of writings for the movement. A number of pieces from the present anthology are from the original manuscript. In 1977 Sharon joined me in New Haven, Connecticut. For the next two years we tried in vain to find a publisher. Mainstream and leftist presses reacted similarly to the manuscript. They could not believe that fat could be other than a sickening condition caused by bad eating habits. No matter how thoroughly we documented the claims cited, they felt, somehow, that we were wrong. Feminist presses were more open to the personal issues raised, but most expressed the view that the book would appeal only to a very small readership, namely, women who "liked" to be fat. Clearly, for the book to be published would require a much better understanding among feminists of the role of fat oppression in all women's lives.

Meanwhile, late in 1978 I selected several of the most informative articles from the original book manuscripts, made photocopies, and began selling them through ads in feminist newspapers. This was Fat Liberator Publications.

Isolated, and lacking support for political action, I turned more toward building up the scholarly basis for fat liberation. Several academic people offered much encouragement. Drs. Susan and Wayne Wooley, behavioral psychologists at the University of Cincinnati, brought the message of fat liberation to their colleagues. So did Dr. Natalie Allon, a sociologist at Hofstra University (and a NAAFA advisor), until a surgical accident late in 1980 left her in a coma from which she has not yet recovered. Karl Niedershuh, a student and NAAFA activist, supplied me for years — at his own expense — with photocopies of hundreds of medical research articles.

While these things were happening, fat women's liberation was growing back. Several members of the Los Angeles movement had become active again, and new groups and individuals were organizing all over the United States and in the Netherlands. Isolation was a problem; and the radical feminist press, for the most part, still resisted taking any stand that might be construed as supportive of fat liberation. Fat Liberator Publications helped to break down the isolation. By 1980 enough fat women had contacted FLP to make it possible to contemplate holding a nationwide conference.

The first Feminist Fat Activists Working Meeting was organized by Judith Stein, Diane Denne, and myself. It took place in April 1980 in New Haven. It was small — only seventeen women attended — but they came from six states and over thousands of miles. The first day we spent meeting among ourselves. The second day we presented a panel discussion and several workshops at the New Haven Women's Health Weekend, which met concurrently with us.

The fat women's conference marked the end of my intense personal involvement in the movement. I gave away Fat Liberator Publications to Diane Denne so that I would be free to concentrate on graduate school, which I started the following fall. Diane managed FLP for a while, then gave it to Lisa Schoenfielder, of the Iowa City Women's Press. Two Iowa City women decided to focus their efforts on publishing a fat women's book. They used some material from the collection Sharon and I had tried to publish years before, and they gathered new material by advertising the project at feminist centers around the country.

Thus, the story of how this book came to be written is completed. The story of fat women's liberation is just beginning. More fat actions have occurred in the last year than in all ten prior years of the movement. It is for the women who are working on these actions now to describe them.

Actually, the statement above is not quite correct. No one knows how many fat liberation struggles took place in the last decade. We have lacked a way to communicate with each other. Under the triple stresses of fat oppression, isolation, and the disinterest or even hostility with which our pleas for support were often met, fat activists have all too often taken the frustrations out on each other and destroyed our own organizations before they could take root. For years, I have heard rumors of fat women's groups in Baltimore, Philadelphia, elsewhere, that formed, then toppled into oblivion with no proof that they ever existed. In addition to the women named in this introduction, I know of dozens of others who worked hard in support of fat liberation who have not yet received any recognition. There are signs that the isolation is ending, and that fat women's liberation will soon be recognized as a distinct yet fundamental feminist voice. As this happens, I hope that fat women who struggled to build this movement in the past will come forward to share their experiences and thoughts with new activists. We will need more than the one anthology we now have. We will need more than a single book, or a single journal, or the support of a single feminist agency, none of which we have now. I pray for an outpouring of fat women's thought, speech, and action to come soon, in our days.

*Storrs, Connecticut*
*April 1983*

# Preface

## Lisa Schoenfielder and Barb Wieser

*Who we are:* We are both white Lesbians who have lived a number of years in Iowa City, a midwestern college town. We both work at Iowa City Women's Press.

*Lisa:* For as long as I can remember, I have been fat. I truly believe that there hasn't been a day in my life that I have not been aware of that fact. I have spent most of my life wishing that I were thin. I have lived, and often still live, in a fantasy world where I am the size I always thought I should be. At times I have been shocked to see my reflection in a store window or to look at photographs of myself.

Nine years ago I decided to have a gastric bypass operation. I had to wait eight months to be scheduled for the surgery, and during those eight months I had no reservations about taking the high risk involved in that kind of surgery. After three days of tests and preparation, as they wheeled me up to the operating room I got scared and decided not to go through with it. At first, I felt as if I had failed and had disappointed family and friends, just like I had done a million times before on diets. But I also felt angry and tired of hating myself. For the first time in my life, I let myself off the hook. I realized that I have always liked who I am and that most of my desire to be thinner was coming from forces outside myself. I started talking with other fat women, and the picture became clear. Most of us stopped dieting and started to fight back against the oppression we were facing.

In 1975 a friend of mine went to California and brought back writings from the Los Angeles Fat Underground. It was a thrill to know that there were other fat women thinking about the same issues. Unfortunately, women in my own community were not taking the issues as seriously. At a lesbian conference in Iowa City a few years later, a friend and I did a workshop on fat politics where only four women showed up, and one of the four thought we were a diet group. The only other workshop scheduled at that time, one on body awareness, drew over 25 women. It was clear to me then that talking about fat oppression was a threatening idea to most women, regardless of their size.

*Barb:* I am not fat and never have been. Like so many other women who are not fat, there have been many times in my life that I have thought of myself as "fat" and have tried to do certain things to control what I saw as my uncontrollable body — "watching" what I eat, intense exercising, going through an extended period of time in which I considered myself a compulsive overeater. I never actually did regimented dieting such as Weight Watchers; but throughout my life, more times than not, I was concerned with my body and how much I weighed.

Several years ago at dinner at a mutual friend's house, I met and talked with Lisa for the first time about fat politics. Or, rather, she talked, and I listened with increasing excitement to ideas I had never heard before, that turned around my thinking on so many issues concerning how I saw myself and fat people.

That night was the beginning of a process of change that I am still experiencing. I began to accept my body for whatever size it is and ceased concerning myself with the amount of food I ate. I also accepted fat oppression as a political issue, an injustice against a group of people. I began to relate to the issues of fat oppression on a much more personal and emotional level as my friendship with Lisa grew through work on the book and at the press, and as I came to know and love other fat women.

*How we did the book:* In the fall of 1980, Lisa took over the distribution of Fat Liberator Publications. FLP consisted of a series of xeroxed articles that were distributed either individually or as a packet via mail order. The cost of producing the articles was high, and the distribution was limited. In January 1981, Lisa joined the Iowa City Women's Press collective. By this time, the press was doing more and more book printing and was considering going back into publishing. Lisa went to several midwestern fat women's gatherings and talked with women there about the idea of putting FLP into book form. She began to talk with Barb about the possibility of the Women's Press publishing and printing it and distributing it nation-wide through feminist and alternative bookstores.

The idea of producing such a book was exciting, the challenge of it pretty scary. This would be the first anthology to come out of the fat liberation movement; and the task of putting it together seemed overwhelming, especially since neither of us is a writer or editor.

We met to begin work for the first time in December 1981. One of the first things that we discussed was our hesitation about doing the book together, because Barb isn't fat. Both of us felt it was very important that such a book be published, and both of us agreed that it would be better if just fat women were working on the book. However, there were no fat women in Iowa City who could work together on this project at that time, and through Barb's work at the press she had developed organizing and publishing skills that would be useful in putting together an anthology. We trusted and liked each other and saw work on the book as a way to become better friends.

Once we began actual work on the book, one of the first decisions we made was that we wanted the anthology to include more than just the work from Fat Liberator Publications. We contacted Vivian Mayer and Sharon Bas Hannah, who had collected material for a similar anthology that they had tried to have published in 1976 (see Vivian Mayer's Foreword). They sent us all the unpublished work they had collected for their anthology. The articles by Lynn Mabel-Lois, Betty Shermer, and Sharon Bas Hannah are previously unpublished works from the original anthology. They also sent us the proposed title from their anthology, *Shadow on a Tightrope,* which we decided to adopt because of the powerful image it conveys.

To try to elicit new writings for the book, we composed a flyer and poster and sent it off to women's bookstores, women's centers, fat activist organizations, and individuals. We also ran ads in several lesbian and feminist publications. Narrowing down the more than 100 submissions that we received to the 35 or so that we have included was difficult. We realized that with the number of good articles we had received, we could have compiled a much longer book than this first anthology.

One problem that we soon recognized and attempted to deal with was our geographical and cultural bias — we live in a mostly white, midwestern town, and our access to women of color and women of ethnic groups is limited. Furthermore, we are both lesbians, and our sphere of contact, locally and nationally, is mostly with other lesbians. We attempted to lessen the influence of our biases, mainly by appealing to women we know in cities, who could open up other worlds to us. Toward the end of our work on the book, we started doing oral interviews. We wish we had begun to use that tool earlier, because we have learned it can gain us entrance to many different fat women's lives.

Perhaps our major misgiving concerning the book is that, in spite of our efforts, it doesn't speak often enough to fat women who survive without the support of political communities. It is mainly a voice from the feminist community speaking to women of the feminist community. However, that is the community in which we live, and what we hope is that the ideas brought together in this anthology will help women recognize the reality of fat oppression in their own and other women's lives, and to find the courage to fight back.

# Acknowledgments

We wish to thank the following women for their help in putting this anthology together:

Carol Wolvington and Nancy Romine for their work with Lisa on Fat Liberator Publications and for their suggestions and advice on various manuscripts. Carol also transcribed the tapes of the four interviews included in the book, a task that took her over fifty hours.

Sue Norman did the original work on the Bibliography, compiling material from many different sources.

Michal Brody took Sue's list and bibliographies compiled by other women and put them into a more final form. Michal also helped us make a decision on one of the manuscripts.

Cindy Cleary taught us how to do oral histories, an important tool in bringing more women into the book.

Joan Pinkvoss, of Aunt Lute Book Company, worked on editing some of the manuscripts and gave us support and encouragement.

A few women donated money at the beginning of the project to get it going. We would especially like to thank Katharine, the women of Bloodroot Restaurant, and Veronica and Dirtbag.

Judith Pendleton, of Annie Graham & Co., put time and hard work into making the book as beautiful as possible.

We would like to thank our co-workers at Iowa City Women's Press — Veronica, Michal, and Mary — for allowing us the time at work and away from work to put energy into the book. We also want to thank them and the women of A Fine Bind, Lorna and Nancy, for the care they put into the physical production of this book.

We want to thank women of the fat liberation movement whose work made this anthology possible. We would especially like to thank Vivian Mayer for her advice and encouragement at the beginning, and for writing the Foreword.

We also want to thank Vivian and Sharon Bas Hannah for the

work they did in compiling the beginnings of this anthology several years ago.

We want to thank the women who worked on the final proofs: Ginny Blair, Claudia Carver, Cindy Cleary, Tina Mazula, Joan Pinkvoss, Steff, Connie Wilson, and Carol Wolvington.

We especially want to thank Veronica Hubbard for her continued support, encouragement and advice.

Finally, we want to thank the friends who gave us so much support throughout the year and a half we have spent putting this anthology together.

# whoever i am i'm a fat woman

## Sharon Bas Hannah

the space of a silhouette
entering the space of a silence

curvatures of silk
caverns flooding
welcome to a canyon:

she's an artist womon
a desert womon
a dancer

she's a fat womon

a fashion hall for dreams

she's a seeker    your lover    your sister
a dreamer    a bohemian    a thinker
your doctor    she's a healer
a psychic    her stories will set you free

a laughter's echo
she's a fat womon
a womon
bound to cut
this earth of the shadows inside her

she's a blues singer
a flautist    a drummer
a hiker    a kite flyer
your shadow on the tightrope
she's a fat womon

leaping on laughter's echo the rhythms of her life.

the womon procured by money
the womon who is heard above laughter

the womon who walks beyond
the streets of desire
the womon who has always walked these streets
with passion
the womon who has taken over the space of
her body
and the womon who has refused to conquer
that space.

worker  bohemian  boss  scholar  aristocrat
roadrunner  sailor  weaver

a fat girl
she's a wallflower
socializer  leader  recluse  wanderer

she's a stallion    a fleet of rivers

feel the womon
whose river bathes in mammoth luxury
tracing the moons
that are inside her

candlemaker
chiropractor
stuck up bitch
fast smiler
on welfare
or could be
she's a fat womon

the silent womon
worn
with a mask around herself

the womon who is challenged to a duel

the womon who is tortured

tied to the bed and raped

the womon who always sleeps in black
the womon who never says "excuse me"
or smiles when she's supposed to

the womon whose existence is in question

rough outrageous dull graceful ingenious

exciting to be alive as being a fat womon

she's a deep sea diver
a windmill climber
a motorcycle mama
and a bicycle rider
she's a fat womon

certain truths
will make your heart beat fast
when you hear them from a fat womon

you'll grow pale
get chills
disbelieve
but she's marching toward you
she's here and she's taking back her life.

# 1. The Fat Illusion: Exposing the myths . . .

# The Fat Illusion

## Vivian F. Mayer

If you have any doubts, a random handful of women's magazines from any grocery store will make it clear that fat is one of the biggest issues on women's minds. Almost every issue of every women's magazine carries an article on how to lose weight. Fear of fat is so entrenched in the American mind that even the most radical women, who have spent years exploring and rebuilding women's consciousness through the Women's Liberation Movement, have failed to spot the fraud.

In gatherings of the highest revolutionary spirit, you will see right-on feminists drinking cans of diet soda to avoid being fat. That they are avoiding fat is a problem but it is not *the* problem: women ought to be free to choose how they will look. *The* problem is the belief that drinking a low-calorie soft drink enables them to choose their figures, the illusion that fat or thin is a matter subject to personal choice and control. They are locked into that old-time religion promulgated by the eleven-billion-dollar sexist industry that has made the lives of fat women a living hell.

> The electrified rat has learned how to control pleasure. When it presses a button, the electrodes that scientists implanted in its head stimulate the pleasure center of its brain. Since it prefers this intense pleasure even to food, the rat will soon starve to death.
> — observed in a psychology laboratory

> I feel good when I feel hungry. Each pang of hunger reminds me that I'm in control, so I feel proud and successful.
> — a woman on a reducing diet

Women on reducing diets are not in the extreme circumstances of the electrified rat. The woman probably will not starve to death. The rat probably experiences much greater pleasure.

Figure control is one of the few forms of control most women are allowed to exercise. The fact that some men also struggle against their weight is overshadowed by the legions of woman-

3

oriented reducing industries:  the hunger clubs, the sweat salons, the pseudo-foods advertised always in the mouths of slender women.  The hunger that average-sized women endure for a few weeks — only to gain back all the weight they lose — fat women endure for months, even years, only to gain back all the weight they lose.  No one talks about the 99% failure rate of *all* reducing diets.  Everyone's too busy talking about the diets.

Even among women who, as a group, have gone the furthest toward renouncing standards of beauty and "health" defined by patriarchal culture — radical feminists and Lesbian feminists — the diet talk continues:

> I know I'd feel better if I just lost about fifteen pounds.

> She was fat as a way of avoiding men.  Since coming out as a Lesbian, she's lost a lot of weight, and you should see how great she looks!

> I really like some fat women as sisters, as good friends.  They just don't turn me on sexually.

Aside from a superficial awareness that fat women are oppressed by looksism, radical women still see fat as a personal sickness: abnormal, undesirable, lamentable, and curable.

The "facts" about fat as known to the woman-on-the-street can be summarized as follows:  That fat people lack "will power," they're fat because they eat more than thin people.  That they overeat to make up for personality problems or because they're not in touch with their true feelings.  That being fat is unhealthy.  That weight loss can be fun, or at least tolerable.  That once the "excess" weight is lost, a slim figure can be maintained by eating as carefully as any normal slim person eats.

These "facts" are learned from doctors and therapists as well as from common knowledge.  We read them in women's magazines in articles written both by medical/psychiatric "experts" and by journalists; we also hear them in televised interviews with diet doctors and read them in the diet books that they are on television pushing into national best-sellers.  All this is astonishing — because the technical medical literature flatly contradicts each of the above popular statements!

Regarding "overeating," the fundamental sin for which fat people are constantly punished,

> When food intakes of obese individuals were accurately assessed and compared with people of normal [*sic*] weights, the intakes were

identical. There are thin people who eat excessively, "He has a huge appetite and never puts on a pound"—and there are fat people who eat too much. Likewise there are thin people and fat people who have small appetites. The average fat person is euphagic."[1]

And when this euphagic (pleasant, moderate) food intake is reduced for the sake of weight loss, a United States Public Health Service Report found that,

> One well-controlled study showed that young women who lost weight on 1000-calorie diets experienced a decrease in basal metabolism rate and in [calorie] intake required to maintain their reduced weights. Follow-up studies indicated that a lower calorie intake than recorded initially must be maintained indefinitely in order to maintain the reduced weight.[2]

Fat people who have endured the pain of starvation to "cure" themselves so that they can live like "normal" (i.e., slim) people find, according to a noted diet doctor, that,

> Those who lose and maintain a normal [sic] weight must accept some degree of hunger and unsatisfied appetite as a way of life.[3]

But since prolonged hunger is a painful condition that all our biological instincts compel us to avoid,

> Review of the literature since 1958 did not reveal a successful long-term study using a diet regimen by itself or in combination with drugs, psychologic treatment, or an exercise program.[4]

There is something grotesque about having to quote from medical sources to defend a liberation movement. Ideally the Fat Liberation Movement will be based, like other liberation movements, upon the assertion of the masses, the reality of oppressed fat people, our lifetimes spent living the contradictions that no one dares admit exist: skipping "fattening" foods like any *Vogue* beauty (but get an eyeful of the difference), contemplating suicide as we gain weight back after every diet (merely by eating like a slim friend—where does the fat come from?), discovering that to maintain the weight loss one must go to bed hungry every night (is this how slim people live?). But who would believe our assertions? Not doctors, who make money and build their professional status selling weight-loss treatments on a basis that is two-thirds cover-up of facts and one-third appeal to emotions. Not the general public, who think we are sick, sinful, and absurd. Not leftists who use our bodies to symbolize the oppressors—the "Fat Capitalist," the "Pigs"—and consider us disgusting and decadent. Not even we ourselves, whose ability to trust our own judgment is naturally undermined by the skepticism with which the rest of society regards us.

Fat and thin, medical and radical, intelligentsia and common people alike, we are all, as a culture, caught in the Fat Illusion. We believe that our bodies' sizes are chosen and reflect personal control, and we ignore or reject all evidence that contradicts this belief. What powerful forces of *social* control make this illusion so dazzling that we cling to it through starvation and spiritual pain, through absurdity and failure of hopes?

We stand at the core of the Fat Illusion, looking out. Layers of confusion and cruelty are piled upon each other like the layers of a poisonous atmosphere. Let us begin with the simplest, most personal experience of fat reality, to work our way out of this illusion.

### #1: The Illusion of Personal Control

OBSERVATION: I eat what others eat. My eating is labeled "overeating," and I am punished for it. The others who do not get fat are not accused of overeating and are not punished.

CONCLUSION: I don't deserve as much food as others do. I am bad, less worthy than others.

Being fat even as a very young child, I naturally saw my condition in such absolute and terrible terms. I don't think I could have internalized such a condemnation and stayed alive. So I, like many fat women of upwardly mobile middle-class background, found it easier to break from reality and believe that the things I saw happening were not really happening. I rationalized away the sight of slim people eating more than I did with thoughts such as, "They'd skipped lunch," or "They plan to exercise the calories off." I did not admit to myself that I felt hungry on the greatly reduced food intake that allowed me to maintain the "normal" body-size I'd starved down to. Or when I had to admit the hunger, I'd rationalize that it was not real because something was "wrong" with my ability to feel hunger. The prolonged hunger eventually led to eating binges, and the uncontrolled intensity of these binges led me to believe that I was crazy. A whole culture's fat-hating forced me to accept the illusion that what I felt in my guts was imaginary and unjustified. Worse, the hunger became perverted into pleasure. Every pang was a spiritual agony atoning for my imagined sin of gluttony and bringing me one step closer to being a "normal" woman. Like the electrified rat, I thought I was in control of my pleasure and pain. Will power — self-control — figure control: these are all illusions. We are manipulated by the men in white coats.

#### #2: *The Illusion of Freedom of Choice*

Regarding aesthetic and economic intertwinement as one aspect of social control, Gudrun Fonfa writes, "Looksism is the standardization of a look (body image) and the discrimination against those who do not meet or conform to the [prescribed] image. Societies set acceptable broad limitations, because it is important to create the illusion that individuals are choosing their personal aesthetics, i.e., which bone to put through your nose."[5]

If you are fat, you can choose to count calories or grams of carbohydrates; to drink Sego, Slender, or Liquid Protein diets; to eat Figurines; to go for Dr. Simeon's Human Chorionic Gonadotropin (HCG) injections; to follow the *Redbook* Wise Woman's Diet; etc., etc. The range of choices hides the fact that you are *compelled* to choose. As for the choices themselves, no matter which you choose you are choosing pain through hunger. If therefore you choose to reject all reducing options, you are punished with ridicule and social rejection. Unfortunately, with almost all attempts at weight-loss failing, the same women who are constantly using one or another diet product are also punished for looking as though they do not use any diet product!

Social control goes beyond simply repressing deviants. Fundamental means of social control affect every person in the controlled society. One might argue logically that the persecution of fat women takes away each woman's freedom to become fat. More accurately, since there's no way to look at a person and know, on the basis of her size, whether she eats a lot or a little, the freedom women lose is the freedom to be comfortable with our appetites.

Most slim women believe that they would become very fat if they "let themselves go." Particularly in the middle and upper classes, this belief is exploited into an obsession by the sexist image-makers. As a result, millions of average-sized women experience nagging terror over every bite they eat, and come to look upon their bodies as barely tamed dragons that could turn on them any moment and erupt with fat. The fact that they can gain five pounds easily over Christmas indulgence seems to confirm this danger, and also leads them to believe that fat women are women who indulge themselves all the time. But the millions of women who are convinced that only their diets stand between them and two hundred fifty pounds struggle against their appetites to no real purpose. Approximately 99% of all attempts to lose weight end in failure; consequently, no more than 1% of the women who are slim can attribute their figures to the success of a diet.[6] Why are they slim? Maybe it's genes.[7] Maybe it's magic. The mechanism is beside the point. It is certainly not the power of will or better eating habits, since most slim women are eating as much as most fat women anyway.

Many believe that lack of exercise is what makes people fat. Here again, the individual who exercises regularly tends to gain some weight when she stops exercising. Furthermore, studies show that some groups of fat women (for example, fat adolescent women) tend to be less active than their peers.[8] However, the same studies show that these less active fat women also eat significantly *less* than their slim peers. Instead of assuming that they are fat because they are less active, researchers should ask whether they are less active because they are underfed; lessened activity and lessened productiveness are commonly observed in semi-starved laborers in Third World countries. Those who righteously harp upon exercise ignore the role of persecution in causing fat people to be less physically active. This persecution ranges from the lack of large-sized gym uniforms for fat high school students to the open ridicule that many fat people encounter when they attempt to jog, swim, or dance in public.

Furthermore, those who blame fat on laziness ignore evidence provided by social class differences. Charwomen, for example, do hard physical labor all day long and frequently are fat. They are poor, rarely have their own cars and must rely upon public transportation, which means that they must walk to and from bus stops, etc. In contrast, front-office secretaries sit in front of typewriters all day and are usually slim. Middle-class people are more likely than the poor to own their own cars. Recently more middle-class people, especially women, have taken up regular exercise—tennis, running, etc. Before this trend they were not all fat—certainly not as fat as typical charwomen. Jean Mayer, one of the best-known researchers in the question of exercise and diet, writes that weight loss for fat people requires ". . . an attitude almost stoic in its asceticism and . . . the deliberate setting aside of time for what will be often lonely walking and exercising."[9] Stoicism, asceticism, lonely walking and exercising hardly describe a *typical* slim woman's life!

The point of all this is that we have much less choice over our figures than we are led to believe. The suffering of women over their figures is meaningless — and that's hard to accept.

*#3: The Illusion That It's "For Our Own Good"*

Surrounding the shame of fat women and the fear of non-fat women is a half-century of medical and psychiatric lies which the Fat Underground calls "gynocidal malpractice."[10] In this writing, I want to devote only a little space to the radical counter-arguments that doctors make fat people sick and psychiatrists make fat people crazy. The gist of these arguments rests on observations such as the following:

Regarding physical health,

1 That serious bodily damage, including that damaged caused by prolonged starvation, is known to occur in fat bodies on diets.[11] There is evidence that atherosclerosis, leading to heart attacks and strokes, is caused by repeated dieting.[12] This fact alone would account for the high death rate of fat people from these illnesses.

2 That all studies claiming to prove that fat is unhealthy were done on people who have dieted frequently and who live in an atmosphere of constant persecution and self-hatred.

3 That the handful of studies existing on non-persecuted fat people suggests that they are quite healthy,[13] whereas studies of persecuted groups other than fat people, such as black people, show these groups to suffer from many of the diseases "characteristic" of fat people.[14]

And regarding mental well-being,

4 That compulsiveness toward food is found in almost all individuals, fat or thin, who are starved or deprived of food, or who are threatened with starvation or deprivation.

5 That since all psychiatric theories are based on the assumption that fat people are fat because they eat more than slim people, this psychiatry contradicts reality and forces alienation upon fat people.

Actually, "our own good" is not the real reason for persecution of fat people. The real reason is looks. When was the last time you saw people who smoke cigarettes denied employment, laughed at when they complain about discrimination, ridiculed throughout the media, rejected as friends and as lovers? — and they are endangering their health and other people's as well.

Looks are always the reason for women's dieting, even when the reasons spoken out loud, and often believed, are health. There is no way that a woman can feel good in this culture if she sees herself as fat. Feelings of sluggishness and of being "weighed down" are at least partially a reaction to the culture's fat-hating, internalized and expressed in the "overweight" person as self-hatred. Keep in mind how many of us had fat grandmothers, and how hard and vigorously these fat grandmothers worked.

Among many women, health is not even a pretense of an issue when it comes to getting rid of fat. At a meeting of fat women in Los Angeles, April 20, 1973, one fat woman admitted her secret fantasy: "I wish I could get cancer or some other wasting disease, so I could die thin." The increasing popularity of intestinal bypass surgery reflects this desperate attitude. In this surgery, all but a few feet (sometimes inches) of the small intestine is surgically shunted aside, so that most of one's food passes out the gut undigested. Weight losses of a hundred pounds are typical. In the months or years while she is wasting away to a slim (if jaundiced) beauty, the patient endures explosive, foul-smelling, painful diarrhea; malnutrition; and related damage to organs. The death rate for this operation is estimated conservatively at 6%,[15] and since it is still new and experimental, the long-term effects are not even known. Yet at least 5,000 intestinal bypass operations are done annually in the United States, about 80% of them on women[16] (and at an expense of typically $6,000 apiece, paid for by the patient — who, of course, is too fat to qualify for health insurance).

To alter her organs as if they were so many cogs and circuits is the natural duty of a sex object. Usefulness (sex-appeal) is the only virtue; pain is irrelevant. The relation between doctors and fat women is sado-masochistic. Believing that she is inadequate to manipulate *herself* as a sex object, the fat woman finally gives up her power to the doctor to manipulate (mutilate) her. Her jaws get wired shut. Her guts get cut apart. Her submissiveness approaches a passive ideal. This is the extreme fat version of the masochism inculcated in almost all women by sexism. We are brought up on the old principle that "you have to suffer to be beautiful." The amount of pain is a matter of degree. According to the rhetoric of sado-masochism, through submission to pain, Woman obtains absolute power. What she really obtains is the illusion that she is in control.

The power that doctors hold to perpetuate or end this misery is not an illusion. Doctors continue to plead that they are puzzled by the contradictions in the obesity literature — but their puzzlement doesn't stop them from practicing as if obesity were just a matter of caloric bookkeeping. As long as doctors practice this way, they are using their power to abuse us.

The discovery that doctors can be women's political enemies is not new to feminism; the self-help movement, the radical therapy movement, and writings such as those of Barbara Ehrenreich and Dierdre English on the history of women as healers[17] represent a taking-back of power by women over our bodies and minds. Fat liberation is the next stage in this women's liberation process.

### #4: The Illusion of Self-Limited Achievement

"If you really want something, you can have it — it's all up to you." How many times we hear this double-edged cliché! On the one hand the cliché urges people not to give up in despair. On the other hand, it is a paralyzing excuse for the status quo, implying that the "haves" deserve their privilege and that the "have nots" are "have nots" because they are not sufficiently motivated to work for and obtain the privilege. By this trick, politics are made to look like personal psychology, and the victims bear the blame. Most doctors are deeply hooked into this self-righteous attitude. How could they respect themselves, how could they avoid demoralizing guilt, unless they believed that there was justice in a system that deprives so many and rewards so few, happily including themselves?

Under "The Illusion of Freedom of Choice" I described how the Fat Illusion tricks individual women into meaningless struggles for "figure control." At the level of the Illusion of Self-Limiting Achievement, those individual struggles become meaningful, making up a system that controls the energies of masses of women.

Women are divided into those who fear getting fat and those who are ashamed of being fat. Through buying weight-loss ideology and products (saccharin, diet soda, *Weight Watcher's Magazine*, etc.) slim women assert that they are motivated to be slim and beautiful. They are rewarded with male approval and with permission to feel superior to fat women. By the same actions, fat women assert that they want to be approved of by men — that their hearts are in the right place, that they accept domination by the Patriarchy — but their reward is only a future promise of male approval, since as long as they are fat, even if they are dieting, they suffer persecution. However, they do get to feel superior to some mythical person who is fatter than they and who goes on eating without shame.

The value and power of male approval is increased by the suffering women go through to earn it.

I have emphasized male approval to show that this is a sexist situation keeping the mass of women dependent upon the mass of men for self-esteem. The same situation exists among Lesbians in a more subtle way.

Money and support which women pour into the weight-loss industry is turned into a whip that persecutes fat women — creating jeering diet and fashion advertisements whose message is that only slim women are worthy of love. The resulting spectacle of fat women's suffering terrifies women into continuing to support the weight-loss industries. This is an extortion racket where each penny we pay to the reducing industry increases its power over us. Women's power is stunted not only by competition to be slimmer than the next woman, but by hunger and by preoccupation with food. The ultimate anti-revolutionary message is that what feels good for us — such as eating what we want — is really bad for us.

The Fat Illusion, in all its levels, must be eliminated from women's lives. There must be no support, and no condoning, of the reducing industries, since these industries degrade fat women. Every can of diet soda that you buy — no matter how much you may "prefer the taste of it" — hurts fat women, and by extension, all women. As women liberate knowledge about fat from the medical monopoly, fat women will come out of the closets of our minds to realize that there is nothing wrong with us. It is time to struggle with the implications of thin privilege and fat punishment the same as we struggle with other social injustices that we've recognized for years. We cannot wait for help and advice from doctors. Aside from the fact that few doctors will risk their careers to debunk a popular medical racket that is, after all, mainly a women's issue, the truth in this case is just not good business.

We porkies may never get to see that "thin man" [imprisoned in every fat man] outside ourselves, but it certainly won't be for lack of trying. As we plod ever onward to that great pie in the sky, we are met, as never before, by "stop" signs that admonish us for our gluttony and direct us back to the straight and narrow. [18]

## REFERENCES

1   A. M. Bryans, "Childhood obesity: Prelude to adult obesity," *Canadian Journal of Public Health* (November 1967), p. 487.

2   U. S. Department of Health, Education and Welfare. *Obesity and Health* (Washington, DC: 1966), p. 60.

3   W. L. Asher, "Appetite suppressants as an aid in obesity control," in Louis Lasagna, ed., *Obesity: Causes, consequences and treatment* (New York: Medcom, 1974), p. 73.

4   Joseph A. Glennon, "Weight reduction: An enigma," *Archives of Internal Medicine* (July 1966), vol. 118, pp. 1-2.

5   Gudrun Fonfa, "'Looksism' as Social Control," *Lesbian Tide* (January 1975), p. 20.

6   Alvan Feinstein, "How do we measure accomplishment in weight reduction?" in Lasagna, ed., *op. cit.,* p. 86.

7   Jean Mayer, *Overweight: Causes, cost and control* (Englewood Cliffs, NJ: Prentice-Hall, 1968).

8   Mayer, pp. 125-126.

9   Mayer, p. 165.

10   Fat Underground, "Health of fat women . . . the *real* problem," 1974.

11   Aldebaran, "Fat liberation: A luxury?" *State and Mind* (June-July 1977), pp. 34-38.

12   *Obesity and Health,* p. 40.

13   Clark Stout, *et al.,* "Unusually low incidence of death from myocardial infarction," *Journal of the American Medical Association* (June 8, 1964), Vol. 188, pp. 845-849.

14   Jack Slater, "Hypertension: Biggest killer of blacks." *Ebony* (June 1973).

15   "Current status of jejuno-ileal bypass for obesity," *Nutrition Reviews* (1974), Vol. 32, p. 334.

16   From a telephone conversation with an office assistant of Dr. J. Howard Payne (an M.D. who pioneered the intestinal bypass surgery for obesity), August 6, 1975.

17   Many books have been written by feminist women on the subject of women and health. A good introductory bibliography (omitting, of course, information about fat women) is found in the Appendix of *The hidden malpractice,* by Gena Corea (New York: William Morrow, 1977). The specific book referred to in the

text is *Witches, midwives and nurses,* by Barbara Ehrenreich and Deirdre English, published by The Feminist Press, Box 334, Old Westbury NY 11568.

18   Frank Bowers, "The wild signal of health," in "101 Ways to Lose Weight and Stay Healthy," *Woman's Day* (March 1975), p. 10.

# The Goddess Is Fat

## Kelly

Fat Hatred. . . . For a society that pretends to be so concerned about our health, we certainly take a lot of public and private abuse. Fat hatred is so strongly felt that when a study was done on two-year-old children, giving them a choice between a fat rag doll and a thin rag doll, most children preferred the thin doll. Another study was done on five-year-old children, and by then 83% of them had gotten the message that fat is bad, fat is ugly. And then by the time children are ten years old, 100% of them had gotten the message.

One of these studies was done in Manhattan. Eight groups of children were asked to rate seven photos of other children, as to who they would most want to be friends with, and who they would least want to be friends with. Seven of the eight groups put the fat child last. Unfortunately, the report that I read on this study didn't describe all of the other photos. Only five of the seven photos were described: one child pictured was in a wheelchair, one was a child missing an arm, one was "normal," one had a facial disfigurement, and one was fat. The one group of children that did not rate the fat child last was a group of working class Jewish children. They rated the fat child third. (This was analyzed by the people who were conducting the study, and they concluded that this happened because in the culture of these children, fat people, fat children, are loved and valued; yet exposure to the mainstream culture had caused them to rate the fat child third.)

These same photos were also shown to groups of adults who were employed in so-called "helping" professions, such as teaching, nursing, counseling. These doctors, nurses, therapists, and teachers all rated the fat child last.

In a similar study with teachers, it was found that teachers gave lower grades to identical papers if they were told that the student was fat. Teachers, along with most people in general, tend to see fat people as lazy and dumb. Fat students receive less after-school attention, and less physical affection than thin students.  More understanding and patience is extended to so-called attractive students when they are having behavior problems.

A poll was conducted among students asking them to assign adjectives to a picture of a thin child and one of a fat child.  Of the thin child, they wrote: ". . . trustworthy, would make a good friend, nice, fun, easy to get along with, smart, happy . . ." About the fat child, they said: "dirty, liar, mean, lazy, tends to get into fights, ugly, stupid . . ."

Now, a lot of people do not dispute the fact that life is hell for fat people in this country.  What they want to know from us is why we want to be fat.  Why don't we just go on a diet and get thin, and then we can get treated just as nice as thin people are treated.

It is very complicated and difficult to explain the biology of fat. The weight that you are is determined internally, and is called your "set-point."  This is how much your body says it's supposed to weigh.  Your natural set-point is determined by heredity.  So far they have only discovered two ways to change your natural set-point:  Weight-loss "diets" push your set-point *up;* vigorous physical activity will lower it; but not by much, either way.

The set-point that you inherited is a result of natural selection. And how much it can be changed is also inherited.  Some of us have the potential to weigh 400 pounds; some of us could not weigh more than 100 pounds under any conditions.

Fat cells are places where energy is stored away for emergency situations, like starvation.  If you came from a gene pool where starvation situations occurred, then you inherited this survival mechanism.  *How much* of this survival mechanism you've got also depends on your gene pool.  The more times a population experienced famine, the more the thin people kept dying out of that group.  When the famine was over, all the fat people *looked* thin for a while, but as they had access to food again, they gradually got fat again, *and* just to be on the safe side, the body pushed the set-point up a little, maybe ten or twenty pounds, to be ready for the next famine.

You get fatter after every diet.  You get fatter because your body thinks that you have just been starved for a while.  And your body is *right*.  Mother nature did not anticipate self-inflicted starvation when she was finding better and better ways to survive.  To your body, there is no difference between a diet and starvation, as far as the effects each has on your system. The World Health Council has set the definition of starvation at 900 calories or less per day for an adult. I am sure many women have been on "diets" of 900 calories or less. Now, people like doctors will say that this is different. That if someone is thin and eating less than 900 calories a day they are starving, that they have no extra fat to tap into, that they will start melting away — muscles, vital organs — and then they will die. But when you are fat and you start eating less than you need, your body will go right for those "awful fat cells" and melt *them* away instead of melting *you*. (As if your fat cells were some kind of invaders, and not a part of you like anything else.)

Well, these are lies.

Your fat cells are emergency survival resources. You do not tap into them one day just because you eat a little less than you need. Not having enough food is a major crisis, and the body reacts only slowly to this crisis. It takes anywhere from four to six weeks, sometimes eight weeks, into a "diet" before your system has converted itself over to digesting fat. Before this happens, your body has to find a way to make up the difference. If it didn't, and you were only taking in 1000 calories, you would fall over dead when you needed just one more calorie to pump your heart. Just like the engine of a car: when the gas is gone, the engine stops. So, what happens? You can't tap into your fat reserves yet, remember, and obviously you didn't die all those days you hardly ate anything. So where did the necessary energy come from? Your body went after readily available energy — your heart, the muscles in your arms and legs, your brain cells. You began to digest yourself, your whole self, except for your fat. So there's no difference in the first four to eight weeks of a diet between you and a thin woman. Both of you starve.

After the first phase, when the body begins to adjust, it does two things. It begins to tap into the energy reserves held in your fat cells, and it also makes an energy conservation move — it slows down your system as much as possible. It is trying to avoid dipping into the reserves, since it doesn't know how long this famine is going to last. For a lot of women, this is the famous "plateau" we hit four to eight weeks into the "diet." What the body wants to do ideally is to slow down as much as possible, and tap into the reserves as little as possible; and suddenly, you stop losing weight for a while, unless you are not eating at all. For example, if you cut back your energy intake by 500 calories, for the first four to eight weeks you *will* lose weight — from your muscles, your heart, your brain, etc. Then when your emergency systems kick in, your body will try very hard to slow down by 500 calories if it can. And then it will turn to the fat cells if it has to. It will seem like you have stopped losing weight. But because of the energy slow-down, you will feel exhausted, irritable, and kind of apathetic.

I can still hear a lot of women who are *so* tired of the abuse, *so* tired of not feeling loved and accepted, who would like to starve half to death anyhow. "Any price is worth being able to be treated like a human being." And if it takes putting our bodies through a near-death experience, what the hell. Well, I'm sorry to shatter your dream, but it is impossible, biologically, to stay on a weight-loss diet. Unless you go totally crazy like the women with anorexia nervosa who very nearly do die because they get so cut off from their bodily sensations that they do not eat at all, or eat very little — just barely enough to lie flat on a bed and breathe. (The body has slowed down to the bare minimum.) But if you manage to stay sane at all, you will feel the furious messages from your body to please nourish it. It will pull out all the tricks it can to get you to take in some energy. It will make you think of nothing but food. (Hence, our "strange" preoccupation with food — most starving people think of little else.) It will churn your stomach. You will give in to it, you must. Not eating is like not breathing: You will die. Cutting back on your food intake by 25% is like cutting back on your breathing. It is not a matter of "just a little will power"; it has nothing to do with will power. Will power is something we use to do healthy things like quit smoking cigarettes, and many many people succeed all the time. But using "will power" to inflict harm upon yourself will, hopefully, fail.

Dieting is starvation, it is self-abuse, it is self-hate.

If you use the standards on the insurance charts as a reference for the definition of "thin," you will find that:

91% of all lower-class women are fat.
81% of all middle-class women are fat.
63% of all upper-class women are fat.

One of the factors that goes into the idea about what body size is proper for a woman comes from white European history. People in many places in Europe experienced starvation conditions over the centuries. The people in these cultures who could afford to feed themselves, even during famines, were the rich people. Among the poor classes, even those who would have been naturally fat had been starved, so that they were thin. It became a status symbol to be fat; it flaunted one's wealth. The phrase "fat cat" comes from this past.

Poor people began to value being fat; it meant survival. They soon learned that fat children were healthy children. Remnants of these values are seen in the stereotype of the ethnic grandmother scolding a girl child to eat, eat, eat, even though the girl child herself may already be getting messages from the new American culture that she is "too fat." Grandmother is depicted as a foolish old woman who somehow is crazy and quaint in her insistence that her already "chubby" granddaughter is "too skinny and should eat more." The survival values the grandmother has learned are pushed aside and treated as a joke, as a kind of folk-ignorance.

The "new and better" American values are based on the myth of the classless society. It became unfashionable to flaunt one's wealth; and instead, efforts are made to appear underfed. The higher up in the class system you go, the more pressure there is to be thin. Rich men chose thin women — thin, young, and able-bodied, if they can manage it.

A fat woman is more likely to drop a class or two than a thin woman. A fat woman has little chance of pulling herself up into a higher class. We share this enforced downward mobility with other physically different women. Rich men will not "settle for less" when it comes to women; and fat women, women in wheelchairs, deaf women, blind women, old women are all women "less than" young white thin physically able women. We know what they mean when they say "attractive" — it's not us.

In many male-oriented societies, the men eat their fill first, while the women serve them; and then what's left is for the women. The "sin" of gluttony is really reserved for those that a culture doesn't want to feed. Even fat men in this culture are seen as "gourmets" by the media; and if they are not seen as well-dressed gourmets, they are still one of the boys, basically okay and acceptable as a friend and husband. Jackie Gleason, Sebastian Cabot, Orson Welles, Nero Wolfe, Rodney Dangerfield, and Santa Claus. All lovable, likeable characters. The few fat women who have been accepted as they are are either lower-class or black or both, and their images are not fully positive. Kate Smith is as often joked about as she is loved. The few fat black women on television are in situation comedies. We laugh at fat women, especially lower-class and/or black fat women.

"Scientists" have long since been aware of the fact that there are more fat people in the lower classes. They are always doing studies to figure out how it is that those of us who have less money to buy food are getting fat anyhow. The assumption, again, being that fat people eat more than thin people. They measure and photograph and chart us to find out how we manage this impossibility. They look at our carbohydrate intake, our mealtimes, our energy levels . . . and completely ignore the fact that if you are ugly they aren't going to make you the president of the bank. We're more common among the poor because we're oppressed and kept there. In a society that sees its women as a commodity, we fat women aren't "selling well."

*In a woman-oriented society, God was a woman, and that woman was usually fat.*

Male archeologists are constantly digging up these round little figures of women, all over the world. They choose to call her a "fertility goddess" and dismiss her as insignificant. But those figurines represent the Goddess herself. In woman-oriented societies, fertility was not a fetish; it was the focus of these life-affirming cultures. Giving life was the supreme act of power, the ultimate symbol of woman's ability to create life.

Round is female. Round females are the visual symbols of strength, of love, of life-giving. When you start getting in touch with the fact that being round and being big is very female, then you begin to understand why the men have asked us to go away. They want us to be little, smaller than they are. We have tremendous sexual energy, we have sensuous soft round soft bodies that just have to be touched. Fat women typically become involved with thin people. This is because we have learned to hate other fat people. But what is it that draws these thin people to our beds? It is that they know what we are beginning to find out: there's nothing quite like making love to a warm round body. Somewhere in the mind of the human race is the memory of who we are and what we represent. The cultures that produced thousands of images of fat women knew this about us, that we represent the ultimate female, full, round, big, strong, soft, warm woman. The moon is round, the earth is round, cycles are round, and so are we.

The woman-oriented cultures naturally assumed that the supreme being was female. When trying to figure out how life came about on the planet, they looked around and couldn't help but notice that all babies came from very round women. It was a natural extention to believe that all life came from a round woman in the sky.

It was an astounding act of cultural distortion when men began to get people to believe that men give birth, that a man in the sky created life — a flat man, at that.

And so, in this culture which has bought this biologically impossible lie, fat women are constant primal reminders that god is female. We look pregnant all the time; round and female as we are, we are visual reminders that their male god is a lie. We are physically intimidating to men who want to feel as though women are frail beings who must either be protected from other men or beaten. The "hen-pecked" husband in classic jokes is always married to a big woman with a rolling pin in her hand. The "joke" is on him, really, because he has failed to tame this woman, and she is bigger than he is, which shows his lack of intelligence for not marrying a woman he can physically intimidate.

This older fat woman with her weapon ready at the doorway is the Goddess herself. We're rated last in the patriarchy because we were first in the matriarchy. To keep fat women down is to keep all women down. A total acceptance of an older fat woman by this culture would mean that many of the fundamental tenets of patriarchy had fallen. We are women "out of control" and we are threats.

Choose to be a threat whenever possible.

## NOTES

The vast majority of the specifics noted in this article were researched, reviewed, and interpreted by the following women of the Feminist Fat Liberation movement:

Susan C. Wooley, "Obesity and women. Part I, A closer look at the facts" and "Part II, A neglected feminist topic." Published in *Women's Studies International Quarterly* (1978, 1979) by Pergamon Press, Ltd. Printed in Great Britain.

Vivian Mayer, "Why liberated eating?," "The fat illusion," "Fat liberation — A luxury?," "The calorie controversy — Who's Cheating?," and other articles published by Fat Liberator Publications.

# To those who use "fat" as a definitive adjective

Marianne Ware

Ah yes, I understand,
you mean to grease perception's path,
evoke an image
you believe is universal,
shades of sneering Sydney Greenstreet,
Greed and Gluttony personified.
Then again, your thrust is rural,
meant to conjure baser creatures —
rough-jowled, mud-bound, trough-tied.

In either case,
you lean upon that narrow word
the way our culture uses "Fuck,"
as if mere emphasis
could speak voluminously
of the impenetrable.

And what is "fat" to you:
a state of mind,
a mindless state,
a crime against some right-flanked
notion of ecology,
perhaps of your own voraciousness —
projected?

Those attitudes I could forgive —
considering their addled source —
but not what's couched, malevolently,
behind those meager letters:
one vowel, two consonants,
as in "old" and "Jew."

# The Questions People Ask

## Vivian F. Mayer

When obesity scientists first noted abnormally high concentrations of free fatty acids in fat people's blood, they were not surprised. The reason for the excess seemed obvious. Free fatty acids are a fragment of the fat molecule. Fat people (scientists reasoned) are so stuffed with food that there isn't even room for all the fat in their overstuffed fat cells, and the excess has to spill over into their blood.[1]

However, this "obvious" explanation could not explain further observations. Why did elevated free fatty acid levels return to normal in fat people who gained weight? More puzzling, elevated free fatty acid levels proved to be associated with fasting and hunger in slim people. If so, why should fat people's free fatty acid levels be high at all? A distinguished obesity scientist, recognizing that most fat people studied by researchers are trying to lose weight, suggested that fat people who reduce "would, in effect, be starving all the time."[2]

Needless to say, social welfare agencies did not rush to put Weight Watchers at the top of their list of people to receive emergency food. To be starving "in effect" is not considered the same as to be starving "in reality." In fact, the evidence that fat people might be starving in any sense at all remains unheard-of by the majority of health professionals and the general public. Throughout media and medical practice the great question about fat people remains, "Why do they eat so much?" Only a small minority of obesity scientists ask a different question, and for them the question is only slightly different: "What abnormality makes fat bodies exhibit biochemical signs of starvation unless they are overfed?"

This evolution of a biochemical question illustrates the typical workings of obesity science. The meaning scientists attach to a phenomenon can reverse 180 degrees, from overindulgence to starvation. Yet the view that fat people are overfed remains unquestioned. The problem so obviously boils down to prejudice that many political activists reject science altogether, putting derisive quote-marks around its name:  obesity "science," like Nazi "science," a rationalization for oppression, a delusion of those in power.  The fat people's revolution will be the ultimate reversal in obesity science.  Questions will be asked that are not yet dreamed of!

However, I think that the distinction between science and "science" is not so real as many political activists suppose.  Ultimately, any science consists of observations, techniques, and opinions, held together by a philosophical world view.  The mystique of "objectivity" enjoyed by sciences like physics and chemistry is deceptive, for these sciences have been through revolutions involving profound changes in world view.  Thomas Kuhn's book, *The Structure of Scientific Revolutions,*[3] examines revolutions in the physical sciences.  Reading it, I was struck by how much his analysis reveals about obesity science.  My view of obesity science has changed as a result.  Although I detest its activities and reject almost all of its theories, I no longer see it as some perversion of the scientific spirit.  It is not so unique as that.  Applying Kuhn's analysis shows that obesity science is an ordinary science going through the sort of confusion and disorder that precedes a scientific revolution.  The birth of revolutionary fat politics has occurred at a time when there is a unique opportunity to link a scientific revolution with political struggle.


*Paradigms and Normal Science*

Kuhn uses several terms to describe the structure and activities of science.  His definitions are elaborate, but I will summarize them briefly (and hopefully not too simplistically).

One of these terms is *paradigm.*  A paradigm is an accepted theory that rules the thinking of generations of scientists.  Examples of paradigms would be Newton's laws of force and motion, Ptolemy's earth-centered universe, and the periodic table of elements invented by Mendeleev.  All evidence that scientists discover is interpreted in terms of the paradigm.

In its earliest stages, a field of science lacks a real paradigm.  Instead, numerous theories compete; they may be based on the same observations of nature, but they do not necessarily agree about which observations are important, or how to interpret them.  At this early stage science often depends heavily upon technology.  Technology provides a lot of information (such as "how to make soap"—even if one does not understand why the method works).

Technology also provides a *motive* for finding out more. And although Kuhn does not dwell on this point, I consider it important to note that technology reflects social needs and values.

Eventually one theory will do such a good job of solving problems considered important by contemporary scientists that it beats out the competition. It becomes a paradigm. Other, less successful theories more or less disappear. The paradigm's strength lies in its ability to guide scientific questioning through the maze of natural phenomena. Kuhn writes that the paradigm is "a criterion for choosing problems that . . . can be assumed to have solutions. To a great extent these are the only problems that the (scientific) community will admit as scientific or encourage its members to understand."[4]

Within the security of the paradigm, the overwhelming majority of scientists practice what Kuhn calls *normal science.* Normal science is essentially a mopping-up operation. Its purpose is to extend the frontiers of the paradigm by using it to solve as many problems of nature as possible. Many answers reveal themselves easily to probing guided by a good paradigm. Those that don't are the challenge to creative scientists. The paradigm provides not only a theory, but a method of experiment and a vocabulary for interpreting findings. This is both its strength and its weakness. Kuhn writes, "Closely examined, whether historically or in the contemporary laboratory, [normal science] seems an attempt to force nature into the preformed and relatively inflexible box that the paradigm already supplies."[5]

Sometimes the fit is awkward. Sometimes it cannot be managed at all, no matter how the paradigm is strained. Such problems may be put aside as unimportant, regarded as due to errors of measurement, or simply left to be resolved later. But if enough of this sort of evidence accumulates, the paradigm enters a crisis. It has evolved as far as it can. The only way out of the crisis is revolution. Now the ultimate vision in which a paradigm is based becomes the center of the conflict.

Kuhn illustrates the role of vision in scientific revolution by comparing two views of the pendulum.

> Since remote antiquity most people have seen one or another heavy body swinging back and forth on a string or chain until it finally comes to rest. To the Aristotelians, who believed that a heavy body is moved by its own nature from a higher position to a state of rest at a lower one, the swinging body was simply falling with difficulty. . . . Galileo, on the other hand, looking at the swinging body,

saw a pendulum, a body that almost succeeded in repeating the same motion over and over again ad infinitum.[6]

Inherent rest — or endless, repeated motion: two radically different ways of seeing the same object. Galileo's new view, and his successful accounting for the pendulum's properties based on this view, was one blow in the scientific revolution that deposed the Aristotelian paradigm and set up the Newtonian. Kuhn remarks, "What were ducks in the scientists' world before the revolution are rabbits afterwards." [7]

*Ducks and Paradigms*

In a sense, there is no such single entity as "obesity science." Instead, obesity scientists study fat people according to the rules of normal science in numerous fields, including biology, psychology, genetics, anthropology, nutrition, etc. They lack a specific unifying paradigm. However, it would be wrong to say that obesity science is totally without a paradigm. The word "obesity" itself (Latin *obesus*, from *obedere*, "to eat up") presents a view of fat people which rules the thinking of virtually all obesity scientists, regardless of their specific field. According to this view, fat people are overfed. From this comes the very general paradigm: a theory stating that fatness is a physical abnormality somehow involving too much food. As stated by George Bray, "Obesity is a problem of energy balance. In its final analysis, too many calories are ingested relative to the body needs."[8] All the questions obesity scientists ask and all the answers they accept must fit the box defined by this paradigm. That is, the evidence must show that fat is abnormal and that fat people eat more than they need.

A further constraint comes from the fact that the motivations and observations of obesity scientists are derived almost exclusively from technology, the technology of weight-loss methods. Therefore, the only problem to which obesity research ultimately refers is how to make fat people lose weight. The allowed questions are variations of the following: What are the differences between fat (i.e., abnormal) and slim (i.e., normal) people? What abnormalities cause fat people to eat too much? How do excess food and fat damage fat people's health? How can the excess in fat people's food intake be reduced? How can fat people be motivated to eat less?

The finding by nutritionists that most fat people do not eat more than most thin people presents a serious challenge to the obesity paradigm. However, most obesity scientists are not aware of this finding. Obesity scientists in different fields are free to ignore one another's key findings because there is no unifying paradigm to protect the status of any finding. Those who are aware of the finding defend the paradigm by creating a specialized scientific definition of "overeating." According to behavioral psychologist Judith Rodin, "Overeating is eating enough so that you gain weight." When members of the New Haven Fat Liberation Front pointed out that chronic dieters have been known to gain weight on 800 calories per day, and asked whether her definition of overeating would apply in such situations, Rodin replied, "That's right, and that's a scientific term defined by the outcome."[9]

A different but related approach was used by nutritionist Jean Mayer to preserve the obesity paradigm in the face of his finding that, "As a group, obese adolescent girls are low calorie consumers; that is, their intakes are lower in calories than that of their non-obese peers."[10] Mayer and his co-workers found that fat teenage women who eat less are also less active than their slim peers. Decreased physical activity is a common trait of underfed people.[11] However, to ask whether fat teenagers' inactivity might be a result of underfeeding would require first conceiving that fat teenagers might be underfed. This is impossible under the guidance of the obesity paradigm, which defines them as overfed. Hence, J. Mayer concluded that, although they eat less, the fat teenagers use up even less calories than slim teenagers and so less is still too much.[12] His conclusion is good normal science, picking and choosing among evidence to elaborate on a paradigm. However, it is not the only possible conclusion.

The next logical question of normal science is to ask what role exercise plays in weight control. This question has been researched exhaustively, and the findings are inconclusive. Readers who feel that this question is worth more time should read J. S. Garrow's very cautious evaluation of the research in his book, *Energy Balance and Obesity in Man.*[13] I want to go on now to examine how the obesity paradigm is applied to fat people's health.

Milo D. Leavitt, who was Director of the Fogarty International Center for Advanced Study in the Health Sciences when the National Institutes of Health held a major obesity conference there in 1973, wrote in his preface to the published proceedings, "While there may be some controversy over the cause-and-effect relationship between obesity and ill-health in man, there can be little doubt that the life-style of affluent America has created new patterns of deranged health and that the malnutrition of obesity is a major indicator of this life-style."[14]

The controversies to which Leavitt refers will be discussed below. It is interesting that he considers obesity an indicator of affluent lifestyle. Census studies find that the most affluent Americans have the lowest percentage of members who are fat.[15] The American socioeconomic group with the highest percentage of fat members is black women below the poverty level.[16]

Regarding fat people's health, the obesity paradigm states that excess food and fat cause illness. One popular form of normal research guided by this paradigm consists of showing statistically higher rates of illness among fat people than among slim people. The problem of locating enough fat people for a statistical study is solved by finding them in clinics and weight-loss organizations. For example, Alfred Rimm's 1975 study of the ill health of 73,532 female members of the diet club TOPS (Take Off Pounds Sensibly, which sponsored Rimm's research) was mentioned to me as the last word on the controversy by a public health official in Los Angeles. The sample size was impressive. Rimm himself points out that it might not be representative of fat people in general. Yet despite this precaution, he states that the purpose of the study was to have general societal impact: to "establish the obesity problem on a firm foundation — in the same way that the cigarette-lung cancer effort in preventive medicine was established by the large American Cancer Society studies . . ." thus leading to the initiation of what Rimm calls "meaningful" prevention programs.[17]

Statistics show that certain diseases are more common among fat people than among slim people, and that very fat people are more likely to be severely ill than slightly fat people. However, attempts to show that this ill health is caused by fatness have failed, not only because of questionable sampling practices, but because many slightly fat people have terrible health and many fat people have excellent health.[18] Diseases correlated with fatness seem to be linked to some third, not identified, factor. For example, high blood pressure significantly increases the risk of coronary heart disease. Coronary heart disease is not correlated with fatness, high blood pressure is. Thus the high rates of coronary heart disease among fat people are seen as due to a third factor, high blood pressure.[19] However, attempts to show that fatness causes high blood pressure have so far failed; still another factor may be involved.

A clearer victory for the obesity paradigm would be to show by exactly what mechanism excess food and fat lead to disease. But one problem is to define the excess food. Most medical researches that I have read use the common-sense definition of overeating, assuming that fat people eat more than slim people. Thus, a recent study attempting to document a positive correlation between high calorie intakes, fatness, and high blood sugar levels (diabetes) anticipated that the more one ate, the more fat on one's body and the more sugar in one's blood. Instead, the researchers were surprised to find fatness and high levels of blood sugar correlated with below-average calorie intakes.[20]

Efforts to document the beneficial effects of weight loss have been even less successful. The situation is well described by a physician, George V. Mann: ". . . treatments of obesity . . . are so ineffectual that their effect on any disease cannot be properly evaluated. Obesity is a relatively incurable disorder. This situation makes proper clinical trials impossible."[21]

Close up, the pattern of sickness and early death among fat people degenerates into confusion. But taking a step back it reappears, clearly and terribly. Cultural reasons, as well as scientific training in the obesity paradigm make health-conscious people defend the value of weight-loss with the added moral conviction that they are trying to save lives. They see the problem. And they see solutions. But the only solutions they can envision are those that fit the paradigm, that define fat as a result of too much food and that lead to weight-loss. Evidence suggesting that weight-loss is a futile effort, or even a health-endangering process, may be seen, but cannot be *seen*. That is, the implicatons do not sink in.

Such "unseeable" evidence forms an important basis for fat liberation's theories, and I will summarize briefly here what has been discussed more fully elsewhere.[22] Repeated dieting has been shown to cause atherosclerosis in rats and is generally regarded as increasing the risk of heart attacks and strokes in humans.[23] Weight loss involves destruction of protein as well as fat tissue, and so duplicates the tissue damage of starvation.[24] Not fatness, but efforts to lose weight, have been correlated with nutritional behaviors called "compulsive eating."[25] Furthermore, dieting and social pressure to hate oneself for being fat are conspicuously absent in the histories of fat people noted for long life[26] and good health.[27]

None of this proves that fat is healthy or that dieting is harmful. Such proof (or disproof) will not be available until a large body of research has been done, guided by a theory that specifically distinguishes between the effects of being fat and the effects of chronic dieting. Such theories are anti-obesity theories, denying any inherent connection between eating and being fat. For this reason, and because they reject weight loss as the solution to fat people's miseries, they are usually regarded with incredulousness and even hostility by people steeped in the obesity paradigm.

*Rabbits and Scientific Revolution*

Anti-obesity theories arise from the view that fat people are biologically normal, meaning not the result of any error in body chemistry, behavior, etc. The obvious misery and sickness of fat people is distinguished from being fat per se, and is blamed upon political oppression, including attempts to lose weight. Thus, looking at fat people who hate the way they eat, who can't keep weight off, and who suffer a variety of disabling diseases, where obesity scientists see "ducks"—sick people killing themselves with too much food—anti-obesity scientists see "rabbits"—political victims of starvation.

The anti-obesity view leads to the following theory of fat people:

> *Theory:* Fat people are part of the natural range of human diversity. Fat and slim body types are determined by genes and only secondarily by influences of environment, including diet and activity. Fat people are capable of the full range of human nutritional behavior and needs, and are subject to the same behavioral, emotional, and physicological consequences as slim people when these needs are not met. The miseries which currently distinguish fat people from slim people are artifacts produced by a climate of ridicule and persecution in which fat people's nutritional and other needs are generally denied.

The anti-obesity theory has implications for every area of present obesity research. To begin with, researchers can attempt to verify (or disprove) the following predictions:

1 The sickness and misery of fat individuals depends not on their weight but on their sensitivity to persecution for their weight, which influences habits of nutrition, activity, etc.

2 Chronic and/or repeated dieting, in a climate of ridicule and frustration, play important and specific roles in causing most of the characteristic "fat" diseases and disorders.

3 Fat people who are born and raised free from anti-fat prejudice will exhibit patterns of health and nutrition that are statistically identical to slim people in those same settings.

4 Fat people who live where fat bodies are considered beautiful

will develop athletics, dance, and other fatness activities specifically suited to fat bodies. The proportion of fat people who engage in those activities will be statistically similar to the proportion of physically active slim people in similar but slim-valuing cultures.

5 In an "ideal" society (i.e., free from nutritional oppressions) the range in human weights will be the same as it is today. The distribution pattern will show a large proportion of weights in the middle ranges, from moderately thin to moderately fat.

6 The high rate of fatness among poor women is a combined effect of several factors: (a) natural female biology, (b) discrimination against fat people, especially fat women, and (c) metabolic compensation for chronic calorie deficits. This last point relates directly to the experience of chronic dieters: the more they try to lose weight the fatter they become, according to mechanisms I have described elsewhere.[28]

7 Fat people who stop dieting and eat whatever they want will gain weight, stabilize their weight, and recover a significant part of their health, sense of personal control over food, and self-respect.

### Radical Scientists and Fat Liberation

Scientists who are also social activists bring a new dimension to political struggles such as fat liberation. The fat liberation movement's first goal is to take the power to define fat people away from obesity scientists and restore it to fat people themselves. Scientists who share fat liberationists' view will be valuable allies. This is especially true of scientists who are also fat people. However, scientists are at present an elite group. Since those who will support fat liberation must learn how to do so by treating fat people as teachers, not as experimental subjects, the involvement of radical scientists in fat liberation is part of a broader social revolution affecting all definitions of elites.

Scientists have always been involved in struggles to improve health and nutrition. But with rare exceptions contemporary socially concerned scientists have been taught to believe the obesity paradigm and view fat people as overfed. As a result, when shown evidence of fat people's suffering, they tend to ask questions and seek solutions that I consider irrelevant, politically backward, and destructive of fat people's welfare.

Consider the following statistics for women aged 18-44, from a 1971-72 survey of health and nutrition by the United States Department of Health, Education and Welfare: [29, 30]

|                      | Below Poverty Level | | Above Poverty Level | |
|                      | BLACK | WHITE | BLACK | WHITE |
|----------------------|-------|-------|-------|-------|
| % who are fat        | 35.0  | 25.1  | 25.0  | 18.6  |
| average daily calories | 1,510 | 1,651 | 1,546 | 1,690 |

The data shows that the group of women that eats the least has the highest ratio of fat members while the group that eats the most has the lowest ratio of fat members. Furthermore, if one assumes (unjustifiably) that the fat members of each group are those who eat the most within the group, the raw cumulative data show that poor black women become fat on 1,750 calories per day while non-poor white women can eat 2,000 calories per day before becoming fat.[31] The common explanation that the affluent are slimmer because more of them eat lean meats and vegetables, while the poor fill up on starches is clearly not adequate: on 1,750 calories per day one is not filling up on anything.

These data were presented to a group of social activists as further evidence that fat people do not eat too much, and that the solution to fat people's problems lies in political activism, rather than in change of diet. But the activists refused to support fat liberation on the basis of this evidence, because they wondered whether the probable high proportion of starches in poor women's diets is what makes them fat.

That question is suggested by the obesity paradigm and can be explored through normal research. The answer is, as usual, contradictory, leaning toward "no." Poor males, for example, have a *lower* percentage of fat individuals than non-poor males.[32] More general research shows no difference in nutrient intakes of fat versus slim people.[33] The situation is obviously extremely complicated in terms of factors such as race, sex, and class, besides factors of diet and activity. What next? Ask another question?

There are always more questions; and while asking more and more complicated questions, it's easy to forget why we are concerned with the matter in the first place. Presumably, the goal of social activists is to see people healthy and happy. No one should be oppressed; everyone should have good nutrition, a chance to exercise and enjoy her body, etc. This goal ought to be shared by fat liberationists and more traditional nutrition activists alike.

In fact, the whole purpose for curing obese people is presumably to make them healthy and happy and free from discrimination and malnutritoin. But—is the elimination of fat truly pursued only as a means to social justice? Or is it really pursued only as an end in itself? The true nature of people's concern is revealed in their response to fat liberationists' call for political support.

For fat liberationists, good health, freedom from hunger, and freedom from discrimination are the *first* priorities, to be pursued directly. There is no vested interest in seeing people stay fat or get fatter. (It only appears this way because fat liberationists emphasize self-love and fat pride.) In an ideal society, fat and thin would not be issues in human relations at all. The only concern is that society should stop forcing fat people to try to live on less food and fewer calories than slim people would tolerate. Asserting on the basis of their own experience that fat people live lives of enforced deprivation is what makes fat liberation so difficult to accept—because this assertion conflicts with the obesity paradigm. (Emotional factors are involved, too, such as slim people's resistance to hearing that there is no real basis for their claims of superiority through better eating habits.)

Returning to the case of the poor fat woman whose diet is low in calories, protein, and other nutrients (whether because she can't afford nourishing food or because chronic dieting makes her crave primarily sweets): What action do you recommend?

I would recommend plenty of good food for her, and political struggle against economic and social oppressions that deprived her of good nutrition in the first place. Whether she loses or gains weight through improved nutrition should be irrelevant. That is a fat liberationist's recommendation.

But obesity science cannot conceive of good nutrition separate from being slim, and in fact it defines good nutrition as causing slimness. Therefore, obesity science recommends more research. First we must figure out why she is fat. We must keep on asking questions. And then, the right question having finally been asked, the answer will cure her and her problems will disappear without political struggle.

I want to conclude with an analogy that puts the present controversy into historical context.

As a result of the American Revolution, the problem of black slavery became a nationwide crisis of conscience. Thinking white people saw the contradiction between their rhetoric of "inalienable," natural rights and the enslavement of other humans. Scientific racism arose out of this conflict, justifying the white bourgeois man's emotional/economic/political/social investment in slavery by "proving" that blacks were not really human. However, not all contemporary scientists were so blatantly racist. One of the most liberal, the well-known physician Benjamin Rush, in a paper published in 1799, declared that "all claims of superiority of the whites over the blacks, on account of their color, are founded alike in ignorance and inhumanity." Instead, Rush saw black people's problems as medical: ". . . the color and figure of . . . negroes, are derived from a modification of that disease, which is known by the name of Leprosy."[34] Believing in medical solutions, Rush refused to recommend emancipation or any other political struggle. His priority was to find a cure for this "leprosy." He was willing to wait for as long as the research took, and once black people were made white, the slavery problem would disappear.

You may laugh (uneasily) and be thankful (?) that this was a minority view and that most educated racists were content to call blacks subhuman. I imagine a day in the 21st century when people will laugh (uneasily) to read that fatness was once called obesity. Unfortunately the medical view and obesity paradigm dominate twentieth-century thought.

The therapeutic responsibility that social activists assume toward fat people is a form of elitism fed by the elitism of the scientific profession. It is part of a historical view of "deviants" in Western society. The questions people ask about fat people have implications for the liberation struggles of all minorities. Thinking people must take pains to be sure that their questions reflect their real political values.

## NOTES

1 Richard E. Nisbett, "Starvation and the behavior of the obese," in G. Bray and J. Bethune, eds., *Treatment and management of obesity* (New York: Harper & Row, 1974), pp. 45-55.

2 Nisbett, p. 47.

3 Thomas S. Kuhn, "The structure of scientific revolutions," *International Encyclopedia of Unified Science,* 2nd ed. (Chicago: University of Chicago Press, 1970), Vol. 2, No. 2.

4 Kuhn, p. 37.

5 Kuhn, p. 24.

6 Kuhn, pp. 118-119.

7 Kuhn, p. 111.

8   George Bray, "Pharmacological approach to the treatment of obesity," in Bray and Bethune, pp. 117-131.

9   New Haven Fat Liberation Front, "The calorie controversy — who's cheating?" (New Haven, CT: Fat Liberator Publications, 1978), p. 6.

10   J. Dwyer and J. Mayer, "The dismal condition: Problems faced by obese adolescent girls in American society," in G. Bray, ed., *Obesity in perspective,* proceedings of the conference sponsored by the National Institute of Health at the John E. Fogarty International Center for Advanced Study in the Health Sciences, Oct. 1-3, 1973, DHEW Publ. #(NIH) 75-708, pp. 103-110. See especially p. 104.

11   *Congressional Record (Senate),* June 12, 1975, Report on world hunger, by Wells Klein.

12   Jean Mayer, *Overweight: Causes, cost and control* (Englewood Cliffs, NJ: Prentice-Hall, 1968), pp. 76-77.

13   J. S. Garrow, *Energy balance & obesity in man* (New York: Elsevier, 1974).

14   Milo D. Leavitt, Preface in Bray, *op. cit.*

15   "Skinny women, fat men means money, study says," *The Daily Progress* (Charlottesville, VA), Thursday, July 28, 1977, p. A7. A report of research by the University of Michigan, under Dr. Stanley Garn. The title is somewhat misleading, as the findings were that "as men go up the pay ladder to the middle range of incomes, they tend to get fatter. Other studies show men with still higher incomes are more slim." Among women, the inverse relation between weight and wealth is consistent for all classes.

16   Sidney Abraham, *et al.,* "Preliminary findings of the first health and nutrition examination survey," U.S., 1971-1972: anthropomedic & clinical findings, DHEW publ #(HRA) 75-1229, p. 16.

17   Alfred A. Rimm, *et al.,* "Relationship of obesity and disease in 73,532 weight-conscious women," *Public Health Reports* (Jan.-Feb., 1975), Vol. 90, No. 1, pp. 44-51. See especially p. 44.

18   U.S.DHEW, *Obesity and Health* (Washington, 1966), PHS Report #1485, p. 23.

19   George V. Mann, "The influence of obesity on health," Part 2, *New England Journal of Medicine* (Aug. 1, 1974), pp. 226-232. See especially pp. 226-227.

20   Harry Keen *et al.,* "Nutrient intake, adiposity, and diabetes," *British Medical Journal* (Mar. 10, 1979), pp. 655-658.

21   George V. Mann, *New England Journal of Medicine* (July 25, 1974), Vol. 291, No. 4, pp. 178-185. See especially p. 179.

22   Refers to materials from Fat Liberator Publications.

23   *Obesity and health,* p. 40.

24   George F. Cahill, Jr., "Obesity and the control of fuel metabolism," in Bray and Bethune, pp. 3-16. See also V. Mayer, "Why liberated eating?" Fat Liberator Publications.

25   J. A. Hibscher & C. Peter Herman, "Obesity, dieting, and the expression of 'obese' characteristics," *Journal of Comparative and Physiological Psychology*, Vol. 91, No. 2, pp. 374-380.

26   Julius Pomeranze, "Recurrent obesity," *New York State Journal of Medicine* (Oct. 1, 1956), pp. 3017-3020.

27   Clark Stout, *et al.*, "Unusually low incidence of death from myocardial infarction," *Journal of the American Medical Association*, Vol. 188, No. 10, pp. 845-849. See also Thom N. Lynn, *et al.*, "Prevalence of evidence of prior myocardial infarction, hypertension, diabetes and obesity in three neighboring communities in Pennsylvania," *The American Journal of the Medical Sciences* (Oct., 1967), pp. 385-391.

28   V. Mayer, "Why liberated eating?" Fat Liberator Publications.

29   Abraham, "Preliminary findings," p. 16.

30   Abraham, p. 38 (diet intake and biochemical findings), Table 5.

31   Abraham, p. 53, Table 16. According to the data, 35% of the sample of poor black women eat more than 1,750 calories per day; 18.7% of the sample of non-poor white women eat more than 2,000 calories per day.

32   Abraham, pp. 16-17.

33   M. Coll, *et al.*, "Obesity and food choices in public places," *Archives of General Psychiatry*, in press when cited in Susan C. Wolley, *et al.*, "Theoretical, practical and social issues in behavioral treatments of obesity," *Journal of Applied Behavior Analysis*, (Spring, 1979), Vol. 12, No. 1, pp. 3-25. See especially p. 6.

34   Benjamin Rush, "Observations intended to favor a supposition that the black color (as it is called) of the Negroes is derived from the Leprosy," from *Transactions*, IV (American Philosophical Society, 1799), pp. 289-297, reproduced in Winthrop F. Jordan, ed., *The Negro versus equality, 1762-1826* (McNally & Co., 1969), pp. 44-49. See especially p. 45.

# Some Thoughts on Fat

## Joan Dickenson

*A woman is hating her body.* Behind all that is written about fat stands that reality, a truth too easy to forget. Women are used to self-mutilation in the name of beauty. The extreme forms of woman-hurting, from anorexia nervosa to surgically stapling the stomach shut, may enrage and horrify us, but we rarely connect them with the things *we* do to our bodies or the self-hatred that makes us do them. We are inured to the horror; women are *supposed* to hate their bodies. Grimacing, a woman slaps at a flap of her belly or averts her eyes from her reflection; she is hating her body.

But a woman is not a two-fold thing, a mind and a body — nor is the body a prison for the mind. We *are* our bodies. Hating *them* is hating *us*. Fat is no trivial issue. The reducing diet is as American as Thanksgiving turkey, and both are symbols of conquest, of the rape of a people. *A woman is hating her body* . . .

First, my vantage points. I am a feminist, a writer, a U.S. citizen: 34, white, Jewish, middle-class, and fat. With a daughter, two sons, and a husband, I live in the woods near a small town. Our income — partly by choice — is below the poverty level.

Cigarettes lead to lung cancer and sperm lead to babies, they say. They also say food leads to fat, but I find that connection hard to see, hard to *feel*. How can a brownie, with its 250 small calories, be a potential morsel of *me?* It takes 3,500 calories to gain a pound.

I think my inability to inknow[1] these connections stems from a universal childhood lesson, a lesson so basic it is never stated. Our bodies, we learn, are unruly animals. They must be tamed. Their urges are inappropriate; their hungers are fed or denied according to someone else's will. Our tutors do not teach us to heed internal signals; instead, they list rules — eat at noon, don't pee in the closet, wear an undershirt between October and April — by which our bodies must perform. *We* are taught to control *them*. Thus we learn the all-important corollary: "I" and "my body" are separate entities, and what is good for one may be deadly to the other. We learn not to trust ourselves.

We also learn that no individual manages every aspect of her life. We give up control. Instead of mixing lard with ashes, we pay Procter & Gamble to make our soap; instead of walking, we let General Motors move us around. Instead of finding out what's happening, we listen to ABC News: thus we know only what that network, a business whose sole aim is to make money, chooses to tell us. We even let the surgeon-general and Dr. Joyce Brothers tell us what is going on inside our bellies and minds.

We call this progress, for who wants to make soap? It's hard work, and the product is harsh to the skin. In an intimacy as cold as dead flesh, we live with faceless others — corporations, media, utilities, governments. We can't keep them out of our bodies, minds, and homes, for we have learned to need what they provide. Acting always for their own benefit and never for ours, they control our life.

Simultaneously we hold the illusion that *we* control it, the peculiarly western and contemporary myth of choice. We think we can choose work, companions, and beliefs; we believe every mouthful of food represents a choice. It seems obvious that I can either sip my coffee or pour it away. And the free-will myth does contain some truth; that's why it deceives us so well.

*Can* I pour away the coffee? *Could* I be thin if I wished? Would thinness make me stronger, happier, more useful? These are the wrong questions. Discussing a hypothetical thin Joan insults the Joan who sits here writing. Look at *me:* fat and needing, fat and hurting. What would Ronald Reagan be like if he were black? Or female? Or poor? It's academic. We must (unfortunately) deal with him as he is. The least we can do is show our fat selves the same respect.

Anyway, the choice — if it is one — to be fat is not a one-time thing but a lifelong series of tiny decisions. If we don't eat the brownie at four o'clock, it will still be here at five. Unlike drugs, food can't be given up; we must eat. Women in patriarchy spend many hours in the presence of food, touching it, smelling it — and fighting it like a deadly foe. That battle is a tragedy. Imagine the benefit if all the womanly strength and energy wasted in that war were harnessed to the fight against racism. Food is our source of strength, not our enemy! Without it, we would die.

Me, I love food. I bake a blueberry crisp. As nutty crunch and plump tart berries turn to glory on my tongue, I wonder: How can something so *good* do me harm? But only my senses tell me the crisp is good. The voice of civilization, speaking from inside my head, says it will bring fat and misery. This is no poisonous corporate product, no Hostess Twinkie: I picked the berries myself, and the honey is from a neighbor's hive. Yet although I enjoy each bite, I know I am doing wrong. Moral wrong. And I'm no Puritan — I don't feel this way about other pleasures, only about eating. I can't help feeling it is immoral to be fat. Despite my rhetoric, I still avoid my image in the mirror.

On the other hand, for the first time in my life *when fat* (my weight is a perpetual yo-yo), I recently bought a beautiful, becoming outfit: russet corduroy, silky paisley. Always before, I chose clothes according to my size: colorful stylish things when thin, cheap drab coveralls when fat. For the first time, I feel the fat Joan deserves nice clothes. This is a landmark in self-respect. At last, I think, I'm getting somewhere. . . .

But that's just me. America still scorns the fat. My husband tells me his co-workers, who assess all women who pass the construction site, say of each fat one, "That object should be put to death." We need revolution — revolution in 300 million sets of eyes, ideas, and gonads — and what do we get? Sops. McCall's pattern catalog now uses fat models for half-size outfits, but beside each photo is a drawing of the same costume on a willowy creature with legs six feet long! A few feminists now allow personhood to the fat (although you don't catch them gorging to join us), but society at large still believes the fat woman is an Offense Against the Right.

*Fat Is a Feminist Issue,* by Susie Orbach, and Kim Chernin's *The Obsession: The Tyranny of Slenderness* are more than sops, although both have shortcomings. Orbach spins a sound theory about women and fat, but then uses it in service of exactly the woman-hatred she deplores. *Fat Is a Feminist Issue* grew from a mutual-help group and is "an attempt to share . . . what we learned . . . with the . . . groups and individuals who shared their compulsive-eating problems with us."[2]

> We stopped dieting. Nothing terrible happened . . . Carol (Munter) raised the central question: maybe we did not want to be thin . . . I decided I did not want to be thin . . . You were more hassled by men, you became a sex object . . . I relaxed, ate what I wanted, and wore clothes that were expressive of me . . . But . . . why was I

afraid of being thin? The things I was frightened of came into vision. I confronted them, always asking myself, How would it help to be thin? As the image of my fat and thin personality conflated, I began to lose weight . . .[3]

Eventually Orbach "stabilized" at an acceptable weight, which "turned out to be rather higher than my Twiggy-like fantasies."[4]

Orbach is not selling anything. She offers women her discovery that "non-dieting and self-acceptance might be keys to weight loss,"[5] but what's wrong with that? For one thing, she discusses only white, middle-class women and ignores economics. I'm dubious about any analysis that leaves out the factor of racism, and not only because it is useless to women of color. Just as I've come to distrust theorists who use "he" and "him" while insisting that what goes for men is true also for women (or, as more often happens, neglecting even to mention that not all "men" are male), I distrust books that say "woman" when they mean "white woman." The same goes for Orbach's omission of class. Food and money are intertwined; an analysis of the first that omits the second is obviously incomplete.

But Orbach wrote in 1978. If she were writing now, she would probably — like most middle-class white feminists — be more sensitive to issues of race and class. Leaving aside their omission, Orbach's offer of help still bothers me, and only partly because it presupposes that fat is bad. I have also come to recognize "We want to help you" as a code for "We are better than you, so — *noblesse oblige* fashion — we'll give you a bit of what makes us great."

This book doesn't come on that strong, but its more subtle signal is no less pernicious: "We want to teach you to help yourself." From workfare programs (supposedly intended to "teach welfare recipients a marketable skill"[6] but actually designed to punish them), to the instruction of African villagers in American farming methods, to weight-loss groups for women, this attitude is arrogant and patronizing and sometimes also racist, classist, and/or sexist.

A feminist can usually discount the nagging of an unsophisticated relative: "You can lose weight — just don't eat so much." It's harder to ignore the experts' theories about why we really want to be fat. We fear sex. We crave size because women are powerless in this culture. The kitchen (or our body) is the only thing we *can* control. We want to recreate a pregnancy. Our fat protects our vulnerable self. We're bored, unfulfilled. And so on.

Patronizing. Sexist: all women are alike. Racist and classist:

the same reasons apply to white women and women of color, poor and rich women. Arrogant. To say, "Aha! *This* is the reason, so women need only do *this!*" is to say, with Tarnower, Stillman, and hundreds of others, "All fat women should become thin, and *I* have found the one way to make them so. All they need to do is listen to *me.*" With diets as with patriarchal religions, since each one declares itself the One True Way, it's obvious there *is* no One True Way.*

But even if you accept that fat women should all shrink (and I don't), Orbach's approach can't work unless one does it. What of the woman who tells herself, "Hmmm — I oughta try that sometime" and goes right on eating bread and butter, feeling guiltier than ever? After all, here — at last — is the key to permanent thinness, and she isn't using it. What is *wrong* with her?

A poor creature, you may say, not worth bothering about . . . but consider. In all the other ways of patriarchal oppression, we feminists assume that the patriarchy is at fault and should change, not the individual woman. Why then, in *this* type of oppression, do we insist the victim change? Why is fat — and only fat, not low wages or incest — the victim's fault?

Take rape, one way the patriarchy keeps us down. We agree that rape must be stopped, both by changing our misogynist culture via various paths (from non-sexist childrearing to writing books) and by making women strong (through physical training, support of victims, etc.). So why don't we respond to the hatred of fat, another repression technique, in the same two ways? Why don't we try to change society's image of beauty on the one hand, and arm fat women in confidence and pride on the other? We do neither. Instead, we try to teach women *not* to be fat! Isn't this like telling a rape victim to relax and enjoy it?

The idea that fat women merely lack gumption, like the notion that welfare recipients are lazy, stems from the American tradition of the individual. "Any child can become president," it says, but we know this doesn't apply to blacks, females, Hispanics, gays, etc. We know the free-will myth is a lie in this context — but our logic fails when it comes to the fat woman. She could better herself, we insist, if she only *tried*.

I agree that fat is a problem — but *whose* problem? By stating that each woman can solve it for herself, Orbach implies — even as

---

*Orbach's approach *is* different in one important respect: it is a *women's* approach.

she lists the cultural roots of fat—that the problem is ours. Thinness is best, she says, albeit a somewhat rounder thinness than the *Vogue* variety. Thinness is best, it is a woman's duty to try for it, and therefore it is her fault if she fails. Blame the victim.

Fat *is* a problem, because it makes women miserable. But why? Not because it is intrinsically best to be thin, but because society hates fat. Women internalize that hatred. Hence our misery: It's horrible to be hated for what one is, horrible to hate oneself. Different oppressions have much in common. It's easy to see that hatred of blackness—racism—is responsible for a black slum-dweller's poverty, not blackness itself. Our conditioning makes it harder to see that hatred of fat works the same way.

Like racism, the hatred of fat is *society's* problem, *society's* defect. How did feminists figure out that rape is not the victim's fault? By listening to women, by believing their words instead of men's. If fat women trusted our bodies and defined ourselves according to our own experience, it would be clear to us that we are not sick. The sickness is in a culture that values women (like cattle, only in reverse) according to their girth. We know this is true for lesbians. *They* aren't sick; the sickness belongs to the society that says they are. (Of course, after a while members of despised groups often sicken. Living among people who hate you is enough to make anyone ill.)

My racism or homophobia is my problem and my responsibility, because it hurts people. But my fat renders me a victim, not an oppressor. Only society's hatred of it makes it a problem for me. "But racism is different," some might protest. "You can't choose your skin color, but you *can* choose to be thin." Applied to homophobia, this argument is obviously specious: whether or not lesbianism is a choice is irrelevant, the homophobic boot in the face is an equal outrage. Whether or not I choose to be fat, I *am*. Choice doesn't make it legitimate to torment me. (If I choose to be a Nazi or join the Ku Klux Klan, that's a different story.) No feminist suggests that blacks bleach their skin, or that lesbians try to love men, so why should we insist that fat women aim for thinness?

HEALTH

All this is very well, you may say, but what about health? Doesn't fat lead to heart disease and high blood pressure? Maybe*—but

---

*In *The Obsession,* Chernin argues that the stress of being fat in a fat-hating society—rather than fat itself—is the cause of our health problems.

that isn't the issue. Americans accept that cigarettes and alcohol can maim and kill their users. But—and it's a big *but*—drinkers and smokers do not suffer the total, derisive condemnation that is aimed at the fat. We may disapprove of smoking, but we don't dismiss the smoker—the individual, the person—as a weak-willed failure. Nor do we bombard the alcoholic with the ostracism and ridicule that make it so crippling to be fat in this society. We make it clear that it is smokers' and drinkers' *behavior* we object to, not the individuals themselves.

This anomaly is so basic to our thinking that it is hard to disinter and examine. The fat woman, by definition, is a slattern, a pig; the hard-drinking man just a guy with a problem, if not a romantic hero. We say of her, "Shame, shame, she's ruining her health," whereas our attitude toward the male drinker is, "Well, it's too bad, but *it's his life* to ruin."

Except in that smoke imperils nearby non-smokers and alcoholism affects relatives, the view is widely held that people should be free to destroy themselves. But not fat people! Eaters are constantly harangued by experts (in print and in person) and friends, all concerned about our health, while people with far riskier habits hear at most a mild rebuke. For every book on controlling one's intake of alcohol and tobacco, there are hundreds that tell us how to stop eating "for your health, if for no other reason." American disgust with the fat is grossly disproportionate to the risk we eaters run.

Every spinster or childfree woman has heard the insulting question, "When will I dance at your wedding?" or "When will you give me a grandchild?" Just as women are not allowed, unmolested, to choose a life free of husband and/or children, we can't choose fat and be respected for that choice. And if we insist it *is* a choice, the response is usually "Sour grapes!"

The irresistible drunk is everywhere—in books from Anne McCaffrey to Dashiell Hammett, on TV, in movies—but how many charming gluttons can you think of? I came up with only Nero Wolfe, Falstaff, and Cannon—significantly, all men. Moreover, drinkers often brag: "First I sucked up a six-pack, and then a pint of gin—boy, was I smashed!" Even smokers do it ("Wow!" Three packs a day!"); but rarely does a woman boast, "I ate a pizza, half a cake, and a can of Redi-Whip, and then . . ." If we do admit such indulgence, we whisper it with shame.

Like the pressures to marry and bear children, the universal, self-styled concern for fat women's health is rooted in the axiom that every female's first desire is to attract males. Forget for a moment the homophobia of this assumption; some lesbians, too, agree that fat is ugly. Leave aside the reason it is assumed (contrary to the evidence) that fat always turns men off. What's left is the idea that a woman may not simply *be* and *do* but must also *appear*. Pure misogyny, this: women are things whose value depends on how well their honey pulls in the flies. (This view doesn't ascribe much humanity to men, either!)

The fat-is-unhealthful argument should not be attacked on its merits. Why let the enemy choose the battleground? We might just as well descend to anti-abortionists' level and talk about whether the fetus is a person — or let racists point to the low percentage of blacks in the Reagan administration as proof that blacks are inferior. First, such questions are loaded; besides, they shouldn't be asked at all. Ask, rather, *why* are racists so eager to prove blacks inferior? *Why* are Americans so determined to prove it is immoral (i.e., self-destructive) to be fat?

## THE OBSESSION

Like Orbach's book, Kim Chernin's *The Obsession: The Tyranny of Slenderness* ignores the economic roots of fat and excludes women of color and poor women.

> . . . a woman I have observed over the years . . . At my daughter's school, in a neighborhood gourmet food store, at the opera, or at the opening of an art exhibit, I would often (see her)[7]

Such calm assumption of privilege! Poor women meet at the discount store, the laundermat, or the town dump — if not in the food stamp line.

Nevertheless, this is a remarkable book. Chernin connects the adoration of thinness with both child pornography and second-wave feminism. It is no coincidence, she argues, that as feminism grew, the ideal American female became younger and thinner: Mae West . . . Marilyn Monroe . . . Twiggy . . and now, in 1980, Christine Olman (at twelve, the hottest model in the fashion industry).[8]

> . . . a culture based on the suppression of women will be inclined . . .
> to turn away from whatever is powerful in women. The image in
> fashion magazines . . . reflects this turning away from female power,
> but so also does the masculine retreat from grown women as erotic
> images. This retreat runs a parallel course to the women's (weight)

reduction movement and expresses an identical fear of female power.[9]

I would take this one step farther. I believe that our culture's admiration of thin women culminates logically in admiration of the *male* body. Chernin says the anorexic girl starves away her budding curves to avoid becoming a woman; I maintain she is trying to become a boy. Who could blame her? We are all taught that "boys are better; girls are meant to be mothers."[10]

> We can imagine . . . what it means to this girl, confronted with the coming of her own womanhood to her body, that the round shape of her mother is never seen in a position of power or respect, that this roundness is only seen serving dinners and this abundance is only known clearing up dishes, and this fullness is only encountered telling people to wear their galoshes. That in our culture roundness rarely speaks in a poetic voice, abundance does not philosophize, nor fullness speculate about the meaning of existence; that it cleans the toilet and nags the children and pesters the husband.[11]

Hatred of fat stems from hatred of women. We're all supposed to strive for a long-and-thin ideal, but who exemplifies this ideal? A man, of course; specifically a young man.

> We are not all supposed
> to look like undernourished fourteen year
> old boys, no matter what the fashions
> say.[12]

Indeed, the whole American notion of beauty reflects hatred of women. Our media all tell us, "Women are not good as they are; women should be dissatisfied with themselves; *women must change.*" Who says a willowy blonde with smooth curls and sooty eyes is more beautiful than a chunky brunette with spiky hair and monochromatic features? Newspapers say so. Magazines, television, movies. But on whose authority? These media are in business to sell. They exist to make a profit. Thus they plug the image that causes women to spend the greatest number of dollars on their advertisers' products. Obviously, therefore, this ideal must be as different as possible from the largest possible number of real women.

American beauty images are racist as well as sexist. Black women (along with most other women of color) have been oppressed by American beauty standards since slavery time. Says Mary Helen Washington:

The subject of the black woman's physical beauty occurs with such frequency in the writing of black women that it indicates they have been deeply affected by the discrimination against the shade of their skin and the texture of their hair. In almost every novel or autobiography written by a black woman, there is at least one incident in which the dark-skinned girl wishes to be either white or light-skinned with "good" hair. [13]

Toni Morrison says in *The Bluest Eye* that the concept of physical beauty is one of the most destructive ideas in the history of human thought . . . the idea of beauty as defined by white America has been an assault on the personhood of the black woman. [14]

Skin color and hair. What of black women and fat? Washington warns writers against trying to counteract the degraded image of black women in past fiction by idealizing them now. Suffering is *not* romantic; hardship does *not* ennoble. But black women do have a tradition of strength, of power in both mind and body, quite unlike the white image of a lady who is tiny, delicate — and physically helpless. Although white writers have romanticized that black tradition, black women's own words confirm that it exists.

Black females are socialized . . . to become strong, independent women who, because of precarious circumstances growing out of poverty and racism, might have to eventually become heads of their own households. Black mothers teach their female offspring to perform adult tasks . . . when they are still in their preadolescent years. [15]

Joyce Ladner is not speaking here of bodily strength alone. However, compared to Chernin's words on "roundness," in which the white middle-class mother is seen as powerless, this passage shows the contrast between the way black and white girls feel about their mothers. Black youngsters have a model of adult female competence — and power is next to size. Compare the way white girls are taught:

> He asks you for a date and you go out for a spin.
> The motor fails and he just wears a helpless grin.
> Don't bat your eyes and say, "What a romantic spot we're in —"
> Just leap out, crawl under the car, say it's the gasket,
> and fix it in two seconds flat with a bobby pin.
> That's a sure way to lose a man. [16]

My point is not that black women are unaffected by the American cult of thinness — they are not* — but that they do at least have an alternative.

In black women's fiction, one rarely finds black counterparts of the pedestaled white lady. Why?

> [T]he black woman was not permitted the dubious luxury of being feminine. She was not sheltered or protected from hard work or the lash. She toiled beside her man in the struggle for existence.[17]

Instead, we find capable heroes like Janie in Zora Neale Hurston's *Their Eyes Were Watching God,* who has enough competence to survive a hurricane and then shoot her beloved Teacake when he gets rabies and attacks her in madness. Janie is thin — but strong.

Many fictional white women have inner strength, from Jane Austen's Elizabeth Bennet and Charlotte Brontë's Jane Eyre to Agatha Christie's Miss Marple and Marge Piercy's Vida — but few have physical power, much less size.** White protagonists are of necessity thin. Not so Gracie Mae Still, in Alice Walker's story, "1955, or, You Can't Keep a Good Woman Down" (*Ms Magazine,* March, 1981). Gracie Mae is *fat.* In 1956, when the story begins, she loses ten pounds because of her blood pressure, but in 1968 she says:

> I'll never see 300 pounds again and I've just about said (excuse me) fuck it . . . Aside from the fact that they say it's unhealthy, my fat ain't never been no trouble. Mens always have loved me. And fat like I is, I looks distinguished. You see me coming and know somebody's *there.*[18]

What white character ever talks like this? In white fiction (including TV and movies), fat characters are bit-parts — mothers or teachers or comic relief — and they are *never* successfully sexual beings.*** When Gracie Mae's feelings change, it is not because she has finally bowed to the patriarchy's contempt but because she defines herself:

---

*See, for example, poems in *Black Sister: Poetry by American Black Women, 1746 – 1980,* ed. by Erlene Stetson, especially "Woman Poem" by Nikki Giovanni and "There Is a Woman in This Town" by Patricia Parker.

**A stunning exception is Araminty Brown, the mother in Enid Bagnold's *National Velvet,* who swam the English Channel in her youth. In maturity, enormously fat, she is one of the strongest fictional mothers I've met — but then, she isn't the protagonist. Constanza, hero of Marge Piercy's *Woman on the Edge of Time* (see Note 1) is another exception, but she's only slightly fat.

***A few examples: Rachel Lynde in L. M. Montgomery's *Anne of Green Gables*

1977 — I finally faced up to the fact that my fat is the hurt I don't admit, not even to myself, and that I been trying to bury it from the day I was born. But also when you git real old, to tell the truth, it ain't as pleasant. It gits lumpy and slack. Yuck . . . Lord such a procession of salads and cottage cheese and fruit juice![19]

Only rarely do white characters even *be* fat, let alone talk about it. Few authors consider a woman's struggle with her weight important enough to write about. In this, Walker is revolutionary. She also created Mama Johnson, hero of "Everyday Use":

I am a large big-boned woman with rough, man-working hands. In the winter I wear flannel nightgowns to bed and overalls during the day. I can kill and clean a hog as mercilessly as a man. My fat keeps me hot in zero weather.[18]

She dreams she is reunited with her daughter on television, where "I am the way my daughter would want me to be; a hundred pounds lighter, my skin like an uncooked barley pancake.[19] The simile screams of scorn for her daughter's wish for a slim, light-skinned mother. This woman respects herself: size and physical strength are good to have. And rare indeed in white fiction is the woman with either.*

---

Writing this has been rich with resonance, with echoes: women's voices reciting recipes, offering food, cheering on the dieter (or tempting her). Food has been the context of every friendship, from the fifth grade, when my pals and I baked peculiar cakes after school, to the cooperative — and argumentative — concocting of curries with my sister (now dead), to my last birthday, when a friend brought me a carrot cake, my favorite.

Other resonances hurt: trying on clothes, a fat child/teenager/adult before the merciless three-way mirror. Gobbling countless

---

series (read by millions of 20th-century girls) and Hattie Allspaugh in Lillian Budd's *Land of Strangers,* both comical, nosy gossips with hearts of gold; Val in Marilyn French's *The Women's Room,* who is fat, outspoken, sexual, and consequently doomed; and Myra Henshawe, in Willa Cather's *My Mortal Enemy,* an aging siren whose plumpness helps illustrate the erosion of her charm.

*Other black novelists portraying fat women positively (or at least neutrally) include Margaret Walker (see the cook in *Jubilee*) and Anne Allen Shockley (see Mattie, the Congresswoman in "Play It but Don't Say It," in *The Black and White of It*).

bowls of ice cream, without pleasure—I might as well have enjoyed them! The despair I felt upon giving away my favorite jeans, knowing I would never be that thin again. It *was* nice to be a size 12, but it didn't last long . . .

Then there's the voice that argues with every sentence I write. "This essay is an elaborate rationalization," it sneers, "a pathetic self-justification. You could lose weight if you tried. You're just too lazy, too gluttonous, too flabby, too self-destructive, too sick." This voice has haunted me since age eight, the voice of authority, of the experts, the cumulative voice of mother husband friend sister magazine doctor children television . . . the voice of a hating self.

Shush a minute, I tell them all. I listen for my own voice. What do I really feel? Well, I love to eat. Eating is my re-creation, one of my major pleasures. I love to cook, too—to experiment with new foods: from homemade tofu (a success) to porcupine stew (the porcupine was free, and surprisingly good) to beet preserves, which I won't try twice. Eating is a refuge; food never fails me. If all this is going to make me fat, well . . . so be it.

I also hear a lifelong resentment: *Why me?* Why can't I be one of those lucky creatures of whom people say, "She can eat anything and stay thin?" Or, more likely, *"He* can eat anything . . ." Not that I wish I'd been born male. If male gender is what it takes to be thin, I would rather have my female flesh, every last pound of it. I have great respect for wisdom, for sight—and these come from being on the bottom. People of color know whites, women know men, and colonized people know their governors better than those in power know their victims. To oppressors, a victim is only that— not human, not like *us*.

It may be a case of making lemonade with an unwanted lemon, but I tell myself that if I were naturally thin, my sight would lack that extra dimension. True, in other ways I am an oppressor: as a white, as a person raised with money, as a U.S. citizen. Those who are victimized by me in those personae can argue, with justice, that I can't possibly inknow *their* oppression. Still, being oppressed in one way opens our eyes to other injustice.

Feminism should help us see the pain of all victims, including those we might rather not know of: the rapist, the Taiwanese who—for a wage of pennies—assembled our lovely new tape deck. And oppressions overlap. Cutting social programs hurts the colored, the female, the poor, the cities, the northeast, the elderly— so if you're a 75-year-old Latina, living on Social Security, in Buffalo . . .

Moreover, conflict among victims benefits only The Man on top. There he sits, delighted that he doesn't have to divide and conquer since we're doing it ourselves. We do it every time we draw back from a woman because she's fat, every time we choose a sexual partner on the basis of patriarchal beauty standards.

No one will be free as long as one Native American child dies from malnutrition, as long as one Third World farmer toils in pain breathing poisons that Nestlé isn't allowed to use here — to grow our coffee. Similarly, we can't escape the oppression of fat women just by becoming thin ourselves — or even by making peace with our own flesh. (Compare the executive who kicks away her sisters' hands on the ladder rungs below her.) No. All oppressions have to go. And oppression will be around as long as one person has power over another, be it power to hire and fire, power to rape, or power to make someone think she's ugly.

Black lesbians argue that homophobia strengthens white patriarchy, rather than the black community.* In the same way, scorn of fat women among feminists (whether or not accompanied by an attempt to "help" them become thin) reinforces misogyny. For if we love our sisters, we love the women they are — not the women we think they should become.

*2 p.m., February 4, 1983*

---

*See *This Bridge Called My Back: Writings by Radical Women of Color*, Cherríe Moraga and Gloria Anzaldúa, eds.; *Top Ranking: Racism and Classism in the Lesbian Community*, Joan Gibbs and Sara Bennett, eds.; and *But Some of Us Are Brave*, Gloria Hull, Barbara Smith, and Patricia Bell Scott, eds.

## NOTES

1 Marge Piercy coins the word "inknow," which I define as "to know with the whole being," in her novel *Woman on the edge of time* (Brooklyn: Fawcett Crest, 1976).

2 Susie Orbach, *Fat is a feminist issue* (New York: Berkley, 1978), p. xv.

3 Orbach, p. xv.

4 Orbach, p. xiii.

5 Orbach, p. xiii.

6 Press release from the Allegany County (New York) Board of Legislators.

7 Kim Chernin, *The obsession: The tyranny of slenderness* (New York: Harper and Row, 1981), p. 77.

8   Chernin, p. 95.

9   Chernin, p. 108.

10   Letty Cottin Pogrebin, *Growing up free* (New York: McGraw-Hill, 1980).

11   Chernin, p. 160.

12   Marge Piercy, "Cats like angels," in *The moon is always female* (New York: Alfred A. Knopf, 1981).

13   Mary Helen Washington, ed., *Black-eyed Susans: Classic stories by and about Black women* (Garden City, NY: Anchor Books, 1975), p. xv.

14   Washington, p. xvii.

15   Joyce Ladner, "Labeling Black children: Some mental health implications," in *Urban Research Review,* Howard University Institute for Urban Affairs and Research (Spring, 1979), Vol. 5, No. 3, p. 3. Quoted in Gloria I. Joseph and Jill Lewis, *Common differences: Conflicts in black and white feminist perspectives* (Garden City, NY: Anchor Press, 1981), p. 95.

16   "100 easy ways to lose a man," in *Wonderful town,* lyrics by Betty Comden and Adolf Green (New York: Chappell, 1953).

17   Washington, p. xxi.

18.   Alice Walker, "Everyday use," in *In love and trouble* (New York: Harcourt, 1971).

19   Walker.

# Writings from the Fat Underground

## FAT LIBERATION MANIFESTO
### Judy Freespirit & Aldebaran

1   WE believe that fat people are fully entitled to human respect and recognition.

2   WE are angry at mistreatment by commercial and sexist interests. These have exploited our bodies as objects of ridicule, thereby creating an immensely profitable market selling the false promise of avoidance of, or relief from, that ridicule.

3   WE see our struggle as allied with the struggles of other oppressed groups against classism, racism, sexism, ageism, capitalism, imperialism, and the like.

4   WE demand equal rights for fat people in all aspects of life, as promised in the Constitution of the United States. We demand equal access to goods and services in the public domain, and an end to discrimination against us in the areas of employment, education, public facilities and health services.

5   WE single out as our special enemies the so-called "reducing" industries. These include diet clubs, reducing salons, fat farms, diet doctors, diet books, diet foods and food supplements, surgical procedures, appetite suppressants, drugs and gadgetry such as wraps and "reducing machines."

WE demand that they take responsibility for their false claims, acknowledge that their products are harmful to the public health, and publish long-term studies proving any statistical efficacy of their products. *We make this demand knowing that over 99% of all weight-loss programs, when evaluated over a five-year period, fail utterly, and also knowing the extreme, proven harmfulness of repeated large changes in weight.*

6  WE repudiate the mystified "science" which falsely claims that we are unfit. It has both caused and upheld discrimination against us, in collusion with the financial interests of insurance companies, the fashion and garment industries, reducing industries, the food and drug industries, and the medical and psychiatric establishments.

7  WE refuse to be subjugated to the interests of our enemies. We fully intend to reclaim power over our bodies and our lives. We commit ourselves to pursue these goals together.

FAT PEOPLE OF THE WORLD, UNITE!  YOU HAVE *NOTHING* TO LOSE. . . .

*November, 1973*

© Copyright 1973 by the Fat Underground

## FAT WOMEN AND WOMEN'S FEAR OF FAT
### LYNN MABEL-LOIS & ALDEBARAN

When Mary went looking for a job, she tried no further than the back office. She did not even bother to inquire about many typical "women's jobs" advertised in her newspaper — the place that wanted a receptionist, or the place that wanted a "gd-lkg gal to run sml ofc," or the place that wanted someone to "type 55 wpm for a honey of a boss," or the place that wanted a "saleswoman able to deal with the public." The wording of all these offers suggested that they required a sex-appealing look, a front office appearance, chic, and class. Mary is fat.

When Joan missed her period two months in a row and went for a pregnancy test, the first thing the doctor said to her was, "Who in his right mind would want to make *you* pregnant?" Then he refused to examine her. Joan is fat.

When Katherine was raped, the police laughed at her and refused to take down the report. Katherine is fat.

Mary, Joan, and Katherine have tried to stop being fat. Like over 99% of others who try to lose weight, they have failed, or regained the weight within a year or two. When they are denied employment, denied medical care, and denied human respect, they blame themselves. They continue to see their fatness as a personal problem, a unique inadequacy. They consider themselves to be failures as women. It is not surprising that, several years

53

ago, the *Ladies Home Journal* published a survey in which they had found that American women are twice as afraid of getting fat as they are of "all the hate and killing in the world." Being fat means a life of ridicule, rejection, starvation, self-hatred and guilt.

The popular belief that fat people eat too much has led to the conclusion that fat people choose to be fat and therefore ought to suffer the consequences. Actually, this public faith that fat people get that way by lacking will power or by gorging themselves on goodies is without foundation. Ample evidence from nutritional, physiological and genetic research supports the view point that fat people are fat by biology, not choice, and can't effectively get thin. But to dwell on this question would be to miss the point of this article. For here we want to show how the persecution of fat people, under the assumption that they *choose* to be fat, is particularly sexist. Society punishes fat men and women by taking their sexuality away. Fat women are punished most severely. For, in a society where women are chiefly sex objects, a woman's sexuality is really all that she has to bargain with in the first place.

It's considered "natural" for a woman to want to look as attractive to men as she possibly can. With all the beauty aids available for a price, one assumes that any woman worth her estrogens ought to be at least "pretty." With all the low-calorie food substitutes and all the reducing aids available, one assumes that any fat woman ought to be able to lose weight and keep it off.

With cosmetics, diets, and charm courses, women are required to make themselves over to please men. Fat in women is considered especially reprehensible because it suggests that the fat woman is more interested in indulging *her* appetites than in indulging a man's.

She who "chooses" to be unattractive to men thereby loses her right to benefit from men's attention. In this, though, is perhaps the essense of justification for the enormous discrimination against a fat woman: *she has no right to benefit from men's attention.* Therefore she has no right to obtain attractive clothes, no right to be seen at parties or other social gatherings where men go to meet attractive women. She has no right to work in offices which are owned and controlled by men. She has no right to be pregnant because she has no right to be loved by a man. She has no right to complain about sexual mistreatment because she has presumably forfeited her sexuality by being fat. Her sexuality is defined as her appeal to men.

This description may seem too extreme, too absolute. It is based not on real life but on media mythology. In the media, men who are shown as successful in sex obtain women who are slim. In real life, men who are attracted to fat women are often ashamed to admit this attraction because people would think that their sexual values are perverted. Fat women are not entirely rejected by men; fat women do get jobs, babies, and breathing space. This is more the case among poorer people, including racial minorities, where men will accept a "lesser" grade of women than the media mythology urges upon them. A middle- or upper-class fat woman's survival is always in spite of tremendous odds. She must work twice as hard as a slim woman, and frequently for scraps.

Thus in the position of fat women is shown the true position of woman in our society. Without the pretense of chivalry — for fat women are presumed not to deserve it — women have nothing but scorn.

Fear of fat is a means of social control used against all women. The current ideal woman's body is so thin that many women with quite average figures consider themselves to be too fat. A woman is warned that if she "lets herself go," her husband will leave her, she will have no lovers, and she will be miserable.

Most people seem to gain weight as they grow older. On men a certain amount of paunch is acceptable, but the typical aging woman experiences her weight gains as a terrible blow. If she must be fiftyish, at least let her not be fat! The message of the advertising media is clear on this point. "Eat on the young side," one ad says. "Keep your youthful figure and keep your husband," is the clear implication. In most cases her struggle against weight is as doomed as her struggle against age. If her husband actually does leave her, she is likely to rationalize that she deserved to lose him, since fat, presumably, is a deliberate offense.

Women are the chief targets of the ten-billion-dollar reducing industry. Pictures of skinny women are on the boxes and cans of saccharined peaches, liquid diet, sugarless soda pop in the supermarkets. Men are never shown, except maybe as admirers of this glamorous woman. Not that men don't go on diets — they do. But the privilege that men have over women is reflected in these weight-loss advertisements. The only weight-loss ads that are specifically designed to appeal to fat men are those advertising medical treatment by a doctor. The message is that fat women are supposed to lose weight by limiting their own appetites, while fat men rate the consideration of "experts."

Women usually quote sex appeal as their goal in losing weight. Men usually quote the more "serious" reason of health. (Sex-appeal is very serious for women — a matter of survival.) Doctors have told the public for years that fat is unhealthy. But what has generally been overlooked is that medical studies suggesting the danger of fat have, almost without exception, been done on fat people who are either dieting, or thinking they ought to be dieting, or hating themselves for not dieting, or any combination of the preceding. There is no clear information: Are the high blood pressure, the cholesteroled arteries, the heart disease, the kidney failures due to being fat; or are they due to the stresses of living a persecuted, hated life, and undergoing frequent and prolonged periods of starvation?

Losing weight is not a body change on the order of curling hair or putting on make-up. It is only accomplished by prolonged starvation. This is an ordeal for any body, fat or thin. It leads to malnutrition and all its known and well-publicized side effects: nervousness, loss of hair, complexion problems, fatigue, debilitation, increased susceptibility to disease, physical collapse and acute depression — not to mention the conditions currently blamed on "obesity" but possibly due more to persecution of obesity. An estimated 27,000 people died in one recent year directly from dieting. Countless others die from related effects.

Women get hooked on diet pills. We've all heard about the middle-class junkie. When they go off the pills, they may experience lethargy, insatiable hunger, and depression, leading to even greater weight gains.

Until recently, doctors in the United States tried to discourage average-sized women from gaining more than a minimal amount of weight during pregnancy. They still try to encourage fat women to lose weight during pregnancy. It's not unusual for such doctors to refuse to treat fat pregnant women altogether. They claim that fat women are prone to difficult delivery and to toxemia. But, as a 1970 U.S. Public Health Service Report pointed out, toxemia in pregnancy is more common in women who do not get adequate medical care, and is completely unrelated to weight (except that fat women are often refused medical care until the moment of crisis). The report went on to blame insufficient weight *gains* during pregnancy as a prime reason for the high infant mortality rate in this country compared with other countries.

Doctors' refusal to treat fat pregnant women on the grounds of high risk during delivery is no more justified than their refusal based on toxemia. Considering the difficulties of losing weight, doctors would be more successful looking for a way to deliver fat women of their babies safely than trying to get fat women to reduce while pregnant. But then the burden would be upon themselves, not upon the women. In fact, feminists working with women's health problems have seriously criticized medical obstetrical practices as harmful to women and based on doctors' convenience only.

It may be hard for some readers to accept that dieting is dangerous. We have been taught all our lives that fat is not only ugly, it is unhealthy. Women who lose weight frequently report feeling better simply because, for as long as they can keep the weight off, they are not persecuted. They feel pleasure in their bodies because they are not ashamed of them. Society makes it almost impossible for a fat woman to experience the pleasures her body can give her. It is as if, because men are not supposed to enjoy our bodies, we are not supposed to enjoy them either.

If dieting were not so much a woman's problem, would the dangers of dieting have been so little publicized? Would the abuses of fat people by medical professionals have been prevented? One wonders. Weight loss is a multi-billion-dollar business, and it's women who pay. Perhaps the media silence about the abuses of fat people is part of a tendency to ignore and trivialize women's health problems, to make them subservient to fashion and custom.

## REFERENCES

Bruch, Hilde. *The importance of overweight.* New York: W. W. Norton & Co., 1957.

Fineberg, Seymour K. "The realities of obesity and fad diets." *Nutrition Today.* July-August, 1972.

Grosswirth, Marvin. *Fat pride: A survival handbook.* New York: Jarrow Press, 1971.

Louderback, Llewellyn. *Fat power.* New York: Hawthorn, 1970.

Mayer, Jean. *Overweight: Causes, cost and control.* Englewood Cliffs, NJ: Prentice Hall, 1968.

*Obesity and health.* US DHEW, 1966.

United States Public Health Service Report (November 1970, Vol., 85, No. 11, p. 964.

# 2. Growing Up: Memories of fat women's lives . . .

# *fat in a blue tu-tu*

## Kate Allen

dance lessons.
it was the thing
for young girls then.
leotards, soft slippers,
toe shoes cotton-stuffed.
i performed
with the rest.
(in a group of whirling
glitter costumes one fat girl
is not noticed.)

then the teacher said "duet."
i, self-blind, trained,
straining to move in unison
with my partner's slender form.

one day, as we twirled
toward each other,
i saw how it would be:
she, graceful, gliding toward me,
me, fat in a blue tu-tu,
waltzing toward her
like a hippo bearing down
on a reed.

i saw myself then —
my sad body
sagging into the years,
and had pity on it:
i stilled the dancer in me
and blinded myself
to her tears.

# "We'll worry about that when you're thin."

## Lynn Mabel-Lois

I suppose if I had been born a few years later than I was, I would have found it very exciting to be the only one in fifth grade legally on rainbow pills. However, having the fortune or misfortune to be in elementary school at the end of the '50s, I was extremely embarrassed at having to take those pretty colored diet pills. I learned to swallow pills without water because I was too embarrassed to ask permission to go to the water fountain. I knew I was not really sick, and I didn't want my friends to feel I was sick because I was fat. If you take pills you are sick, if you are sick you are "different"; to be "different" is to be as good as dead. Children are programmed by the adult world very early to be critical of and stay away from "different" people. To be fat and taking pills makes you twice removed from the world. I was not a particularly savvy child, but it didn't take a lot of savvy to know that I was left out of activities and friendships because I was fat, and, to extrapolate from that, that if I were to be any more "different" I might scare off the few friends I had.

I took diet pills off and on from age six or seven to age twenty. I spent most of adolescence either climbing walls with the nervousness the pills gave me or deeply depressed when I went off the pills. I have had almost every kind of diet pill there is, including "thyroid" pills given to me at age nine by a clinic doctor who for some unknown reason decided to give me placebos. I know they were placebos because at age nine I was so tired of the diet merry-go-round that I tried to commit suicide.

It happened this way: I had paid my weekly visit to the clinic and seen my doctor. I hadn't lost any weight since the last visit, and I knew for a fact that the "thyroid" pills he was giving me were not helping me. By that time I had had enough experience with pills to be extremely aware of their effect on my body. Those "thyroid" pills had no effect whatsoever.

In my nine-year-old innocence, I told the doctor that the pills weren't doing anything, and that I was still hungry. That was the day I discovered what doctors really think of fat people. This adult white male began screaming at me, called me a fat pig, told me that I was hopeless, that I was weak, a stupid animal, that I deserved to be fat, that it disgusted him to look at me, and didn't I even realize how disgusting I was, was I that stupid? It was a vicious, screaming tirade that paralyzed me with fright and guilt. I believed every word he said. I had been hearing much the same, although spoken more calmly, by every doctor I had been to since I was four. I saw my life was set out for me: to always be hungry, to always be an object of disgust, something less than human, and to always be a failure. I had been trying unsuccessfully to lose weight for six years and I was still in elementary school. How could I expect to ever live a normal life?

The crowning blow came when I got home and my mother and I had a fight over my friends. She considered them unsuitable because they were much younger than I. I couldn't find the courage to tell her that none of the older kids would play with me because I was fat. I went up to my bedroom, crying uncontrollably, and took my entire month's supply of pills. I thought that if I died I could finally be rid of the guilt of being fat, and I hoped that my mother and, mostly, my doctor would feel guilty at causing my death. I lay down on my bed and waited to die. Two hours later, I didn't even have a headache or an upset stomach. That day I learned what the word "placebo" meant, and I learned that doctors lie.

I continued to go to different diet doctors because my mother, a fat woman, knew how difficult life is for fat women and she wanted me to be spared the kind of persecution she had gone through. I had little interest in losing weight again until I was fifteen and began to feel completely locked out of the social scene because my fat, of course, prevented me from having a boyfriend. I went to my G.P. and got a little number called Adipex. My mother also went, and we got identical prescriptions. This time I lost 85 pounds, most of my friends, my resistance to disease, my entire nervous system, and my personhood. I was thin and pretty and high as a kite all through ninth and tenth grades. I took five or six pills a day, more on "difficult" days, i.e., days when I woke up hungry or had a party to go to. My mother took one-half a pill. I took her pills, so that we both had to get our prescriptions filled three times as often as should have been necessary. The doctor noted that we were using up the pills very rapidly but said, "It's more important that you lose weight. We'll worry about the pills when you lose all your weight."

Finally, I could stand it no more. I stopped taking the pills completely and spent several months so depressed I cried almost constantly. Without the pills, I got hungry like normal people, and ate like normal people, which was death to me, since my body was so messed up from years of starvation and pill-taking that if I went over a thousand calories a day I gained a pound.

I started gaining back weight and went to a doctor who was very popular among my classmates. If you didn't lose weight every week, he yelled at you until you cried and promised to be good. I, however, was too sophisticated for this to be effective. I had had several screamers since that first one when I was nine. However, he had an incredibly good stock of pills, and when I told him about having been hooked on Adipex, he found a suitable substitute. I'll never forget his back room — it was literally crammed with huge plastic jars of brightly colored pills, lining the shelves, sitting on the floor, the desk, everywhere. I got my pills and lost weight, got hooked again, began to lose my hair, stopped going and gained weight.

In my senior year, I got nervous when prom time began to be talked of, and paid $100 to a doctor for shots I was to get every day, which would magically make me lose weight. The shots were to be combined with a 500-calorie diet and — you guessed it — more pills. I lost weight, got a date for the prom, and got dizzy a lot in school.

I decided enough was enough — I was not going to take any more pills. I went to a psychiatrist, since I learned from my more well-read friends that as a fat woman I was by definition mentally sick. The psychiatrist said he would work with me only if I went to a diet doctor in addition to seeing him. I agreed, determined to lose weight without pills. The diet doctor immediately offered me my choice of pills and I, firmly but with great shame, told him, "I've been addicted to pills. I cannot take them any more without becoming addicted again, and I fought too hard to break that dependence to go back to it."

He said, "We'll worry about your being addicted or not when you get thin."

"I don't think you understand. I've been through this before, losing weight on pills and then having to deal with the horror of being without them."

He said again, "We'll worry about that when you're thin."

I felt my anger rising, and as I opened my mouth to tell him what I thought of his methods, he cleared his throat and said, "I see you've been referred by a psychiatrist." The put-down was unmistakable. The reason I got hooked was that I was unstable, disturbed, crazy. Guilt. He was the doctor; he was right, of course. I moved out of the area before I could become "cured." I was still fat.

College was a bad time in my life. I was having trouble at home, trouble with my boyfriend, money trouble, and I hated the school where I was. I developed headaches so severe that I literally couldn't move when I got one. I knew it was a reaction to stress, but I had no money for a psychotherapy "cure." I went to a doctor to get a prescription for tranquilizers or Darvon, a pain-killer. The doctor gave me prescriptions for both and emptied all his diet pill samples out of his drawers and gave them to me, unasked.

"Am I supposed to take these and the tranquilizers and Darvon at the same time?"

"No, take the diet pills in the morning and the tranquilizers later in the morning, and the Darvon as needed."

I had taken great pains to give this man my history of "addiction," at great cost to my self-esteem. I had admitted a "weakness" and now he was ignoring it.

"These diet pills are uppers. The tranquilizers and the Darvon are downers. So you're telling me to take uppers and downers."

"Yes."

"I can't do that. It's dangerous, physically for one thing, to mix these drugs. Secondly, I told you once before that I've been addicted to diet pills."

"We'll worry about that when you're thin."

"If I'm not dead first."

I paid my bill and took the pills and the headaches went away and sometimes so did the feeling in my extremities. The day I left college I threw away all the pills. The weight came back but the headaches never did.

The only benefit I ever got from diet pills was that when the drug scene became popular, I was already hip. I knew all the slang and what dosage was good for a high, and I had developed such a tolerance to the pills that I could go to parties and pop them all night long and remain apparently unaffected. I got a reputation for being very cool. I was also very useful, because, although by now I rarely took amphetamines, I could walk into almost any doctor's office and get a prescription for any upper we wanted. If we were traveling anywhere, I carried the pills, on the theory that, if we were ever caught, my weight would justify their possession. I never understood what my friends got out of taking amphetamines.

# Fat Memories from My Life

## Terre Poppe

Today I know I am a beautiful, strong, fat dyke and I really love myself at least 70 percent of the time. (Given I'm 33 years old, this 70-percent recovery is wonderful after so many years of self-hatred.) I have learned that my story is shared by other wimmin and that I am also unique. Because of this, I am sharing some of my fat memories in this article. Realize that these are only *some* memories — for each one I share here, there are many, many others in my active and inactive memory. Know also that I was afraid to write this, but that in the writing, I am beginning to accept and love who I was in the past, which is only increasing my self-love now.

---

I was a big baby, weighing almost 10 pounds at birth. This pleased my Iowa rural town and farm relatives for they saw it as a sign of healthiness. I was encouraged to eat. In my Swedish-German family a fat baby was a form of wealth and prosperity. Since we were fairly poor, and my older brother had been tiny, I was especially appreciated and loved.

This sense of love and appreciation lasted for several years, probably until my immediate family moved from Iowa to Santa Fe, New Mexico, the summer between my 1st and 2nd grades. Santa Fe is the first place I remember being called "Fatty." There was one other girl in my class who was even fatter than me. I used to join the others in tormenting her; I wanted desperately to fit in and make friends. Instead, the kids would often switch from taunting her to taunting me.

One of my worst experiences in that school had to do with the special education class. There was one class of kids with various mental and physical impairments — all ages put together in one special classroom. I was frequently told that I should be in that class because I was so fat, and I was shoved into the line of special ed kids when we'd line up in the playground to go back into the building.

It was during those years that I toughened up, started beating up other kids, shut down my own feelings as much as possible, and was generally quite unhappy.

My parents split up when I was in 4th grade. My dad moved to Albuquerque, and my mom had even less time to give attention to any of us kids. (She had to work two part-time jobs because she had no marketable skills and no one would hire her full-time.) My older brother was smart and got attention for that. My younger sister was cute, thin, blonde, and innocent-acting and got attention for that. I was none of those things and the only attention I got was when I was bad, so I became good at being bad and mean — lying, stealing, and beating up kids.

The rest of the time of living with my family was very migratory, between towns, within towns, following the various men in my mom's life, moving before the rent, trying to get into better apartments. I ended up going to 15 different schools in those 12 years of public education. And, starting in the 2nd grade, they were years of misery as a fat kid.

Because we were poor, we couldn't afford to buy me the more expensive chubby-girl-sized clothes. Instead, I started wearing cheap, large-women's clothes at a young age.*

My mom clung to the belief that my fat was baby fat and would disappear as I became a teenager, so she didn't give me a real hard time about being fat. However, I was generally being impossible to live with and she was seriously considering putting me in juvenile hall, for being "incorrigible."

At this time my dad agreed to let me live with him and his second wife. I spent 7th grade in the prison of their home. My life and activities were so restricted that I wrote a 200-page hand-written novel, in which I was the heroine, thin of course, and did many brave and wonderful and exciting things. My dad's wife, a petite five-foot-tall woman, immediately put me on my first diet — Metrocal, carrot sticks, and celery, every meal. When I took Metrocal to school for lunch, it was in the Metrocal can, not even in a thermos. The humiliation was enormous, as were my hunger and shame. My dad and his wife refused to give me any kind of allowance — they were sure I would spend it on candy and food. They did, however, let me be a member of a paperback book club and, as soon as I had read the books, I would sell them to other kids and use the money to go for sodas and junk food after school with the neighborhood kids. That year I also had to take home economics in school, and my dad's wife made me take the sewing section both semesters because she didn't want me to have access to the food in the cooking class.

I did lose a lot of weight—down to a ladies' size 12—but I was so generally miserable that my newfound thinness did not pave the way to popularity as I had always thought it would. I begged to be returned to my mom and promised I would behave better if I did get to go back home. The summer between 7th and 8th grades I went to Florida to rejoin my mom, brother, and sister.

Immediately the pounds piled on. I was no longer starving. I was much happier with my mom now that I had seen another life. And I did try harder to behave. My life settled into a pattern of school, reading, writing, eating, and housework. I read for escape, always fiction—something to take me away from my reality. The public library was a haven I escaped to as often as possible.

My major social activity, begun in second grade, was Girl Scouts. I was the one United Way paid for, providing my uniforms, and once I went to Brownie daycamp in the summer. Girl Scouts was a way to make some kind of contact in each new environment; it was a way of knowing—at least superficially—someone when I moved. And though we didn't get close, they were nicer than the other kids, especially as I got older. I had some good times in Girl Scouts, although no real friendships were formed.

One of my defenses as we moved around, and as others weren't quick to offer friendship to the new fat girl, was to withdraw and act as if I didn't want or need anybody. Because I was responsible for keeping the house clean, cooking, and ironing, I had good excuses to give my mom for not being involved in school activities. The efforts I did make to try to fit in had developed into me being a comedienne as well as a smart-mouth in school. I took to heart the saying that it's better to get them to laugh with you than at you. If I was being funny, maybe their laughter wouldn't hurt so much. And so I fell into the jolly fat stereotype.

I spent 9th grade at a junior high school in Pensacola, Florida; 10th grade at a high school in Pensacola; 11th grade in Denver, Colorado; and 12th grade in Sheridan, Wyoming. As I look back, it's mostly a blur. Every time I made a tentative step toward being involved in something, we moved. I had such a fit when my mom and her husband decided to move between my 11th and 12th grades that they packed me off to my aunt and uncle's in Iowa for the summer. After the move was completed, my grandparents drove me to Sheridan. When my folks moved the middle of 12th grade, I totally refused to go. Fortunately, it got arranged so that I lived with a woman who had worked with my mom's husband—I was on my own at age 16.

I had a real attitude those years. Between moving a lot and being fat and poorly dressed (and poor), I tried to make sure that no one could reject me—I didn't give them the opportunity. I had a wall so thick no one could get through—I couldn't get out. The real me was well hidden and protected from the world. The teenage years are hard on everyone, but if you think about those years being spent as a poor, transient, fat girl, perhaps you can better understand what I mean about thick walls and what one fat girl went through.

POST SCRIPT

Fortunately some of those hardships in my life gave me the strength to change and grow—the walls are smaller and smaller. The DC area has been my home for more than eight years. During those eight years I have been involved in such activities as writing (*off our backs* collective), anti-racist work, anti-nuclear groups (Spiderworts, Women's Pentagon Action), a working-class Lezzie writing CR support group (Palms Read), a Wicca coven (Power to Wimmin), and a fat liberation group (FATSO—Fat Sisters Organizing). By the time this book is out I will be relocated in the Seattle area. I'm looking for someplace to really call home, not an easy task for a nomad.

# *Sanctuary*

## Leah Pesa Kushner

Where is the sanctuary?

    creeping    crawling through corridor walls
    to avoid the fat talk
    and the crude cunning remarks
    i rerouted to avoid the pain

    feeling like that fat freak forgotten
    by the other children at recess
    always alone
    tough and tearless

    finally being able to get revenge
    and join in with the other kids on
    ganging up on Ellen.
    "Ellen, Ellen big fat watermelon."

Where is the sanctuary?

    captured and cornered at home
    while my mother weighed out her food
    and mine
    as i watched her fat dangling between her thighs
    and tangling torturously in her mind
    each pound adding to her disgust and depression

    locked behind the door of my bedroom
    i lay wondering
    not locked behind my father's threats of my life alone
    i lay wondering
    how i would manage living my life alone
    loverless
    my mother was fat and she had boyfriends and danced and
        married my father

---

This piece is part of the FatLip Readers Theater manuscript, from Berkeley, California.

Where is the sanctuary?

> shutting the lite before i took my clothes off
> when i made love
> for fear that my lover would see my stretch marks and leave me
> taking the first person who wanted me

> in the nite
> afraid to sleep
> hearing the echoes of my sister's voice turning and twisting
> > toward me
> "You are not just fat.  You are obese."

Where is the sanctuary?

> running from the fear of fat
> behind broken zippers
> and shaken heads
> of people in the street
> seeing every rejection as because of my fat
> my only identity is being fat

> running from the word fat
> the word obese
> avoiding every conversation
> pretending i do not hear
> acting like you were not talking to me
> it does not bother me
> the words drill deep within the dungeons
> of the memories
> with the diets
> where i locked myself before

> i say nothing bothers me
> i say nothing bothers me
> i said nothing bothers me

> i am toughened
> like the manufactured tomato
> seedless
> never to ripen
> or ooze

> i said nothing bothers me

and then
the tears fall and i ooze
with the seeds cast and growing
into a movement so strong
carrying giant pain and anger
within my pretending
to feel body

i will not be moved

when i move i shake
when we all move together we shake so big and loud and fat
clearly cast

you will have to see us
and you will have to hear us
and you will be moved

# Interview with Darla

*Darla is a 15-year-old fat woman growing up in a small town in Iowa. Like many fat kids, she is harassed by schoolmates and teachers and has had to fight to survive her school years.*

Darla:  I was born in Iowa City. We lived in Iowa City until I was maybe 6 or 7. Then we moved to South English and I went to school there from second grade until now.

*Barb: How old are you?*

Darla:  Fifteen.

*Barb: What do you remember about being in grade school?*

Darla:  Well, all the teachers always picked on me.

*Barb: Why?*

Darla:  I know that I used to be a troublemaker, but I wasn't that bad.

*Barb: What kind of things did you do?*

Darla:  One thing is that I used to mouth off a lot to the teachers. And another thing was I used to pick on some kids who thought they were really cute and really smart.

*Barb: Were you always a pretty big kid when you were little?*

Darla:  Yeah, I'd say so.

*Barb: Did you get hassled around that?*

Darla:  Well, maybe three or four kids did hassle me — there was one that did it constantly. He doesn't anymore because he's sorta big too now. Nobody likes him.

*Barb: What kind of things did he say to you?*

Darla:  Oh, he'd say, "You big fat blob," or something like that.

*Barb: Have you had other kids say things to you?*

Darla:  Yeah, one kid, but she's big, too. I mean, she's BIG.

*Barb: Bigger than you?*

Darla:  Yeah.

*Barb: What kind of things would she say?*

Darla:  Oh, first thing that she would say would be "Oh, I'm bigger than you and I could beat you up." And I'd say, "Well, try it." And she goes, "Well, I don't want to waste my time on you, you big fat nerd." But most of the kids didn't pick on me 'cause they really looked up to me, 'cause I would be their friend. Except for one girl. She's in my class now. She was a really skinny girl and I asked her if I could play ball with her and she said no and I got really mad and I almost killed her.

*Barb: Why wouldn't she let you play ball?*

Darla: Well, I don't know. She said that she was playing ball with other friends and so what I did—I took her head and I rammed it up against the wall. I was pretty much a bully to some kids. It depends on what they did or said. I didn't know how to control my temper then. But it was mostly by the teachers that I would get hassled.

*Barb: Like what kind of stuff?*

Darla: One teacher would get mad at me and she'd slap my stuff on the floor and do things like that. And another teacher used to call me "Sherman."

*Barb: Like "Sherman Tank," was that the idea?*

Darla: Yeah.

*Barb: What grade was that?*

Darla: I think 5th or 6th grade.

*Barb: Linnea told me about some problem you were having with a teacher who seemed to be really hassling you a lot.*

Darla: That was last year when that happened.

*Barb: What grade are you in now?*

Darla: I'm a freshman now.

*Barb: What kind of stuff did he do to you?*

Darla: He lets people go to the restroom, right? But he doesn't say anything to anyone else. I go up there and ask him if I can go to the restroom and he goes, "Yeah." Then as I was walking out, I thought I heard him say, "If you can set your fat ass on the toilet." When I came back, a bunch of other kids told me about this, so I knew he said it. I was really mad because I didn't do anything to make him say that.

And he has done other stuff like that, too. I usually have my work, but one day I forgot and I thought I had it in my math book. Just one day. He came up to me and asked me to answer a problem and I said, "Well, I can't find my math. I forgot it in my locker." And he goes, "Excuses, excuses." I said, "Well, that's not an excuse, it's true." Then I asked if I could go get it and he goes, "No, I want you to get a big fat zero, just like you." And so then I got up and I said, "God, I hate you. You make me so mad I could just . . ." I don't know, I said one word I forget. Then he told me, "I don't want anybody who's crying in my class." Because I was really mad and when I get mad I start to get real red. So he said, "Get outta here. Go to the office. I don't want you around here." So I went to the office. I told the principal about it and he didn't believe it. 'Course nobody does. Then I had to talk to the guidance counselor for about two weeks, and then I had to go talk to the teacher. And try to figure it out.

*Barb: Did your mom or other people say things to you about losing weight?*
Darla: Yeah, especially my grandmother and my aunt. They want me to lose weight so I'll look better. They'd ask me, "Why don't you lose weight so you could look real good and have boyfriends?" And all this.

*Barb: Did they say stuff to you a lot?*
Darla: Yeah. Every time we go to see them. They go, "It's about time . . ." But lately, I've been trying to lose weight 'cause I want to. Not because anybody is telling me to, but because I want to.

*Barb: Why do you want to?*
Darla: Well, because I'm really getting tired of people saying stuff to me.

*Barb: Is this the first diet that you've been on?*
Darla: No. I have been on I don't know how many—one in 7th grade when I was going out for basketball. You know they had hot lunches. I didn't eat all my potatoes, my cookie or anything. I'd give it away. And then I lost about 20 pounds. Now we've started on a diet that is really strict.

*Barb: You and your mom?*
Darla: Yes. We can only have a certain amount of juice, like one-half cup of milk or one-half cup of this. Really strict.

*Barb: When you were in grade school, did you do any kind of dieting?*
Darla: Well, I played a lot of sports. That's about it. I wasn't really big, big in second through maybe fifth or sixth grades, you know. I was just broad-shouldered. That made me look like cavewoman. Some people would call me that.

*Barb: Cavewoman?*
Darla: Caveman, something like that—'cause of my shoulders, that's all.

*Barb: Do you talk to your friends about going on diets or anything like that?*
Darla: Yeah. Someone who is really close and usually I don't want anybody to know who'd go off blabbing it. Like I would tell a close

friend. They would tell me to keep doing what I'm doing and don't stop.

*Barb: Do you think you have gotten treated differently since you've lost weight?*
Darla: Yeah, probably.

*Barb: How?*
Darla: Oh, the kid that called me a fat blob or something like that, he doesn't call me that anymore. Actually, I think HE should lose weight, he's really getting up there.

*Barb: Is it hard to diet?*
Darla: Yeah, sort of. I can do it. It's just that when I see my sister not on this diet and eat desserts or a brownie, then it's kinda hard.

*Barb: Does the idea of getting real fat scare you?*
Darla: No, I've never thought about that. 'Cause I don't want to end up that way.

*Barb: Do you think that if you hadn't gotten hassles and stuff, you'd be wanting to lose weight?*
Darla: You mean as in nobody ever called me anything?

*Barb: Right, nobody ever said anything to you about it at all.*
Darla: Yeah, probably I'd still want to lose weight no matter what.

*Barb: Why's that?*
Darla: I know I'd look better.

*Barb: How do you think you'd look better?*
Darla: I don't know really. I have a certain goal to get down to. I want to lose about 30 more pounds. Get down to a hundred and ten. 'Cause that's what the normal size range is around the school.

*Barb: You played a lot of sports, right?*
Darla: I went out for every sport that there was. One year I went out for track, but the coach wouldn't let me do anything really. He'd use someone else. It was like, I was just there for practice. If you got second or third or first place, you get a ribbon or something like that. And I went out for track and I didn't even get to try out for anything.

*Barb: Why not?*
Darla: 'Cause the coach said, "Oh, we'll let Angie do this. If you want to quit, go ahead." So I went to the coach and I told him, "I'm going to quit if you're not going to use me in anything." He goes, "Well, don't quit, I'll use you in the next one." So I believed him. I thought he would use me. Sure enough he didn't. So, I just went on 'cause there was only one more track meet to go to so I just stayed on. And this year I didn't go out.

*Barb: What other sports did you play?*
Darla: Just softball and basketball.
*Barb: Now that you're in high school, have kids hassled you?*
Darla: I think one thing that really got me mad was this one kid, Joe, the same kid who called me a fat blob. He used to hang around these guys who thought they were really cool and they were a year ahead of him. Joe told one of these guys that I had called him a dirty name. They asked me, "Do you want to fight about it?" And I go, "No and I didn't call you any name or anything." And then the guy said, "After lunch I'll meet you outside." And I said, "I don't want to meet you outside 'cause I'm not into fighting." So then I ate lunch and then I was just going to forget about it. I thought maybe they would have forgotten about it. I walked out the door and they were standing there waiting for me. Seven kids against me.
*Barb: All boys?*
Darla: Yeah. And one was Joe. What they did was just kind of pass me around and push me from one person to another and make me fall down and get scraped up. My sister was there and she was trying to stop it, but she couldn't. So she started walking up the walk to go get a teacher and they stopped. And then I left and sat up against the wall of the school building and Joe came up to me and goes, "You gonna tell on us?" And I said, "Well, if I did, I wouldn't be here." And he goes, "Well, are you gonna tell on us?" And I go, "Well, I'm not a ratfink." So I didn't tell on them.

*Barb: Do you remember being angry?*
Darla: Yeah, a lot.
*Barb: Have you had a lot of friends?*
Darla: Yeah, I had a lot of friends in grade school, but I don't think they were friend friends. They were just friends in hiding behind me because boys were chasing after them. You know how they're scared of them so they'd come to me for help.
*Barb: Because you were bigger?*
Darla: I guess.
*Barb: Did you have best friends?*
Darla: Not really. I just had friends that came to me for help.

# *Outrages*

## Lynn Levy

age 8 . . . . . At Goldenberg's, a small guest house in the Catskill Mountains, Lilian Goldenberg rushes my mother into the kitchen to stop me from eating more than the allotted number of cookies.

age 10 . . . . I am already a practiced liar. Knowing my mother will always ask me first when any food is "missing" (she somehow keeps an exact tally), I have a long-standing agreement with my brother to cover for me. He is 8 and skinny. "When Mommy asks who ate the malomars, say you did, ok?" And he always would. And she always did.

age 14 . . . . I am taken to the family doctor, Dr. Lieberman, for shots and pills. I think he is a quack and refuse to go to him when I am really sick, but I have no choice now. I dread the weekly visits to his office in Sheepshead Bay, sitting in the waiting room full of people, ashamed, fearing they all know why I am here, my fat worse than the most awful, unspeakable illness. I wait through the muzak to enter and be weighed. I have already known this tension too many years, the sinking feeling in my gut when I approach a scale.

age 15 . . . . My mother threatens that she will not buy me a dress for my sweet sixteen party if I do not lose weight. And again, I am close to desperation. In my neighborhood, in 1962, in Brooklyn, a sweet sixteen is the upwardly mobile working class equivalent of a coming out party (as in debutante, not dyke). We rent the Jewish Center, a juke box, the food will be catered. How can my mother threaten me so? She knows I must have a dress — a semi-formal dress. But she thinks that if she hurts me enough, embarrasses me enough, scares me enough, makes me desperate enough, I will lose weight. She never dreams that if I am desperate enough I will kill myself.

age 25 .... My husband tells me my fat turns him off. I have been steadily gaining weight since we married four years ago. Until now, he never seemed to care. Once again, I am filled with desperation. If I do not lose weight, he will leave me. And until then, the anguish of being undesirable. I am frantic with fear and disgust, never at him, always at myself. When we are in bed, I cry to feel so unwanted. Within a year he does leave. He is involved with a thin woman, seven years older than we are. I fall in love with her. We kiss once. She tells me she is attracted to me, that she has dreamed of our being in bed together. I am so excited I can hardly contain myself. She tells me she fears my losing weight because then he might not want her anymore.

age 27 .... My first night with a woman who calls herself lesbian. When we awaken she asks if I am planning to lose weight. "I am usually not attracted to fat women," she says. I am again frantic. I begin a diet that day. I never see her again.

age 29 .... I am having an affair with a woman ten years older than I, a psychologist. Whenever we go out to dinner, she tells the waitpersons all about the 70 pounds I have lost. I want to crawl under the table, but she continues. She drinks too much, and with each scotch talks more about the weight I have lost, the weight I have yet to lose. Finally she tells me I will be beautiful once I'm thin. She is sincere, but I know, even as she says it, that this is no compliment.

age 33 .... My lover threatens to leave if I do not lose weight. Again, I think, I have heard this before, but you, my trusted love, are the first to use the words. So there it is, I can choose between being fat or being loved. It is no choice. I again try to diet. It takes me a year to feel the full frustration of failure one more time. I finally tell her she had better move out, because I won't live with the tension any longer of not knowing when or whether she'll leave.

age 36 . . . . I am getting off a bus. While one man yells "cow" at my back, I hear others laugh. And I am outraged. Enough to kill!

I am a fat woman. I was a fat child, fairly thin through high school and college because I dieted and did pills a lot, then fat again from age 22, when I married and went away to graduate school. I got fatter still after 1973, when I came out. It wasn't until 1980 that I heard about Fat Liberation and, for the first time in 34 years, was able to let go the desperation I had always felt around being fat and needing to lose weight. I had first thought of titling this piece, "Is there life after liberation, or, What do you do with the memories?" when I was rudely reminded that the outrages are not all memories — they continue, even after I refuse to play the game. My "liberation" does not prevent a man from harassing me on the bus, it does not prevent airline seats from being too narrow, it does not prevent my being unable to find clothes that will fit in the styles and materials I like. Passing cars, passing strangers, I harden myself to words I have trained my ears not to hear, hurled at me on the streets. It all continues, and I look forward to the day when I can no longer control my rage.

# Interview with Deb

*Deb is a 31-year-old Black lesbian living in Minneapolis. Steff is a 40-year-old white lesbian living in Iowa City.*

*Steff: I know your mother is fat. How does she feel about you being fat?*
Deb: Pressure. A lot of pressure to be thin. And there was even more pressure because her and my sister were thin together at one point, and so they sort of ganged up on me, which just made me freak out even more about food. I remember that there was a lot of emphasis placed on clothes when I was growing up. My sister and mother used to go clothes shopping together, and I always felt like this outcast. I hated the fact that I didn't have any clothes. My mother would make us clothes and, because I was fat, I'd just bust out of them before my sister would, so consequently she would have all these clothes and I wouldn't have any. And then when we were in grade school, my mother dressed us exactly alike. People thought we were twins. There's nothing like her being in a dress and being thin and me being in the same dress and being fat. It felt like something was wrong.

Even after I grew up, there was a lot of stuff with my mother about inappropriate clothing. One time I came over and I had on a pair of parachute pants and a loose top and I felt real comfortable and she said, "You look like you're wearing your pajamas. You have to wear tight clothes so you can remember that you're fat." I looked at her and I said, "What?" I said, "I want to be comfortable." You know, I ran around in girdles for so long. I'm not going to wear tight clothes so that I can remember that I'm fat.
*Steff: What was it like when you were growing up?*
Deb: We were very poor. On welfare. But because my grandmother had been middle class and her mother had owned a boarding house and my grandmother had everything she wanted, we were raised pretty middle class, even though we didn't have any money, and there was a lot of stress put on getting an education. 'Cause if you got an education, you could succeed.
*Steff: There's seven kids in your family?*
Deb: Uh-huh.

*Steff: Most of whom I've ever heard you talk about is your sister, Ronnie.*

Deb: Yeah, that's because Ronnie and I are 18 months apart.

*Steff: And she's younger than you?*

Deb: No, she's older. But it doesn't feel that way. Seems like I'm older.

*Steff: Are any of the other kids fat?*

Deb: No. Victor and Michael are real thin. Kimmy is kind of plump, but she's getting older so she's getting just round. She's started jogging and all this other stuff, and my mother says to her, "Oh, you're so fat." And me and Ronnie say, "You are not fat. You are NOT fat." And we just keep telling her, "Don't get stuck in that, just don't get stuck in that because you are not fat." And I look back at pictures of myself when I thought I was just this little pig, and I'm not. I am not. And I was told I was ugly. I wasn't. I was a cute kid. I was real cute. I can't believe I was told that.

My sister Ronnie is in this constant battle with her weight. When we were growing up, I thought my mother liked her better because they were confidants. That was really hard. In just the past eight years or so, Ronnie and I have become friends. We still are really worlds apart as far as politics and styles of clothing and all this other stuff, but we are a lot alike. We like each other now, whereas before, she could have died and I wouldn't have cared.

*Steff: So you're out to your whole family?*

Deb: I'm out to Ronnie and Al, her husband, and my aunt, who also has some Lesbian experiences. My mother knows but we don't talk about it. It has never been formally acknowledged.

*Steff: How do they feel about you now when you're so physically, visibly different from them?*

Deb: Oh, they think I'm real zany.

*Steff: Do they like you?*

Deb: Yeah. I think my mother especially likes me. 'Cause I'm not doing anything normal. And I know my sister and my brother, Anthony and Kim, I know they like me a lot. Victor and Michael, well, who knows, but they always treat me special when I come over, which is a treat. And my mother always wants me to stay. "Oh, why don't you sleep here tonight? Why don't you come over for the weekend?" Or else she'll invite me over for dinner.

I love it. And just recently I found out that if I don't call her at least three times during the week, she calls my sister and asks where I am, what I am doing, has she seen me.

*Steff: Now you're okay with being fat?*

Deb: I'm okay.

*Steff: What about your family?*
Deb: Well, it's real interesting. It's like they know about fat dykes.
I don't say fat dykes, I say I'm going to a fat women's conference.
I told my mother I was going to Iowa City to be interviewed for a
book about fat women. "Oh," she said. So they know that I'm involved in this fat liberation stuff. Every once in a while, they still
get on me about it, but not like they used to 'cause they know that
it just doesn't work anymore and that I don't freak out about it
when they try to do that stuff. They know that I feel comfortable
in my clothes and that I look great. And that freaks them out because I'm fat. How could a fat person look nice in clothes?

I'll come over and sometimes my mother will say, "Let's go get
ice cream." And then she'll say, "Oh no, no." And I'll say, "Well,
why not?" She needs a conspirator to go do stuff like that, so then
we'll go get ice cream and then she'll say, "Oh God, why did I go?"
And then I'll say, "Well, look, if you're gonna do that, then don't
ask me to go get ice cream with you 'cause I don't wanna hear
that stuff. Either you do it or you don't, you know, one way or the
other."

And also my sister will come over and I'll have ice cream in the
freezer and she'll say, "Can I eat this?" It's like she's not allowed
to eat that stuff at her house. And I'll say, "What's with you?" And
she'll say, "How can you keep ice cream around and not eat it?"
And I say, "It's 'cause I'm not obsessed with the fact that it's in the
freezer." I'm not thinking about it all the time, that it's sitting
there, all chocolaty and good, waiting for me. And I said, "You
are and you come over here and you go crazy." And then she'll
say, "Let's order chicken from Chicken Delight," and she knows
she can come over and that she can do that kind of stuff because I
don't diet and I'm not real freaked out about food. It's like she
needs a conspirator too.

*Steff: How was it for you in school?*
Deb: I was the bad girl. I always got in trouble in school. I always wore inappropriate clothing to school. I ran with the girl's
gang. We used to wear real short skirts and, like, two or three
pairs of socks and our legs would look real thick 'cause boys liked
thick big legs. They like women with big thighs and big legs. I
was always getting expelled. And Ronnie was the good one. She
was on the Student Council. And I was always fighting and carrying on and getting a lot of attention that way. That's how I got

the attention. Till I found out there was an easier way to do it without antagonizing everybody.

*Steff: Tell me about grade school. What you were like in grade school?*

Deb: Precocious.

*Steff: Smart?*

Deb: Yeah, I think I was pretty smart, but I was pretty obnoxious 'cause I wanted a lot of attention and I remember teachers just either liking me a whole lot or thinking I was this obnoxious little child, that I was really awful. Also, I remember getting beat up a lot when I was in grade school. And then, when I was in 5th grade, I decided I wasn't going to get beat up anymore, that I was going to be the one who was going to do the beating up. And so I started being that one, and got a reputation as a bully, which wasn't so much fun.

*Steff: Were you fat then?*

Deb: Yeah, I was a fat little kid.

*Steff: What was your family's attitude about school?*

Deb: You were supposed to strive for good grades and go to high school and go to college and if you went to college and you got this degree and then you'd get this wonderful job. Sometimes it was learning to do something practical. My mother wanted me to learn how to type so that I could get a job as a secretary and have something to fall back on. When I dropped out of high school and just fooled around for a couple of years, and then decided to go to vocational school, my family was just scandalized. They called it bum's college. I thought they'd be happy that I was going to go back to school and try to get my GED* and try to do something, but they weren't, they were really unhappy about it. So there was a lot of double messages.

*Steff: How old were you when you dropped out of high school?*

Deb: Fifteen:

*Steff: How come you did it?*

Deb: I hated it. There was a lot of pressure to fit in. I tried to fit into every clique I could — I tried the hippies, I tried the greaser white girls. There weren't many Black kids in the school, but the Black kids that were there were divided into two classes, the lower class and the middle class. The lower class kids were just too far out there for me and the middle class kids were very straight-laced and dressed in preppy clothes and didn't want to have anything to do with anyone who didn't have money, so that sort of left me just floating around and I decided that after doing all this work

---

* General Education Diploma

and being this rotten kid, I was going to make one last stab at being real good.  Also, I was following in my sister's footsteps, and she was real smart and got A's all the time so they automatically expected me to be just like her.  Well, I hated her so I tried to do everything in my power not to be like her and I remember just before I dropped out I made one last attempt at being like everybody else, and I went to school and I had on stockings, and flat shoes and a straight skirt and a belt and my blouse was tucked in, and my hair was fixed and for about a month I tried to be like everybody else.  I tried to answer questions in class.  I felt like I was being forced into a tube that was too small, and I remember at one point I went out to lunch and there was this park by the school that I used to walk in and I went into this park and I kicked off my shoes and I took my blouse out of my belt, messed up my hair, and sat and cried.  'Cause it was like I couldn't do it.  I could not do it.

So I stayed home and I read and went to the library and hung out and that was more education than I could have ever gotten in high school.

*Steff: Were you fat in high school?  Did you hang out with ones that were fat?*

Deb: Yeah.  I hated the fat girls in high school.  I hated them.

*Steff: How come?*

Deb: They were the victims.  They were just dragging themselves on through life.  I just hated them.  But like birds of a feather, the fat girls stuck together, right?  We sat at a certain table in the lunchroom.  I just hated it.  I wound up not hanging out with anybody.  Just being alone a lot.  I remember just spending hours and hours alone.  And sometimes liking it, and sometimes hating it.  Wanting to belong so badly that I would just reject anybody who came near because I thought, "No, I'm gonna hurt you first."

It was awful.  I didn't have the clothes to compete in high school, and that was a real thing.  That was one of the reasons I dropped out of school — I didn't have any clothes.  I was wearing the same clothes all the time, alternating, trying to make them all look different.  That was a real problem, because everybody was so clothes-conscious.

*Steff: Were you taking shit from other kids for being fat?*

Deb: Oh, yeah.  Somebody always wanted to beat me up.  Which after coming out of junior high school and being in a gang and feeling like I belonged and kicking ass right and left, and then going to a place where there were mostly white kids who had money who were supposedly sophisticated and thought you were an animal if you got into a fight. It was real hard to pull back my anger and try to pretend like I was like everybody else. It was real difficult.

There was this boy who sat behind me who used to call me "Frankenstein" all the time. And I remember walking down the hallway and kids saying things to me and looking at me strangely and just being disgustingly rude.

*Steff: Was there a difference in the way Black kids treated you and the way white kids treated you?*

Deb: Yeah, the white kids ignored me. I hung around with some Black kids, and then there were always some Black kids who wanted to fight me for some reason and were always trying to get me into fights with them and I wouldn't do it. I just wouldn't do it. I felt so angry I thought, if I get into a fight with someone I will kill them. If I get my hands around their necks, I will kill them, so I better not get into a fight. And they all thought I was scared. And I wasn't. I remember sitting on the bus and looking out the window and some girl getting on the bus with her friends who just hated my guts and starting to ridicule me and I just kept my face turned to the window and smiled. I thought, I don't want to do anything because if I start I'm not going to be able to stop.

*Steff: So grade school and junior high were mostly Black and high school was mostly white?*

Deb: Yeah, and that high school now is just about all Black.


*Steff: What was your first job?*

Deb: Working for my aunt when I was 13 in a restaurant for 90 cents an hour and thinking I was making big bucks. That was my first job and it was a drag, but it was easier working for her than somebody I didn't know.

*Steff: Pretty much your paid jobs have been cooking jobs?*

Deb: Yeah, a lot of cooking jobs, all restaurant-related. It's cooking and waitressing and doing prep work. Stuff like that.

*Steff: Was stuff about food and cooking and serving important in your family?*

Deb: Yeah. Sometimes it was fun because I learned so much about cooking. What foods to put together. I'm not talking about correct food combining, I'm talking about how to make it look lovely on the plate. One of my mother's favorites was meatloaf, grits, and corn. Two starches, right? I know that's not cool. But it was lovely on the plate. And the gravy would be just right. And how to make things look real petty and taste good and lots of seasonings. But she would cook vegetables to death. She would just cook them to death. Cooking was a real important thing. The time when I could feel close to her was around the cooking or when she was braiding my hair. And I remember her being pregnant and me leaning my head up against her stomach and her braiding my hair.

We didn't have any food for such a long time. And then we had County food — shit out of the cans and out of the boxes — and I remember thinking, "Gosh, I can't wait for the time when I'm going to be able to have food — as much as I want and when I want it. And to be able to have two helpings of something instead of only one."

*Steff: Did you expect that at some point in your life cooking would be your career?*

Deb: I don't know. I thought that there was something special about me that I wouldn't be doing this forever, that I should be doing something else. Which sounds pretentious, but I always felt like that. And it felt like all those jobs were just temporary. And I could never take any of them real seriously. There was never anything that I did that I felt real good about doing. It was just a way to get money. There was a minimum of pleasure in it. Just lately at the last place I worked at, there was a lot of pleasure in the cooking.

*Steff: How did being fat affect your work?*

Deb: The only problem I had was sometimes, I knew I didn't get a job because I was fat. I wanted to get a job at the phone company — I can't remember how old I was — and I put down this weight that was maybe twenty pounds thinner. This woman said, "Well, are you sure this is what you weigh?" And she got into this whole questioning of my weight. She said, "We have a scale in the other room, and we can weigh you, and I think you weigh more and if you do we can't hire you because you're overweight." And I said, "What difference does it make?" Like, I was going to be a telephone operator. She said, "Well, because fat people tend to be sick more than thin people," which I knew was bullshit. And then I came home and I was really upset. And then I told my mother and she said, "You know, that's true, if you're fat you do get sick more and you will probably have to take more days off." I couldn't believe that she was on their side.

So that was one big disappointment. Sometimes I wouldn't get a job because I knew I intimidated somebody because of my size and I figured if you're that intimidated by me, then I don't want to work here anyway 'cause you have a problem.

*Steff: Working with food, being Black, being fat — how does that tie?*

Deb: Well, sometimes I got the feeling that there was this Aunt Jemima image and at the last place I worked everybody came dressed in costumes on Halloween and one of the waitresses said, "Oh Deb, you should come dressed as Aunt Jemima." And I looked at her and I thought, "Gosh, I thought you had some sense." Everybody around me was going, "He-he-he." And I said, "I don't think this is funny." And everybody just sort of looked down, and she said, "Oh, I'm really sorry." I just looked at her and I thought, "you be sorry, you just go ahead and be sorry." And then she was wimpy toward me the rest of the time, and I thought, "I'm not giving you any room."

*Steff: Outside of that very obvious stuff, have you had to educate the ones you worked with about fat stuff?*

Deb: Sometimes. When they say dumb stuff. When they think that women are fat because they eat a lot. And I think there are very few women who are fat because they eat a lot. I mean, I think that's a minority. Women just saying real dumb stuff about another woman's body. I remember at work, I got into an argument with a woman who was saying that some other woman's ass was just too big. And I said, "Too big for what?"

It seems like it was okay to be fat and work in a kitchen. It seems like it was almost expected that the people in the kitchen would be fat. A lot of the women that I worked with were fat, and a lot of the women were Black women and there didn't seem to be any problem with someone being fat.

*Steff: If you had a choice of all the jobs there are, what one would you do?*

Deb: Oh, acting, of course. I would do that. If I thought I could live off the money, I would do that. I wouldn't do anything else. That's my favorite. Cooking is secondary. I mean, cooking gives me a thrill, but not like acting.

*Steff: Who are you most comfortable around?*

Deb: I'm more comfortable around women who are working class and who are fat. But I think I'm most myself when I'm around women who are Black and poor. 'Cause that's where I come from. And I really like when I'm at my mother's and it's just me, my mother, my sisters, and we all start talking, and sometimes there are certain things that I can say to a Black person that it's like this coded message that they will *immediately* understand what I'm talking about, whereas the white person I would have to explain it more intellectually until they got it. Recently I was sitting around thinking, "Oh, you know, I just want to fit." And then I thought, "You're never gonna fit in. You're not gonna fit in. You might as well stop thinking that because, for all the absorbing that white culture has tried to do to Blacks, it's like we ARE different. We DO eat different food. We DO talk differently. We ARE different. And that's all there is to it." So I feel I'm most myself when I'm around Black women who are from the same background.

*Steff: What were the most frustrating parts of your life?*
Deb: I think some of the most frustrating parts has been when there were friendships that I've had to abandon because I kept changing and my friends didn't. That's been real frustrating. And then to run into those women again and see that they're just about the same as they were, to know that we had some real good times, but we're not going to be friends anymore. In the past few years, I started to realize how important my friendships are and to align myself with women who are loyal and who are true, who I can count on and who I know that if anything happened to me, I could fall back on them and vice versa. I wanted to be a real true woman. I wanted to be someone that somebody else would want to be friends with and would feel safe with and know that they could count on me. I strived to be that and it seems like it cost me a lot of friendships. I've lost friends in the past couple of years, but the friends that I've gained have been real good ones, REAL good ones who don't bullshit and who aren't afraid and who I can have fights with and still come back and know that we can be friends.

As far as lover relationships, I don't know. The last relationship that I had, I made a lot of breakthroughs in it in realizing that I could have a fight with a lover and not hate her forever after having it. I also realized that you don't just go into the relationship and if things start getting rough you just split, 'cause that's what I had always done in the past. And in this last relationship, every time things got rough, we would stick it out. We would just weather it and we would go through it and it was real good. I learned a lot about loyalties.

*Steff: What are your views around relationships?*
Deb: Something that I'm just starting to realize, which is real

hard to know about myself, and really annoys the shit outta me, is that I need a lot of devotion. I need someone to be real adoring to me.

Also, finding out that sometimes I can take someone or leave them, that even though they're real important to me, if they start getting in my way, I won't be with them.

*Steff: You want to talk about the dieting stuff?*
Deb: Sure. Something I can't seem to get across to a lot of women who are fat and really hate themselves is that my worst times was when I was thin. I felt indecisive and really unsure of myself. And the way I covered it up was by picking up men because I knew that men were just suckers for women who they thought looked good, and it didn't matter if you could talk or you were smart or anything like that, 'cause they didn't care. So those were some of my worst times. Those were some of my hardest times, and also when I was thin I never got thin by eating diet foods or eating less or anything like that. I got thin by doing drugs.
*Steff: Speed?*
Deb: Speed. Yeah. And the drugs really fucked up my body, but I was thin. And I was real miserable. And one time I lost about 50 pounds by eating just one meal a day and doing speed. And being real crazy. I knew a fat doctor in Milwaukee and you'd go in and he'd pretend to take your blood pressure. And look at your tits and tell you you were cute but you needed to lose weight, and give you black cadillacs.
*Steff: Do you want to talk about the Black/white differences around being fat?*
Deb: I think on some levels it's more acceptable in the Black community to be fat, especially concerning men, because there's a certain kind of fat that's okay. This sort of, you know, large, rolling woman, who's really comfortable in her body and with her sexuality. And I notice that in my community a lot of Black men really liked it when a woman had big thighs, big hips, and big legs. They REALLY liked that. In America the emphasis is placed on the breasts — if women have big breasts, that's a big deal and they are sought after. But in a lot of African cultures, it's if women have big thighs and big behinds, that's something to be sought after. And I think the reason being, is that it's for childbearing — they think women like that are sturdy, they can work, they can have babies, and if they're pear-shaped, then that's like a real good shape

as far as bearing children. It seems like it's just carried over. I know that some of my white girlfriends that were going out with Black men were pear-shaped, and these girls couldn't understand why these Black men were just ga-ga over their legs, 'cause they thought they were fat.

I know some Black lesbians who are fat, and they don't seem to have any problems finding women to be with, but I don't know — I don't know if that's true or not. I've never had any problems finding women to be with. I think if I was fifty pounds heavier, that might possibly be a problem, but it seems like in the dyke community, there's a certain amount of heftiness and heaviness that is allowed and if it goes over a certain point — I'm not sure what that point is — then you're not looked upon as this big strong dyke, you're looked upon as this fat woman.

*Steff: Do you want to talk any about getting involved in fat politics?*
Deb: Yeah. It was really good. I knew that I was starting to feel okay about my body, and that it was other people who had a problem with my body, but I wasn't sure and I knew I was angry about all the image and body stuff, but I didn't have any words for it. A friend of mine turned me onto a fat dyke weekend. I was really ignorant of all this stuff, so it was kind of hard, but it was kind of good because after I found it out, it was like, "How you gonna keep 'em down on the farm," and I REALLY liked it. And then I was picking up on all this fat oppressive shit and there were times when I thought, I don't want to know this.

But it really helped me to understand why maybe a woman was acting strangely to me, and also, I looked back on other relationships and friendships that I had and understood why women said certain things to me and treated me a certain way and it was because of my weight. Which gets into the whole butch thing — women thinking that because I'm Black, I'm fairly aggressive, I have short hair, and I'm fat, that I'm butch. I am not butch; I am femme.

*Steff: How do you feel about being a separatist?*
Deb: I think that I knew I wanted to keep being a separatist in spite of losing two real good friends over it. And I thought, if women aren't talking about this and they're so freaked out about it, that it must be something real important. What has happened is that I've lost the wimps along the way and gained some really

strong friends through it. I thought I was gonna be out here in the wilderness, but that's not how it's been. It's been real good. What's really funny is that, because I came out with it in such a public way — I wrote an article that was published in AMAZON — I got this reputation of this real tough-assed hard woman. And also there are a lot of white dykes in my community who are not dealing with their racism, so me being Black and being a separatist and being fat made me pretty awesome. Which I thought was hilarious. Because they don't know that I'm this pussycat.

So I just played on it. Sometimes I would use their own bullshit just to make them keep their mouth shut, you know, their own racism. I would just turn it around back at them. Or turn around their fear of separatism or their fear of fat. And what has happened is that, instead of this being this big burden, it's been something good, because it's really divided the women from the girls. It's like, when a woman is friends with me, I know that she likes me and wants to be my friend. It's real clear.

*Steff: If you had a daughter, how would you like her life to be the same as yours and how different from yours?*
Deb: Well, I'd like it to be the same in that she would take chances. She would take chances and she would have adventures. She would be able to have the audacity to tell someone they were full of shit instead of just thinking it and going along with what they were doing — being able to say it and walk away and feel good about it. And if she was fat, I would want her to be able to do anything she wanted, whether she was fat or not, and feel okay about being fat or thin or in-between or whatever, and not be freaked out about her body. And really like the way she looked and like clothes and feel comfortable and know that she was attractive and be able to be with a lover. And not be weirded out by it.

3. *"I stilled the dancer in me":*
   *The struggle of fat women to*
   *be outside, to exercise, to*
   *participate in sports . . .*

# Rec Center

## Susan J. Norman

I go. I swim. I sit in the sauna. I take a shower. Change my clothes. Leave.

I go. I walk to the Rec Center after class. My spirits are high or I wouldn't go. I may sing the happy songs of my past; I may whistle because I love to whistle.

I change into my swimsuit. I stay close to the lockers and preferably in a corner. I talk to no one and no one talks to me. I change from black eye patch to adhesive. I quickly put on my goggles.

This is me. I am Susan. I am five feet five inches tall and weigh one hundred and ninety pounds. My swimsuit covers the hair on my chest; the patches cover an error of nature: a birth-defect tumor, removed, scarred, eye removed, muscles damaged and removed. At the center of me, I know myself to be strong, a survivor.

I change into my suit. I pass the ever-present mirror and look quickly at the rolls of fat on my back that are not hidden by this suit. I looked everywhere for a suit. I wrote to major companies and they wrote to their local dealers. These people would not talk to me when I first went looking but were willing to bend over backwards for me now. One man ordered two suits for me; they came and didn't fit. He reordered; they came and didn't fit right. Two men behind the counter seemed to laugh when I suggested that the suits didn't fit the way I wanted them to. I couldn't stand at the counter and cry so I paid for them and left. I waited until I got outside to cry; these suits that are unsuitable.

I see the rolls of fat in the back that is cut too low and my legs ballooning out of the tight legs of the suit. I pass the ever-present mirror and the scale.

I get into the pool. I push myself until I can push no more. Years of cigarettes have made this nearly impossible. I quit for six months but lately I have been cheating, a lot. In the pool, I catch myself on the brink of drowning; I change strokes to keep the water from rushing further into my brain. I am thinking obsessively of the crush that just ended: "What did I do, why don't you love me anymore, what can I do to go back to those times that were dear to me, why did you leave me? See, I am trying to change, trying to be healthy and happy, strong. Why won't you accept me as I am?" I realize that I am not going to drown. Again I realize that I am not going to drown; too many years of being totally at home in water, hidden and blending with the water.

I get out.

I sit in the sauna in my suit and breathe in the hot air in an attempt to obliterate all that is in my mind. To ease, to erase, to listen to the rhythms of my heart that I am not quite sure is beating. I listen to the women talk of this boy, that boy, this formal, that formal, this roommate, that roommate; I want to scream at them, "You are not Others, you are Whole People!"

I have heard them snicker at the hair on my legs and I have almost laughed out loud thinking, "This is only the beginning, kids."

I take a shower. I go to showers with vinyl drapes for those of us that cannot bear to be seen out in the open, for whom the snickers and jeers are just too much. The hair on my legs is mere sarcasm compared to the hair on my chest. No matter how much I try to change and alter, alter and change, certain inescapable facts about me remain: the fat, the hair, the birth defect. I have dealt with all of them concurrently, separately, until I have been unable to deal with them at all; I am not just imperfect, I am very imperfect.

I go back to change. Once again I pass the ever-present mirror, this time red and flushed. My fat red legs are in sharp contrast to the small white towel; my heart sinks. The crush would have preferred any one of the thousands of bodies that have passed through this place over mine; I think of suicide. How did I gather the courage to come here? How can I get out of here as quickly as possible? The center of me wants release, to be let out, to explode. I hate in my guts the crush, the snide comments, the women in the sauna, the cute suits that stare down their noses at me.

I leave. I walk quickly and I stop for nothing. I no longer have to hold back the tears; I sing the death songs of my past and then slowly work my way back from the brink. I implode, I gather the broken pieces of me and I go on.

# *Summer*

## Veronica Hubbard

This article is about summer and how it affects me because I'm fat. Everyone likes summer, especially on one of those perfect summer days when the sun is shining brightly and it's not too hot. I'm no different. But the quality of my life during the summer months is so much lower than women around me who are not fat, that about all I seem to feel during the summer is anger, bitterness, and a sense of being left out. I have noticed this summer that I have wanted to be around women who are my safe friends, mostly other fat women. Being around friends who were not fat just reminded me of all the reasons I was so miserable. One of these reasons is softball.

In my community, softball is the main reason summer keeps coming back each year. Everyone is united through softball—the women that play and the women that watch. Being a softball player is like having a Diners Club card, it gets you in everywhere. You meet all kinds of new women, you get praise for playing in the game, women come especially to watch you and your teammates and to cheer you on. But because I'm fat, I don't feel like I can be a part of softball. I'm sure more than a few people—players and spectators—would find it a very funny sight to see a fat woman running the bases. This kind of harassment makes it impossible for me to feel like I can participate in softball, or any other sport, for that matter. In fact, harassment from the people in the bleachers is what keeps me away from just going to watch softball games.

And it's hot out there, right? We watch men all summer long go around with no shirts and we all envy them. Well, that's how I feel when I see thin women wearing shorts and a skimpy tank top. Even if I wanted to wear clothes like that and put up with a hundred times more harassment, I can't get clothes like that. You'll see me in heavy jeans or overalls and shirts, and T-shirts with sleeves, usually a couple of shirts at a time to hide my body as much as I can without suffocating. And you can always count on one of those thin, skimpily clad women to say, "I'm cold, let's turn off the air conditioner/fan, close the windows" while you're there sweltering.

Take those skimpy clothes a little farther and you have swimsuits and swimming. Swimming is one of the hardest things to deal with in summer. If you're fat you will have a hard time finding a suit. If you're very fat, all you'll find are ridiculous suits made of the worst kinds of materials, with skirts on them and ugly flower patterns. After that you're stuck with T-shirts and shorts that make swimming much less enjoyable because they get too heavy on you. That's if you can find a place to swim. Somewhere that there's no little kids comparing you to a whale or adults looking at you as if they can't believe what they're seeing. Even thinking, as I write this, about the humiliation that goes with swimming makes me sick at heart. And I can't swim around other lesbians either, because to be that vulnerable I have to be with someone I trust an awful lot, probably another fat woman. So for me, swimming is limited to the one or two freak chances I might get to be in a place that's safe.

And because I don't swim, I don't get a good tan, which is what everyone in the white culture seems to strive for, along with being thin. If you're tan, then you look good, sexy, healthy. You become more attractive. And if you're not tan, you look bad and unhealthy. But if you can't stand to be outdoors for fear of harassment, then you're certainly not going to get a tan. And so I feel like women look at me and think that I must be lazy because it's obvious I stay inside a lot. I do stay inside a lot, but not by choice, and certainly not because I am lazy.

One way that I do try to enjoy the outside each summer is on my motorcycle. I love riding it. But I get harassed so much more on the motorcycle that many times it is just not worth it, and I don't go or I go in a car. When I am out on the motorcycle, people will look and laugh at me. They get the people they are with to look, and I will see them turning around and craning their necks to look as long as they can as they drive away. Men will see me on the motorcycle and yell, "Hey Mama, you need a Harley for that much weight." Another thing that people seem to do when they see me on the motorcycle is to get mad. People don't like seeing fat people having fun or being happy. If you look like you're having a good time, they will harass you much more and in a meaner way than if you look miserable like you are supposed to be.

This is how I felt a lot last summer. I spent most of it inside, continually feeling worse and worse. I ached to just go out and run around and do whatever I wanted, but I didn't. I spent a lot of the summer being depressed and bitchy. I had trouble with some friendships, which I know was partly caused by the stress of all that you've just read about.

# Fat Women as Dancers

## Sharon Bas Hannah

*When building a new world and creating new people, one must fight against the false conception of beauty. I am glad that I was young in a day when people were not so self-conscious as they are now . . . in those days too, thin-was not equivalent to spirituality.*

*— Isadora Duncan*

Fat people have little opportunity to become dancers today because the development of modern Western dance has left us out. This is not true in other cultures, where there are dance styles that even seem to offer advantages to people with heavier, non-linear frames. Examples are the more grounded, close-to-the-earth forms of some African dance, belly dance, Polynesian and Baltic folk dance. And in the past, too, fat dancers were not only accepted, they were admired.

Today, most Western dance teachers will say fat people cannot dance well or move gracefully. These cultural and aesthetic prejudices are fostered by a system of dance that does seem to work best for thin people, and they are the ones in control. Western dance has long been a major aspect of thin people's privilege over fat people. Thin people have more freedom to develop themselves through dance and exercise.

For most fat people, attending a conventional Western dance class or going dancing socially can be an unpleasant experience. What we lack are dance/movement classes and social dance spaces that provide us with opportunities to explore, express, and appreciate the uniqueness and strength of our bodies. This is what I mean by development of a fat dance consciousness.

As a fat woman I have gone to many dance classes, searching for such encounters. It took me years to find a space where I could go to exercise my body free from judgment and ridicule.

My search to find what should be a basic right (a place to exercise and dance) was long and painful. I went to various classes, in different cities, and always felt rejected, resented. It took lots of courage. If I hadn't had the support of friends in fat liberation it would have been impossible. Another reason was my aunt, a woman in her seventies, who first invited me to attend a tai chi chi class (an ancient Chinese form of movement) at her local senior citizens center. I also went to a yoga class there. The people were energetic, high-spirited, and accepting of me. Nobody had a perfect body, and no one could care less what anyone looked like. They had more important things to worry about.

In exercise classes with my peers I had been at a great social disadvantage, being with people who would not speak with me or look at me. They'd spent years within a thin ghetto world of dance. The sight of my body offended and shocked them, and their behavior reflected this. Certainly, it didn't help when I heard other students constantly talking about their efforts at weight loss. Whether or not they claim to be "only talking about themselves," such comments reinforce the idea that fat is bad and that such dance or exercise as they are taking will take off weight. I resent the assumption that I am there to lose weight, resent the assumption that someone cannot be in good physical shape except when she has a slim body: I know slim people who are physically inactive.

I would often end up discouraged. The psychological effort of will required to enter the room, and once there, my awareness of the stares and unfriendliness, left me with a feeling of depression and exhaustion for hours afterward. Yet I remained committed to this ancient form of physical expression and enjoy the feelings of strength and control in my body that I get from participating.

Slowly I discovered that in beginning level classes I do the exercises as well as, and sometimes better than, some of the slim students, and I know I'm getting stronger. I realized that slim people also have hang-ups and judgments about their bodies. But they still have the privilege of being slim, of having slim role models, being able to buy leotards that fit, and knowing that if they learn to dance well enough, commercial opportunities are available to them.

When I first started dancing, none of these things existed for me as a fat woman. Slowly I researched where to buy large-size leotards. Gradually I found fat dancers in herstory, such as Virginia Zucci, who danced with the Russian ballet, was famous for her pirouettes, and weighed 200 pounds. Or Isadora Duncan, the free-spirited woman who radicalized modern dance.

I met fat women who teach physical education and creative movement. I heard about Meredith Monk, a large woman who performs in dances around the country. I found out about Judith Jamieson; although not fat, she is about six feet tall and dances with the Alvin Ailey Dance Company. I worked with an improvisational theater group where a fat man had a major dance role, and that was an inspiration.

I found that I was copying the movements of smaller women in classes, and I had to go back in time to redeem my own intuitive body patterns. I located an old photo—a proud and confident me at age three, standing naked on the beach—and she became my vision to reclaim. My main role model. Through the years, I've had some positive experiences and become less judgmental about myself. The years of energy I've put into this seem to have paid off in that I can enroll in a new class with a degree of self-confidence and self-acceptance that I didn't have in the past.

People of all classes and ages need the opportunity to exercise. There are many other groups who tend to avoid dance classes, and cultural attitudes provide limited chance for them to get needed exercise or to participate in the performing arts.

For fat people and others interested in attending classes I suggest:

1 Make sure you have comfortable clothing to wear, such as a leotard, or loose draw-string pants.

2 Observe or participate in a class before signing up.

3 Try to find a supportive friend to go with you.

4 The more you go to class, the more confident you'll be; as you study you'll be able to move as well as others in the class.

Conventional Western dance classes have been structured to suit the particular talents and needs of thin people. Keeping old techniques as well as forming new ones, we can work to alleviate our second-class status in the world of Western dance. We can work to create a new dance consciousness and body-awareness, opening up the social environment so that fat people can dance in public openly, free of slim people's judgments. Consider the future: fat people working and performing as dancers, fat people on beaches and at public social dances.

Cultural expression through dance and exercise is a right that belongs to everyone, not only those who are privileged because of their class or physical qualities. In pre-revolutionary Cuba health spas were the exclusive domain of the rich. Now exercise is considered a basic, essential right for everyone.

---

The author has taught creative movement workshops. As a poet and playwright, she has been developing a fat artistic perspective, creating positive role models for fat women in the performing arts.

# On Getting Strong: Notes from a Fat Woman, in Two Parts

Judith Stein

*Part I: July 1979*

Last fall, almost despite myself, I took a self-defense class from an area women's school. The class met for eight weeks, two hours per class, with one hour of intensive stretching/exercise, and one hour of self-defense skills. Our teacher had studied Tae Kwon Do, and she taught us out of that tradition. None of the other women in the class were fat, except for the teacher. Each and every week of the class, without fail, I would have to argue, plead, and make deals with myself to go to class. I would get to the door of the building and have to fight turning around.

I know some of my resistance was what most women go through when we begin to learn to fight back. We are taught to be victims from our earliest childhood, and most of us are encouraged to remain physically weak. But I knew also that, for me, being fat was the biggest part of my resistance — I have a lifetime of being told that I should be ashamed of my body, that I should not make myself conspicuous, and besides, I was too fat to be good at anything like that anyway. The teacher's tangible support, her patience, and her belief that each of us could develop these skills were major reasons why the class was a positive experience for all of us. But for me, her fatness and her skill combined, her skill as a fat woman teaching karate, meant that *I* could do it too, that I could get strong.

When the class ended, we talked about a second-level class for the next term at the school, some months away. During that vacation, the teacher was hurt in a camping accident and so was unable to teach. I didn't know of other women's classes, I was unwilling to study with men, and it seemed easier to let my interest slide than to keep fighting the voices inside me, which said I had no business doing that anyway.

In March, at a rally to mark International Women's Day, some women from a women's karate class did a demonstration that was incredibly inspiring to me. Their strength, their discipline, and their obvious caring for one another were powerfully moving to me, and I took seriously the invitation for other women to join their class. I began the next week, and since that first time, I have known that learning self-defense, learning to be physically strong, and learning from the discipline of studying a martial art are central to my well-being.

In the beginning, several friends of mine began the class with me. That initial support, from women who were aware of my struggles as a fat woman to do physical exercise, was really essential. Our class is actively supportive of all the women in it: it is collectively run, and non-competitive (non-ranked). Although only one other woman in the class is fat, and she and I haven't talked with each other about being fat women, I have found that my raising the issue of fatness and fat oppression has consistently been taken seriously and dealt with respectfully.

One of the earliest times: we were doing warm-up exercises as a group, and a woman was instructing us on an exercise which involved a kind of stretching which I was unable to do. She instructed: "Do it *this* way." After the exercise, I said to her that it was important that women instructing talk about each woman doing the exercise as well as possible. She listened, apologized for defining one right way to do things which excluded me (and several other women); and since that time, women leading exercises will present them as they "should" be done, but encourage women to do the exercise to the best of their ability. For me, this means I can do the best that I am able, without feeling incapable or ashamed of not being as strong as others in the class. I have found that I am getting much stronger and am more willing to push myself to *my* limit, instead of giving up in despair at not doing things "right."

My favorite karate story: In June (1979), our class was invited to do a presentation at a halfway house for drug-addicted women. When the request first came up, I didn't volunteer. Later, after thinking more, I decided I really did want to participate, for two reasons particular to me: I wanted women to see what they could do after only a few months of study (one time a week), and *I wanted women to see that fat women could learn and get good at karate*. At the next class, and at our planning meeting on the day of the demonstration, I brought up both of these points. The women I spoke to were excited that I wanted to do it, and extremely supportive. I was incredibly nervous!

We decided that the demonstration should be short and informal, and that we would present what we did in our classes so that women could see what it meant, for us, to "study karate." We began by introducing ourselves and saying something briefly about why we studied karate and for how long. I spoke last, and started by saying that I was very nervous *and* very excited to be there. I said that I wanted to do the demonstration because I had only studied a few months and wanted women to see what we could do in such a short time. I also said that I really wanted to do the demonstration because I had been fat all my life and had been told in a million ways that I could never get fast or strong, and that I ought to be ashamed to try. I was learning that this wasn't true, and that fat women could learn these things.

I was so nervous that I was looking down at my feet, but after I spoke, I glanced up quickly and saw a fat woman there nodding and smiling. The connections were clear and real for her, and I was pleased that I'd said all that.

The actual demonstration was wonderful! I did very well — felt strong and connected in my moves, and felt fluid and powerful throughout the whole thing. After the demonstration, we shared some basic karate skills with women. They were really open to us, learned from us, and taught us plenty as well. Afterwards, I was amazed at my bravery, and energized and high for hours.

I am physically stronger now than I have ever been before. I now study with the same class twice a week. I know that studying karate will be part of my life for a long time to come. I am deeply committed to women fighting our victimization, and I feel like I have begun to take that fight seriously for myself. Karate is a tangible way for me to clear out the self-hatred I have for my body. The support I have gotten from a few close friends who study karate, their commitment to me as a fat woman studying karate, and their sharing of their own struggles around learning to fight back have been growing for us all.

My favorite karate fantasy: Part I. Other fat Lesbians start to study karate in my class. Every time I go to class, I see more and more fat women working out. Together, in growing numbers, we reclaim our strength.

Part II. Each year, there is a weekend-long National Women's Martial Arts Special Training. This year there were no fat women there. Next year, many fat women, from my class, and from all over the country, will be at this training. Our grace and our power, our size and our strength become clear to each other. We become our own proof that women can triumph over our isolation, that we all can be strong.

*Part II: October 1982*

I still know very few fat Lesbians who are consciously, regularly physically active, and fewer still in the martial arts. The longer I have been involved with a martial arts group, the more I have gotten to know the women's martial arts movement. The more I know what goes on, the less I like it. Almost more than any other "institution" within the Lesbian community, the martial arts movement perpetuates fat hatred, able-bodyism, and the development of the "strong Amazon" (never fat!) as the Lesbian cultural ideal, despite the fact that this standard excludes more Lesbians than it includes. Hierarchical structures within the women's schools; a star system of "famous" women martial arts teachers (none of whom are fat); ranking based on standards that most fat women (as well as many other women) find difficult or impossible to meet; the equating of thinness (or at least lack of fatness) with being a strong woman (read: "good Lesbian"); the requirement of uniforms which are not available to women who weigh more than about 230 pounds; required exercises which are impossible and humiliating for many fat women (example: the yoga plow — feet over your head while you rest up on your shoulders); all of these things contribute to a movement which idealizes the strength of women while excluding most of us.

The National Women's Martial Arts Special Training of my fantasy has become a hotbed of authoritarian teaching styles, competitive workouts between women and among the various martial arts styles; and a showcase for the black-belt "stars" of the women's martial arts movement. Workouts are strenuous past the point of being grueling, and concern that the Training be available to a wide range of skill and ability/disability levels has almost disappeared. Groups such as my own, without ranking and with little interest in the formalities of martial arts etiquette, are included only as the lunatic fringe, and only because we refuse to be excluded.

We know of almost no other ongoing martial arts school in the country which retains a commitment to non-competitiveness and non-ranked teaching along with a political perspective on violence against women. What this means is that it has become harder, not easier, for a fat woman to find a martial arts or self-defense class in which she can determine her own pace, set her own limits, and be dealt with sensitively and respectfully. Access to fighting skills which all women need is becoming harder to get if you're not a jocky little Amazon. In 1982, as attacks on women escalate, this is dangerous.

My own karate skills have improved enormously in the three years since I wrote the first half of this piece. I am well-muscled and stronger, and I feel much more secure on the streets. I know that I am very good at some kinds of karate moves, even while others remain difficult. I think constantly about how being a fat woman fighter helps me, and also about how being fat hinders me. Sometimes I know how being fat adds to my skills. I have learned how to punch well, to make a tight fist, to aim and to connect with a target. I know when all 250 pounds of my energy is behind a punch, that punch will injure my attacker. I know that same thing in blocking an attack; the energy flows out into my arm, and my body weight adds strength, power, grounding and centering. I am an aggressive sparring partner, and my size makes me an intimidating opponent.

More fat dykes have joined my karate class now. We are definitely a presence within the class. When the collective decided to print T-shirts with our logo, there was no question but they would have large-size T-shirts—up to xxxxl and larger. The T-shirts are beautiful, and we all wear them with pleasure. Our class has written out certain guidelines for women joining our group, and these include attitudes we expect from new women. This includes a respect for the variations among the women in the class, and a commitment to creating a non-competitive supportive environment for all women.

My fantasies now have more to do with seeing the changes fat women go through as we learn to get angry and love ourselves. I love the feeling when, after a workshop or presentation about Fat Liberation, women coming up to me say: "I never knew anyone thought that, I thought I was a freak for loving my own body. I am so angry at being fucked over all of these years." If that happens only now and then, it still makes the effort worthwhile. When it happens for a lot of fat women, then I know change is coming.

*My newest fantasy:* Someday, not too long from now, we will have so many fat women doing karate, dance, movement, and other athletics, that we will hold a huge "Moving Women" celebration. As we gather together, powerful women, we will indeed feel our strength and beauty.

# 4. Ordinary Hassles: Living with harassment and isolation . . .

# *Ordinary Hassles*

## Doris K.

I went to the diet group because my friend brought me there. We were best friends through high school, and we lived together for two years before I got married. She knows what a struggle I've had, what I've been through.

People have given me a miserable time about my weight. I give myself a miserable time too, because I don't want to be fat. At other diet groups I had heard people talk before about how unhappy they were because they were overweight, but mostly they worried about their diets and not about their lives. At this particular diet group, for the first time, I really heard people talk about the pain of being fat, of being overweight. Of course they want you to lose weight, but they also really want you to learn to like yourself and to be able to live your life not just constantly worrying about being overweight and what you can and can't eat.

Eating problems — that's the story of my life. When I'm feeling sad, there's not enough food in the world. I don't eat in front of people too much. Sometimes I'll go out and hit Howard Johnson's at 2 o'clock in the morning and have a breakfast or something like that. Sometimes I'll just stay in the house, don't get dressed, don't get cleaned up or anything, all day long, and just sit there and eat, until I feel really sick. I can remember a lot of times eating until I was nearly unconscious, drugged or drunk, but on food. And the feeling is so terrible. I felt, and do sometimes now, so worthless, so ugly, just good for nothing — because how could a person that's worthwhile just sit there and eat?

When I was growing up, any time that I took a mouthful of anything someone in my family would say, "You'd better watch it, you're going to be fat." I think that's when I really started all this secret eating, and probably the binging. If you want to eat, just make sure they don't see you. You have to stuff it in when no one is looking.

Going back through the years, so many people put the thought that I'm worthless into my mind. They say, "Look at that fat slob," when they're talking about some other person who's overweight. So I know they're thinking that about me. And they *do* say it to my face.

When I was pregnant with my second child, I was about fifteen pounds overweight by the charts. The doctor told me not to gain any weight with this pregnancy, so that when I delivered, I wouldn't have the weight problem. So I tried to go along with it. I would starve myself for days, knowing that I had to go to the doctor to weigh in. I can remember a few days when I didn't eat anything, or maybe just had a cup of coffee — that's no way for a pregnant mother to carry a child! But still I gained five pounds. One day, after seeing that I had gained a few pounds, the doctor blew up at me. He threw the chart down. He kept shaking his head and telling me how disgusted he was with me. As he was cursing at me, I sat there crying. The tears were running down my face. To hell with me, I was nothing to him, I wasn't a person, I was a big fat blob that happened to be carrying a baby. He finally said, "I don't give a damn about you. But I *do* care about that baby. I'll get rid of that weight."

So he put me in a hospital and on a very low calorie diet, about 700 calories per day. And after two or three days he came in to check on me, and I hadn't lost any weight. He said, "Who's slipping you candy?" I said, "Honest to God, I'm not cheating." He said, "You have to be, because you're not losing."

So he cut the diet down to 500 calories per day. And he had the nurses watching me to make sure I didn't cheat, as if I was such a mess that I couldn't even be trusted inside a hospital, let alone the real world. And after a week I had lost *one pound*. And he looked at me and said, "Well, you surprise me. I guess it is hard for you to lose weight, isn't it?" And I never saw him again.

A man once asked me how many pounds I'd lost. I said, "Probably a couple of hundred." And he laughed. But really, I've lost more than two hundred pounds, easily! Because I'll lose ten pounds and put back on twelve, and lose ten and put back on fifteen. That's what I've done all my life.

If I'm happy and things are going well, I can stay on a diet for a couple of weeks. If I had twenty pounds to lose, I could probably make it. But I've got a hundred pounds to lose. After a few weeks I get so tired of doing without things that other people normally eat without even thinking. They don't even stop to think that they can't have that bread on their sandwich. They just have it, like they would take a deeper breath. And here I'm always having to say no, I can't eat that because I don't want to ruin my diet. After a few weeks of dieting I go off onto a binge.

Usually I'll just want a sandwich, a real sandwich, not a little diet thing. Or I'll want something sweet. Then if I eat it, I feel I've messed up today, so I might as well mess up real bad and have everything I've been hungry for. As soon as I have a taste of that forbidden food, I'm just gone. If I don't have money to buy food, I'll search through old purses and pockets, get bottles and cash them in, break the kids' piggy bank open — do anything, just to get enough money to buy food, so that I can feel disgusted with myself later on. It's really sick. I'll wake up in the middle of the night thinking, I've got to go back on that diet tomorrow. But then, if I'm going to go on that diet tomorrow, I've got to hurry up now and eat while I can — and I'll go to the kitchen and start binging all over again.

My husband's always on my back to lose weight. But a few times when I did lose weight, I could tell he felt threatened. He'd bring home chocolate cakes, for mama. He'd say, "You've done so well, look at the reward I've brought you." He wants me thin, and yet he wants me fat. He wants me to look skinny and glamorous for him. But he wants me fat enough so that he knows I'll be too self-conscious to leave home and run around. What he'd like is for me to have a "fat suit" that he could put on me, so no one else would look at me. So he could run off and do whatever he wants, and I'm stuck at home.

He used to be tactful about it. He'd say, "I don't want to hurt your feelings, but . . . " and then just let me have it. But the last few years he's been really cruel about it. He'll just say, "Do you know how disgusting you look?" He'd always be nice to me around other people. But, for example, if we were going to a party, just before we got out of the car he'd make some comment like, "You look awfully big in that dress." And for a shy person like me, that would ruin my whole night. I'm very self-conscious. Surrounded by all those size fives, I sometimes feel that everyone is looking at me, I feel like I'm on the wrong planet. And there's no place to hide.

Sometimes I'll be at a party, having a good time, and suddenly I'll become conscious of other people measuring me up in disgust. That finishes me. Most of the time I can't even talk any more.

And inside I feel panic. I'm smothering, being crushed, under all those terrible feelings. Once in a while I find someone at a party who's nice, and I tend to forget that they're small and I'm big. That's how I wish I could live — everyone forget about size. Let what's inside come out. If you have anything in common, fine, you'd get along.

When I see a person who is overweight, I really feel sorry for that person. I know, because of all the problems I've had, that they're really catching hell.

The lady who lives upstairs from me was five months pregnant before she knew she was pregnant. She's always been heavy. Her husband has been giving her a really bad time. He's laid down the law: either she lose that goddamn fat or he's leaving. I talked with her last night. She sounded desperate. She said, "This has been my whole life, trying to lose weight. I don't know what's going to happen. Do you know what I find myself doing now? I go into the kitchen when he's away, and I'll start eating things — anything — just eat, eat, eat. And I'm so disgusted with myself. I feel so bad. I don't know what I'm going to do. I'm so worried."

Society thinks of fat women as disgusting, as very unsexy. But fat men? . . . "He's heavy, but he's a good boy."

Recently I've been re-evaluating my opinion of myself. I've been measuring myself up to a lot of other people and deciding that I do a lot of things well. The women's movement has helped me a lot in this. I used to think I had to let my husband take the credit for things I did. Now I'm starting to realize what a good job *I've* done taking care of my family, straightening out my husband's life. I'm getting to the place where I can think, "I like me. I like to be with me." I'm usually nice to people. I must be a pretty good person. Sometimes I look back and think I've almost been a super-woman to have handled the problems I've handled, as well as I've done.

Now that my marriage is breaking up, I'll be looking for a job. And that scares the daylights out of me. In the first place, I haven't worked for many years, except for my husband, when he had a business — I handled the office. So I can do the work. But I have a nightmare of walking into an office for an interview and the people looking at me — because most places really discriminate against people who are overweight. I've never looked for jobs when I've been this heavy. And I can't stand the thought of that rejection.

All things considered, I think that being fat has ruined my life. I can't do the things I really want to do because I'm afraid people are putting me down for being fat. For example, just this past weekend I went out with two women friends to the theater, then for dinner. After dinner they wanted to go to a discothèque. And I couldn't face that. I told them I wanted to take care of some other things and didn't really want to go, so they should go on to the discothèque and meet me afterwards. But I really did want to go. I was too self-conscious about my weight — being seen by all those thin people in a place where someone who's overweight just doesn't belong. Many times I've passed up things and pretended I don't want them when I really do.

Some people say that the problem is all in our heads — that we should just learn to feel good about ourselves. That we shouldn't care about other people not liking us because we're fat. But those people don't know what they're talking about. They don't know how it feels to be stared at with such disgust. It's not the fat that's held me down, it's the opinion of other people.

Often, now, I hate to get involved too deeply with people. If they want me to lose weight, or if I know that they're going to keep an eye on what I eat, I know I'm going to disappoint them. I'm so tired of disappointing people, I'm so tired of fighting. I just wish everyone could just relax and let me be. And I'll let them be. I wish people would just get off my back.

# *A Day in My Life*

## Judy Freespirit

The question is, "Given the prevalence and virulence of fat oppression how do you manage to get through the day? How do you
survive?" I think about a typical day in the life of Judy Freespirit
before I answer.

I get up in the morning and get ready for work, take my asthma
medication and dash out in time to catch the bus. Since I get on
the bus near the beginning of the line there are a lot of empty seats
so I take one of the empty double ones. I'm aware as the bus fills
up that all the seats are being filled except the one next to me.
Finally, when there is only the one seat left I see the woman get on
the bus. I'm aware of how she looks around before taking the seat
next to me. I'm aware that she is uncomfortable and thinks I'm
taking up too much space. I tell myself that I am not too big, that
the seats are too small. I tell myself that the boys who are jabbing
each other in the ribs and laughing at me are ignorant little creeps
and I send them an itch where they can't reach it, hoping that my
magic works. I walk the 2 blocks from the bus station to my office.

When I get to my desk I ignore the discussion between the three
secretaries who sit nearby talking about the latest diets they are
on, and about how many miles they jog each day. I ignore the
prick attorney who ogles them and I'm glad that he ignores me. I
make sure that my expression is neutral, that the hostility I feel
does not either show through or get co-opted by an attitude of
charm and ingratiation.

I make sure that when I walk to the xerox machine I breathe
evenly and heavily so they will not interpret my asthma as the
huffing and puffing of a fat slob. I tell myself that I'm all right,
over and over again. I tell myself that I'm in control of deciding
where I will put the energy to educate and I choose not to do it
here in the office where there is little chance of succeeding.

I make sure that I work hard and well. I can't afford to have any complaints about my work because the chances of getting another job are not good. The tighter the job market the less possible it is to get work if you don't look like a fashion model.

I relieve the switchboard operator for her lunch hour and pick up her copy of *Cosmopolitan Magazine* to kill the boring hour. I look at the articles on how to lose weight, the "Doctor's Advice on Dieting." I note that they are full of shit, and think about how I really should write an article, but know they would never publish it. These readers don't want to hear the truth. They want to believe they can all look like the woman on the cover. I look at the ads for slim cigarettes advertised by slim models, the ads blaring out "Lose Ugly Fat," and "Results guaranteed without tummy wraps," and "I lost 110 lbs. in 20 weeks and my husband loves me again." I remember that it is a lie, remember the motive is profit.

I go to lunch. I sit on the high stool at the counter in the coffee shop. I'm careful about how I get on and off the stool so I won't give the folks a chance to see me as a clown. I prove myself capable of looking graceful as a ballerina. I force myself to eat slowly. I remind myself that I have a right to eat, to eat in public, to eat what I want. I ignore the covert glances and blatant stares and eat anyway. I refuse to hide from them and let them control me. I leave with a knot in my stomach.

After work I look over my notes on fat liberation, then drive over to KPFA radio station. I grit my teeth as I plod up the steep stairway to the second floor, pausing just before the top to catch my breath so I won't be panting when I reach the receptionist. Without asking who I am she tells me Toni Gray, the moderator for the women's health show, has been looking for me. I wonder how she knows who I am. Toni introduces herself by telling me that this is the first time she's done a show on fat and that she doesn't know much about fat liberation but her roommate told her we have a lot to teach her. Toni is very thin, maybe 100 lbs. I wonder if I'm going to be set up again on the air.

My co-guest speaker is an average-sized dietician with good fat politics. She gives the correct medical information and answers Toni's questions and speaks from a fat liberation perspective as a professional, giving credibility to my position as a fat activist. We work well together, as we have done in the past on many occasions, and after 15 minutes of discussion the phones are opened up to callers. All women. The first one thinks we must have the facts wrong, the second one says there are new articles she's been reading about some new weight-loss method and do we know anything about it; The third one thinks people in fat liberation are *pathetic* because they have given up hope. The fourth one has just lost 35 pounds using affirmations and knows that if I would just learn to love myself and affirm myself I could do it too. The last caller wants to know something about whether or not fat floats. I get one minute to rebut, to make a final statement. I do the best I can in an impossible situation.

Toni is freaked out. She's never done a health show before with an oppressed group of people where every single caller was hostile, where nobody appeared to have heard anything that was said, where the fear and self-hatred of the callers was so clear and pervasive. I give her a ride home and try to explain about internalized oppression, about the righteousness of women who manage for periods of time to "pass," the fear over the possibility of failing, the self-righteousness at the momentary victory. She is freaked out. She feels responsible. I end up having to take care of her.

I go home. A friend who heard the program calls to tell me that the callers were off the wall and I was fine. I cry. I feel alone. I want to be held but have no lover, and when I have no lover I don't feel loved. Even though I *know* I'm loved by my friends, I don't *feel* loved. It's because I'm fat, because I'm aging, because I'm an incest survivor who learned that to get love was to be sexual. I tell myself it's not true. My friends love me. I am lovable even if I'm alone in bed. I think about the show, about the process of the day. I go to sleep sitting up because I'm wheezing.

So the question was, "given the prevalence and the virulence of fat oppression, how do you manage to get through the day? How do you survive?" The answer is, it's a struggle, day by day, hour by hour, minute by minute. It's keeping on because there's no other choice.

# Interview with Martha

*Martha is a 41-year-old Lesbian living in Iowa City. She has been in a wheel chair for the past twenty years.*

*"I don't want the women who read this to feel that I spend all of my time being bitter and angry, but to realize that these are the hardest parts of my life in a concentrated form. Also I worry that the wheelchair part will be hard for some to put in perspective, so I would like to add that sometimes being in a wheelchair is awful, but that most of the time it's pretty ordinary."*
— *Martha*

*Lisa: Were you fat when you were a little kid?*
Martha: I was told I was. As I look at the pictures now, I realize that "chubby" to them meant I was 5 pounds overweight. Probably in seventh grade I did start getting fat. But I had been hearing that I was fat since I was about five.
*Lisa: What kind of stuff did they say to you about it?*
Martha: They always kept saying, "Well, Martha's got baby fat. She'll outgrow it one of these days." It was constant. "Oh yes, she'd be such a pretty girl if she wasn't so chubby."
*Lisa: And when did they start knowing that you weren't going to outgrow it?*
Martha: I think probably in eighth grade and then early high school. I started dieting then.
*Lisa: When you went on diets, did your whole family go on them with you?*
Martha: Pretty much. One of the things that was happening was that in grade school you got a quarter for lunch money and what I ended up doing, because I was never allowed any spending money, was that I took my lunch money and I spent it at the candy store at noontime and bought all this shitfood. I know that mostly came from seeing other kids having spending money. If I'd had my choice, it would've been nice if I had eaten lunch and then maybe had a dime or something. My folks were really tight with money.
*Lisa: How were the kids in school about you being fat? Were there other fat kids?*
Martha: I don't remember too much about grade school. I got

along pretty well, so I didn't get too much teasing for being fat. I'm not real sure why. I think I was always considered the athletic one. I wasn't into boys, so by eighth grade the girls were starting to change and have different interests. All I was interested in was playing volleyball and baseball.

Lisa: *And you were pretty good in sports?*

Martha: Fairly good. I was also in band and played the accordion. After school when the other kids were playing, I was home practicing the accordion. I was really quite isolated. So the kids probably didn't know me well enough to make fun of me when I was getting bigger. In eighth grade I was starting to get pretty chunky, as they say. I was probably twenty to thirty pounds overweight.

I think in high school it started getting real bad. It was really evident that I was starting to get out of step because I wasn't doing the boy trip. But there I was fairly lucky again, because I got in band and I was still known as a good athlete. The other thing was my cousin Don was a year ahead of me, and he was very popular. And so I had a lot of girlfriends because they wanted to get to know him through me. That was why I had girlfriends pretty much. Basically, I read through high school. Every place I went I had a book, and I tried to stay inside of myself as much as possible.

Lisa: *How did you feel?*

Martha: How did I feel? Well, it was real hard to get involved with the crap that was going on at school because there was so much crap going on at home. It was just real hard. I didn't care. I mean, when there's life-threatening shit going on at home, who cares about school — school was a joy. I was never sick a day. Who the hell wanted to stay home?

Overall I kept thinking to myself, maybe if I get a little bit fatter, people will finally get off of it. There's got to be some point when they will finally shut up. But it's like, I'm at 300 pounds now, and they still haven't shut up.

Lisa: *When you were in high school and were pretty aware of being fat, did you every once in a while go on a diet?*

Martha: I can't remember dieting a lot in high school. I was different from the other women in high school because I like athletics. I never worried about it too much. I always figured it was just part of being an athlete. That doesn't mean that there weren't times when I wanted to be skinnier, but dieting just didn't occur to me a whole lot. I remember before I went to college my mother instituted another diet. That one worked pretty well. We got me down pretty skinny so I was presentable for college.

But mostly, I wasn't skinny in college. I was in phys. ed. and some of the instructors were not too happy about it. They never really said a lot. I think they were more worried about me being queer than they were about me being fat. I don't know how they did it, but they would not let one woman I knew graduate until she lost weight. They actually threw her out of the program until she could lose weight. I'm not sure that she ever came back.

When I got here and was in phys. ed., I became the class clown. During a field hockey game I was running and running and finally slipped and fell and lay down on the ground and just sort of wheezed. I exaggerated the wheeze so people would laugh. And the same thing—we had a tumbling class and when it was my turn to do a flying sommersault over a human pyramid, I would yell, "Okay, girls, are you ready down there? Here I come." How I got through was to try to be the class clown. I made people laugh at the stuff I couldn't do and, of course, the friend I picked was totally skinny. She probably weighed about a hundred pounds dripping wet and was taller than I, so in modern dance class, it was sort of like Laurel and Hardy.

So that's basically what I did—I tried to be less self-conscious about being heavier than a lot of the women by trying to make them laugh.

*Lisa: What did you feel would have happened if you hadn't done that?*

Martha: It was real evident that I didn't fit in and that was the only way that I could sort of fit in. I really didn't know how to make close friends very well because I was just real shy and I was drinking a lot. Being the class clown was the only way I could make friends. And that wasn't making friends, that was just hoping that you would be accepted.

*Lisa: And you felt it came from being self-conscious about being fat . . . maybe not being able to do some of the things . . . ?*

Martha: Well, I think it came from two things: one was from being fat, and some of it came from just being really naive and not very worldly. I didn't know how to make friends. When I was going to high school, I would get up at six in the morning, and I had to practice the accordion for an hour in the morning and then when I got home from school, I had to practice whenever band let out—from 3:30 on to 5:00. So, there was no time for making friends.

*Lisa: Tell me about the accident.*

Martha: It was my senior year in college. It was winter, January, and real cold. About midnight we came up over the hill and a truck was jackknifed across the highway and there were no flares out. We ended up in the ditch. Nobody was killed, but there were some bad injuries. I broke my back, which I knew. They did surgery on my back and they said, well, they didn't know if I was gonna walk or not. They wouldn't say absolutely not. They started having me sit up and get used to a wheelchair and then they were gonna have me walk with crutches and braces, which is a laugh except that it's good exercise. I don't know of any women paraplegics who walk with crutches and braces. If you see any women walking with crutches and braces, chances are they are polio victims. With polio you at least have the sensation of where your legs are. Whereas with this, not only can you not control them, you don't know where the hell they're at. Walking with crutches and braces, you fall a lot.

I got real strong. But they were busy watching my weight. I started putting on weight as soon as I got well and started eating again. And then I started drinking again very heavy, even drinking in the hospital. I was underage, but what were they gonna do . . . you know, they couldn't throw you out. By the time I left the hospital I was drinking real heavily and I was putting on more and more weight. That's what I did for twenty years. Finally, I don't drink anymore. Now I weigh probably 330 pounds. I don't mind being fat. I've been fat or thought I was fat all of my life. And if other people would forget about it, I wouldn't mind it.

I've been trying to think that I'm just the right weight, instead of thinking that I'm fat. Because thinking that you're fat means so many crummy things, you know, that if you just think that you're all right, then you won't have to worry so much about doing what other people want you to do or what you have been told that you should do.

*Lisa: So, who tells you what you should do?*

Martha: The doctor tells me every time. He does everything but sneer. I put in my catheter, and he is amazed that I can get my legs spread apart and get a little tube in there. "I just don't know how you do it." My dad started bringing me articles, trying to get me to join Overeaters Anonymous and Weight Watchers. When I was working in pediatrics, they made all of their doctors who were overweight go to Weight Watchers. You read ads in the news-papers about insurance companies saying that fat people are making your insurance rates go up, so it's no wonder people feel they can put down fat people.

The pressure from the doctor comes down in the form of: if I ever need surgery, my being obese would cause a greater chance of morbidity. I love how they put it. Some of it is that they're just not willing to operate on people my size.

*Lisa: How many years has the doctor been telling you that?*
Martha: About five years. Another thing — he's been trying very hard to fix me up with a surgeon who will do stomach stapling. Cutting my kidney, that's real risky; but cutting my gut, that's not? I'm just not up for dying. I'd rather be fat than dead.

*Lisa: Where did you live after the accident?*
Martha: In Iowa City. There was nothing back then. You couldn't use the pool. There weren't any curb cuts. There was nothing to do, no place to go. All you could do was go to a bar and go to a restaurant. You couldn't go to the movies — you were a fire hazard in the movies unless you transferred over to one of the other seats; and if you transferred over to the seat, then the usher would take your wheelchair and put it out in the lobby. So if there was a fire, you knew damn good and well you were going to burn to death. Now there are theaters with the back seats out. I've gone to more movies in the last two or three years than I did in the last twenty years.

*Lisa: What was it like at your job at the University?*
Martha: I have always assumed that if I was skinnier I would have been more popular at work. In my older age, I'm not so sure that is true. I think I would have had a better chance at it. I think people would have been more accepting. 'Cause then I was pretty heavy. It was real evident that I wasn't going to be included. I was not only in a wheelchair, but I was fat. I was really pretty lonely.

There is a part of me that is afraid to be skinny 'cause I'm afraid I'd get mean. I think it would be real hard if I did get to be size 12 and people'd start being real nice to me. I think it'd make me real angry. I don't know if I could handle that. I fantasize that I would just use them and throw them away. Fat woman fantasy number one.

I never wanted to get a promotion to be a private secretary. I never even tried for it, because I knew that, because I was overweight and in the wheelchair, none of the doctors were going to want me. The doctors were into real pretty secretaries. Some of the doctors were known for being lechers. They even fired a woman because she complained that her doctor was making passes at her. He wasn't asked to leave, she was. So I didn't really want any part of that, and as I became more and more aware of the politics of working there, I became more and more closed to myself. I became the head of the typing pool; that was about the best I could do. They didn't want to lose me because the turnover was so great in that typing pool that they just wanted somebody who was going to work there constantly, who wouldn't cause any trouble, and I fit the bill perfectly.

The people that I worked with treated me pretty good. And they had reason to — I think I treated them pretty good. Eventually I started coming in to work later and later. By this time everybody probably knew that I had a drinking problem. A lot of people probably wondered why I didn't get fired — even *I* wondered. I felt bad, working with the people in the office that I did, 'cause I knew that they were having to do some of the work that I should be doing. But at that point, you know, you're just trying to survive, and you can feel ashamed of yourself for it, but there was nothing I could do about it.

I think I was trying to be fired. And I was getting sicker and sicker. They had me on antibiotics for about ten years, for kidney infections. Finally they said, after I'd been on the medication all those years, "Oh, yes, by the way, that medication causes your hair to fall out." And I said, "Well, gee, I could have told you that."

I started thinking seriously about going on disability and that's what I eventually did. But it was hard — the pride of working and this sort of thing. I'm still lower middle class enough that that was always important to people that I grew up with. So it was real hard to do that. Even now, at times, I make work so I can feel proud of the things that I do. I know that I'm much more healthy now that I'm not working. I can take better care of myself. And it's like living a lie — I mean, I don't know how people manage it, working in the institutions like that — the things that are rewarded are incredible. If you can lie, cheat, and steal, then the prospects are good for becoming high management in institutions.

*Lisa: While you were working, did you ever think about trying something else?*

Martha: No, I was too afraid. By then, I knew I was an alcoholic, and, with my work record, I couldn't get a job any place else. I didn't think anybody else would hire me. During all this time, too, people in the office were real diet-conscious. There were a lot of diets going on.

*Lisa: If there was something that you wanted to do, what would it be?*

Martha: There's nobody I want to work for. I think that most people are tired out from working an eight-hour day. But when you're in a wheelchair, it is incredible. To be at work at 8 AM, I had to get up at 6, and that's a matter of not even getting to work on time. If it's winter, that means I gotta make sure that one of the kids in the trailer court is gonna shovel the walks for me. It's just incredible worry. The worry of even being at work, in a public place where you have to be every day.

There were no bathrooms in the University where I worked that I could get into. Even when they finally got around to making some handicapped bathrooms—and I had worked there for ten years before that happened—they were quite a distance away. There was a bathroom right next to my office, but it was still not one that I could use. On the days when I had diarrhea or something like that, I could be there but I was real uncomfortable. I worried every minute that I was going to go to the bathroom, because I don't have enough sensation to know whether I'm going to go or not. I think that's my biggest relief from not working. I have shit in front of a whole office full of people. And let me tell ya, it's real mortifying. After the first time you get mortified, it gets easier. Maybe nobody would even see me dirty myself, but I'd have to get transferred into my car, and then I'd go home and jump in the tub and just cry. That's one of the reasons why I don't want to work for someone in a public place anymore.

*Lisa: Are there other ways you are uncomfortable in public?*

Martha: I'm not real social about food. I know that I'd much rather eat all by myself. It's much more comfortable. I don't feel like anybody's watching what I eat. I can eat whatever I want without trying to be impressive by eating a lot of salad when I really don't want salad. There's this pressure when you're in public to eat reasonable foods, and I'm sure that I would eat reasonable foods anyway, but I always feel the pressure.

*Lisa: I know that at different times you've talked about the natural foods co-op here not being a great place to go . . .*

Martha: It's hard to get in and out of there. For the most part, it is basically a self-serve type of place; and because I can't reach a lot of those things, I feel like I'm putting people out. And the floor is uneven and I almost fell out of the chair once when I went down in that dip. I feel more comfortable going to the grocery store, where I run into a lot of old people, a lot of fat people. If I go to the co-op, I'm going to run into skinny hippy-dippies with their jeans and soft shirts, and I feel real out of place. All those skinny young people make me feel like it's a joke that I'm trying to eat health food.

There were times when I wheeled past the co-op restaurant. You had to be tall, because the counter was way tall, and there was sort of this following from the store into this narrow place. With the wheelchair, I blocked everybody. Nobody could get past me. So, there was no way that I could sit there and feel comfortable.

*Lisa: Maybe you should talk about when you came out, and when you used to go to a lot of the dances.*

Martha: It was real painful back then when the lesbian community sort of came to be. And I wish I could say that things got better for me, but they didn't because the community mostly consisted of college women with real middle class to upper middle class backgrounds. I can't tell if it was because I was so shy or felt so conspicuous or uncomfortable and that's why I wasn't very popular, or if it was because I was drinking or because I was too intense. I had a feeling that a lot of it was the wheelchair and a lot of it was being fat. It was a real painful period. I was hurt a lot. I mean, there were parties upstairs. I had a girlfriend, and she thought nothing of going to a party that I couldn't get to.

The other way that I used to communicate when I was a walking person was that I loved to dance. I didn't have to talk much if I danced with somebody. Where I grew up everybody told dirty jokes to be social, but I soon realized that that was no way to be a good feminist, and I would edit what I was going to say. So for a while there—about three years—I stuttered. I look back on that time now, it's funny: I had a couple of real close girlfriends—not lovers, just friends—and every once in a while I'd pull one of them aside and say, "Quick, quick, I just gotta tell somebody a joke."

And she would listen and roll her eyes and then go back inside to the party. I needed a joke fix every once in a while.

At the dances I found that what I did was I drank and I played with the kids. We had some youngsters, and that's who I would spend my time with. They used to push me around in the wheelchair at the dances and stuff like that. I could sort of dance sitting in the wheelchair, but I felt like I had to be drunk before I could do that. And I felt like I was fat and just sort of bouncing around in the wheelchair. I didn't know what it looked like. If I got drunk enough, I didn't care. Another thing, too, is I never had mirrors in the house. I used my bathroom mirror just to comb my hair. Now I have a full-length mirror, and I like it. I really look at myself. I've even danced in front of the mirror, and it's really not bad. I like the way I look when I dance, and I'm thinking that I could try it again now without drinking, since I don't drink anymore. But back then, I was too scared to have a mirror. I mean, even if I could have, I don't think I would have. It was real evident that I wasn't very popular. Nobody much asked me to dance, and when they did, I always felt like they were asking me to dance because of the wheelchair.

The few girlfriends that I did have didn't seem to have much patience as far as making love. I got so I would make love to them and I wouldn't let them touch me, because back at that time I didn't have any sensation. I still don't, but I have sort of learned to come. And it took ten to fifteen years to learn how to do that, and I feel like basically I had to learn it all on my own, because the women that I was with, none of them wanted to have anything to do with that. They just didn't understand. I think part of what made it more difficult was that I was heavy, and I felt like I wasn't very lovable. It was a hard time. I feel real bitter about back then. I can't tell how much of it to put on the wheelchair, how much to put on being fat, how much to put on the people I was seeing then. I don't know if it's anybody's fault or everybody's fault.

There weren't many things I could feel good about—making love was one of them. If anybody asked, I probably would make love to them, just so I could say, "Hey, well at least she wants me to make love to her." My priorities are certainly a lot different now than they were then. The reason that I went along with it is that it at least made me feel good to tell myself that I was a good lover. Now, I don't care. Now, you better be a good lover or buzz off.

It's kind of interesting that most of the lovers that I've had have been real pretty. I don't quite understand. There was this one-night stand, and she said that she used to be real fat, and she was one of the first people that made me aware that it might be real nice to have a lover who was fat. I got to thinking about it, and I thought, "Yeah, gee, it would be real nice to have a fat lover and one who was in a wheelchair." I got to thinking that that would be just all right, whereas before I'd gone along with the rest of the mystique that everybody wanted a lover who was skinny and pretty and this sort of thing. That was a worthwhile one-night stand. Now most of my friends are fat, and that helps.

Things have changed. I used to feel primarily that I was a lesbian. Now, I feel primarily that I'm a woman in a wheelchair. When I was twenty-two, I didn't know any other lesbians. Now, I don't know any other women in wheelchairs. There are a few around, but they're not very friendly. I ran into one in the store and tried to make conversation with her, but it was real evident that she just wanted me to kiss off. So, I just sort of did, ya know?

*Lisa: Why do you think it's that way?*

Martha: Oh, there could be a lot of reasons. It could be because I'm fat and ugly and in a wheelchair. They may feel like I make it hard for them to be in a wheelchair because I'm fat. It could be that they're not used to being crippled yet themselves, and they really don't identify with being handicapped. And so, being approached by another person who is handicapped can be difficult. It takes a while to get used to that.

*Lisa: Have you ever run into another woman who is fat, and your eyes meet, and it's that same kind of thing?*

Martha: Yeah, it's like they don't want to look at you 'cause they know that they are fat. It *is* the same thing. Also, I find that Black people and I have a lot of eye contact. We seem to have this back-and-forth feeling. I'm sure it's the wheelchair and not necessarily the fat. They know that I'm oppressed, wheelchair-wise. I've figured out that I get off easy being fat and being in a wheelchair, because people feel that I'm fat because I'm in a wheelchair, and they figure that if I was a walking person I wouldn't be fat and so that frees me from some of the shit that they would normally throw on me.

*Lisa: In the early days of the community, things were pretty hard. Were there some people who were your best friends?*

Martha: Yeah, I hung around with Paula and Sue. They were pretty much my best friends for quite a few years.

*Lisa: Did you talk to them about all this kind of stuff?*

Martha: No. In fact, one of the things that we had arguments about was that Paula and Sue liked being over at my house because they could be touchy-feely with each other, and it was real painful. I mean, I certainly wasn't included . . . maybe I'd get a hug here and there. But I wasn't included, and finally I said, "Hey, you know . . ." I think they did attempt to change. Paula wasn't too happy about it, but I think Sue understood and so she helped Paula to understand.

At that point in time, I was really drinking a lot, I was drinking a whole lot, and people would come over. That's the other thing that has been hard: most of the people I know, I can't get into their houses. It's been so long that, even if I had the chance to get into their houses, I wouldn't go. It's like, I don't know how to act in somebody else's house. With the wheelchair, I feel like I can't move around because I nick furniture. I nick furniture all over my house. I feel like, in other people's houses, I gotta be real real careful. So between everything, it makes me real uncomfortable.

*Lisa: Things could have been better. Ideally, we would have more Lesbian space that's accessible to everybody.*

Martha: Yeah, I agree. I think that things could have been done. Now that I'm sober and forty, I'm starting to understand that nobody gave a flying fuck. That was basically where it was at. I could say, well, they were having their own kind of troubles, but the reality was that I was the only one in the community in a wheelchair, and I wasn't making any noise about it. And it's always the same thing: if you shut up, if you don't make people aware of it, they're not going to do anything. Ya know? It's not their problem.

*Lisa: How come you don't go to dances anymore?*

Martha: Most of the people that I want to see, I could see in other circumstances. And I've got a lover, so I'm not out beating the bushes for a lover. If I didn't have a lover, I'd be more inclined to show up at one of the dances here and there just to see who's around. But the main reason that I'm not going to the dances is that I absolutely refuse to be carried down the stairs anymore. I wear skirts a lot. I don't want to be tilted back and have everybody that's standing out on the stage to be able to look up my skirt while I'm being carried down like a sack of potatoes. The hell with it. Ya know, it's not worth it. They're not that much fun, anyway.

But if they were accessible, that might be different. I can't go to the bathroom. If I gotta piss, that means I gotta piss in a beer can or a bottle in the middle of the kitchen with everybody watching. I get tired of that. I'm not willing to put up with those kinds of indignities anymore.

It sounds like things are gonna sort of change around the coffeehouse and be made more accessible. I'm not positive, because some of it has to go through the landlord, but if the bathroom gets changed and if I get a parking space, I think that will make me feel a lot better.

*Lisa: How have you felt about going to concerts?*

Martha: Well, the concert place is fairly accessible. There isn't an easy bathroom to get into, but it's only for short period of time. The nice thing about it is that I can come and go as I want. They have got an electric lift there, and so if I want to I could come with my roommate and she could stay and I could leave. And I don't need anybody to "help" me out the door.

*Lisa: Would you feel like talking about that one concert that you and I both were at several years ago?*

Martha: Well, that was a real crucial time in my life. The day before had been the first day I had stopped drinking, and Sue and I were broken up for the time being, so I was kind of alone. When I went to that concert, one of the neat things was Meg Christian talking about her alcoholism, which came at a real good time for me. She couldn't have planned it any better. I'm sure that one of the things that helped me recover was that, when she talked about it, somehow I got it that this is Meg Christian, and I could see that she is a good person, so that means that *I'm* a good person. I never got it before that I could be an alcoholic and be a good person. I always thought that I was a real bad person, that there must be some character flaw that made me an alcoholic. I hadn't gotten it that it was a disease, and that I was a good person.

At the concert, we ran into a lot of people that I hadn't seen for a long time and they were saying, "We'll see you at the dance afterwards." Well, when I drove to the dance, I was kind of shaky. You [Lisa] could see that I was kind of shaky and you didn't want to go into the dance that much yourself, so we sat outside in the truck and talked.

*Lisa: I sort of remember some other things about that night . . .*

Martha: What do you remember?

*Lisa: I remember that a lot of the stuff that Meg Christian was talking about was this certain kind of togetherness that Lesbians had. I felt that it was pretty hard to enjoy the kind of stuff that she was saying becasue I didn't feel part of it.*

Martha: That was probably going on for me, too. I never did feel part of the community. I've never felt a camaraderie . . . I think one of the things is that most of the women feel togetherness by working together. And there's never been the ease with which I could comfortably work with other people. About the only thing I could do was encourage women to be as independent as they could be or support them in their work. But, I think that the kind of closeness that Meg's talking about is what you get from working with women, and I never felt included in that. I don't know if it's the wheelchair or being fat or both, but I'm sure that wasn't me she was talking about there.

# *untitled*

## Sue McCabe

I walk at night feeling safe in the darkness. My hands buried deep inside my pockets, I can go anywhere, and I have.

It is only when I walk in daylight that I am afraid. I am afraid of the children who pass me on the street and yell, "fat ass." I am afraid of the insults that echo off car windshields. I am afraid of my reflection in storefront windows.

How can I describe this feeling of always wanting to hide. To become invisible. To go deeper and deeper into myself, where I am safe.

I walk and feel my pulse inside my throat and remember to hold my stomach in.

# The Human Potential Movement: Judging People's Humanity by Their Looks

## Sharon Bas Hannah

Family Synergy is an organization for the study and practice of inner emotional growth, extended families, and communal living. I went to one of their meetings because I have similar interests.

The meeting was held at the local Unitarian Church. The facilitators would take turns saying phrases like "One thing I fear in a relationship is . . ." "One thing I'd like to experience but am afraid of is . . ." And we would each, in our little groups, repeat the words and complete the sentence according to our experience.

The exercises were designed to help us open up, to let down our defenses. I was pulled into this, and felt safe enough, or daring enough, to express what I felt about my body. I can remember listening to the people in the group and perceiving them as sensitive, flexible, responsive. I believed this group encompassed listeners who would be eager to hear yet another insight into the realm of value changes. I felt sure they'd react kindly and appreciate my words.

So when our next completion sentence was, "One thing I've decided I like about myself that I don't need to change is . . ." and we were going around the circle in my little group, I confidently stated, "One thing I've decided I like about myself and don't need to change is that my body is fine the way it is and I don't need to lose weight."

The other fat woman in the group, a woman my size, when her turn came, said, "One thing I've decided I like about myself, something I don't want to change, is that I want to continue to try losing weight." Oh well . . .

But as the evening progressed, the questions got more and more intimate, until the facilitators told us we had to go around the group, individually, and tell each person in our circle something we liked about them. Then we were instructed, "Tell each member of the group something you don't like about them." "I'll start," said a woman who'd smiled and chatted with me before the meeting had started. I was the first one she spoke to, and this is exactly what she told me: "Sharon, I'd like to tell you that your body is repulsive, and it's especially repulsive to me because you have such a nice face."

I immediately stated to the group that no one else had my permission to mention anything negative about my body. One woman in the group supported me, saying she didn't judge people that way. Another woman said she liked the way I looked. They seemed sincere.

(In this sort of group, I doubt that a gay woman would be told her gayness was repulsive, a person with a large nose told to get an operation, an Afro-American told her skin color was ugly, someone who wasn't blond enough told to look more Aryan. Liberals no longer feel permitted to say those things. But it is socially acceptable to speak against fat, because fat is seen as a personal fault, rather than as a natural physical manifestation found in all species).

When the completion exercises were finished, the facilitators wanted to know our feelings about the program. Most felt it was a good way to "warm up." A man in my group was amazed that people took the opinions of total strangers so seriously. I was shaking inside, but I raised my hand and said, "It seems to me there's a lot of looksism here tonight." I explained what looksism means: Judging someone as less important because he or she doesn't fit a stereotyped idea of beauty . . . physical chauvinism.

I wanted to say, "You're all a bunch of hypocrites! You talk about struggling and searching for inner growth and new ways of living, you supposedly accept the unconventional, and yet you judge people by Hollywood, and slim supremist standards of attractiveness."

Then someone said she wanted to say what no one had yet said that night, and what she wanted to say was that we should all thank the facilitators for this wonderful experience of learning to relate more directly and honestly with each other. And we all applauded.

The woman facilitator said if we are hurt or angry we are somehow responsible for that hurt or anger; we have partially caused it; and we can control our feelings, for we are responsible for the energy we receive and for all the things that happen to us.

Her words embodied what the others seemed to agree on: if we are unhappy, it is connected to our own faults and failures. I find small comfort in this exaggerated emphasis on personal changes and personal relationships as the ultimate vehicle for social change, for our pain is more than personal — it is social, it is political: I get jeered at on the street, have difficulty buying clothes, am judged physically and emotionally ill because of a fat appearance.

Afterward I was speaking with a man from our group. In the group, he'd said I "hid my beauty" and I asked him what he meant now, thinking it had something to do with shyness. It just never occurred to me that a person in this situation, in this kind of organization, would say what he did: "You should do something about your appearance, and even though I know you didn't like it mentioned, your (repulsive) weight." I had worn jeans and a shirt to the meeting, not worrying about dressing up or camouflaging my body in a caftan, as I'd actually felt this would be a sincere, unprejudiced group. So he was also attacking my lack of femininity. I confronted him by saying that we were here at this gathering to form new values and to free ourselves from such prejudice.

As I was leaving the crowded room, the woman in the group who'd called me repulsive (and even as I type this an inner critical eye says, "not you, your body") rushed over to me, telling me she also had a weight problem. I blurted out that I didn't have a problem, that it is society that has a weight problem, with the other fat member of the group joining in, saying, yes, that's true, but if she didn't try to diet, she couldn't ever hope to get a job, clothes, etc. . . . Still too much in shock to mention Fat Liberation or medical statistics, I made an analogy to racism and quietly removed myself from the meeting, feeling too mad to stay. In the lobby I posted a note on the bulletin board about our Fat Underground meetings.

When I got home and called my friend Sabina, I was relieved. S/he said, "You've cracked open a new space in their consciousness. You were there tonight and that's why it happened." Yes, I did get satisfaction after hearing that, and a feeling that I had given them something to think about.

Contemplating the future incorporation of fat politics into the human potential movement intrigues me. Their self-acceptance recognition of diversity, and self-actualization concepts already include seminars on physical health, sexual preference, and feminism. Yet growth and health centers continue to give healthy fat people information on ways to exercise and control eating habits in order to lose weight.

Growth centers may one day have seminars advertised as "For people who *choose* not to diet!" (Since everything is so personalized, you are therefore still "choosing" to be oppressed!)

The basic social assumptions about femininity and fatness haven't been dealt with by the human potential movement: judging people's humanity by their looks.

---

This essay was written nearly seven years ago. Since then, many of the people involved in counseling and holistic health have taken a somewhat more compassionate view of fat women's problems. In consulting health professionals involved in homeopathy, yoga, psychology, polarity, and nutrition, I have found that if I search carefully I can find healers who work with me without assuming I must lose weight in order to be physically and emotionally healthy. However, I'm also very much aware that the incident described in this article could happen to me again.

# Fat Women and Clothing:
## An Interview with Judy Freespirit

### Cynthia Riggs

*Cynthia: What does it feel like to go to find clothing at a "fat women's" clothing store?*

Judy: Well, the truth is I don't even go to buy clothing in fat women's clothing stores anymore.

*Cynthia: Why not?*

Judy: Because it's really painful to look at things you can't have. When I go to a fat women's clothing store, I find that even there there's nothing or very little that fits me. What there is is generally way beyond my ability to afford. If I find one thing that I can afford and they've got the same thing in several colors, or even several in the same color in my size, I'll sometimes buy them all. But that's so rare that I'm usually not able to get myself to go and put myself through that pain and that energy. I end up feeling like I don't belong in the world. There's this whole feeling that there's nothing made for me and therefore I don't fit, and that I shouldn't even be here. There's all kinds of unspoken messages when there's nothing that's made for you. You're not supposed to exist. I'm not supposed to exist. And what I've done in terms of that is that mostly I don't go into these stores anymore. I used to do my shopping in Lane Bryants and then I found I could avoid a lot of that by shopping through their catalog. But even the catalogs that are in existence like Roamans and Lane Bryants have very little in natural fibers, and I'm allergic to polyester and other synthetics, so I can't even wear most of the clothes in big women's stores even if I like them. And even if there's something that I like, it's generally not available in my size.

*Cynthia: What size do you wear?*

Judy: In a top, about a 54. They generally stop at 52, sometimes at 48. In a coat, I need a 56. They generally stop at 52 or 54 or smaller, and this is in the large-size catalogs. In pants I don't even know, because I haven't bought pants in so long, but I think about a 50. They generally stop at size 46 or 48. So in the catalogs I'm able to buy a few things. There's usually one kind of underwear in cotton in an entire large-size catalog that comes large enough for me to wear. Lane Bryant, which has probably the largest catalog with the most things, doesn't have even one cotton flannel nightgown in my size. Roamans has one. They have two coats, too, that go up to a size 60. All the others stop at 52. So even there . . . but at least I'm sitting in the privacy of my own apartment with a catalog that I'm looking at, seeing what I can't have, rather than having to go out someplace and be confronted with all these actual things, rather than pictures of things I can't have. I hate having to try things on and go through that whole process. And a lot of my clothes I'm getting made now. Luckily I've found a woman who has consciousness around the fact that fat women have a hard time getting clothes, and she's been making affordable pants for me. She does them the way I want them . . . with pockets. I spent probably 20 years of my life wearing pants with no pockets. All the catalogs used to have were polyester pants without pockets, so I have her put four pockets on every single pair of pants, because I'm just so thrilled to have pockets.

*Cynthia: Why do you think that you can't find clothes?*

Judy: It's a real puzzlement to me, because I think that at this point historically, the manufacturers and the retailers are aware that there is a market, that they could make money, but the fact is that there is some sort of stigma attached to fatness that is so abhorrent to people that they don't even want to admit that they cater to people beyond a certain size. I think there is a very strong genocidal societal attitude toward anybody who's really very different, but particularly fat or disabled people. People don't want to see it. And I think that it comes from a very deep-rooted fear that it could happen to them. And if they don't have to look at us, they don't have to face that. And that goes for disability as well as fat. In that sense, I think beyond a point that someone is a certain weight she is disabled. Because accessibility becomes an issue. You can't get clothes, you can't go places. The message from the world is, "You don't have a right to earn a living. You don't have a right to do anything. How dare you even ask? You should die." And so that's why I don't go into clothing stores, even large clothing stores, because I get that message again that I don't deserve to live.

So it's incredibly painful. People often unthinkingly say things like, "Well, I get my clothes at the Goodwill. Why don't you go down there and see what they have." And it's just laughable. Everything I have that's decent I wear until there's nothing left of it. I know anybody my size would not be giving away wearable clothing.

*Cynthia: Haven't you ever gotten anything secondhand?*

Judy: Somebody once found me a jacket, and another woman found me a couple of blouses. Once a lover found me a velour shirt. But that's over a period of ten years that I've found four items. There have been very few times in my adult life when I could shop in a regular store. And there's that kind of stigma of only being able to shop in one store. When I was in my teens and early adulthood, I could find things at Lane Bryant, which was the one store in the city that I lived in that carried my size. It was the only store at that time.

*Cynthia: What size was that?*

Judy: Eighteen or twenty. They didn't have eighteens or twenties in a regular store, at least they didn't have much to choose from. And there was a stigma to having to go to Lane Bryant, having that be the only shop. I felt bad about myself because I couldn't go to the stores where my friends went. The attitude of the sales-clerks and management in those stores was very patronizing. They had a corner on the market. You know, you had no place else to go.

*Cynthia: And they knew that in the stores?*

Judy: Yeah. And you got shoddy quality and you didn't complain too much because you were glad to have anything. In fact, I would buy three dresses or three skirts in exactly the same style or design in each of the colors that they had it in. Usually that meant one in black, one in brown, and one in navy.

*Cynthia: Maroon, if you were lucky.*

Judy: I don't think I ever got that lucky. And there was never anything in pretty colors or pretty styles. Larger sizes were made in styles designed for older women. They were cut differently and were made of different materials than those the other kids were wearing.

So for the first time in my life now I have some clothing that fits in with my friends' styles. That's because I'm getting them made, and because some of the T-shirt people are making larger sizes, finally. So I have political conference T-shirts, and I'll buy three or four in different colors, if they have them in my size. I have a drawer full of T-shirts that fit me, that have bright colors, and are really nice.

*Cynthia: What about work clothes? You work as a legal secretary in an office in San Francisco. How do you deal with that?*

Judy: Well, I can't dress up to everyone else. I suppose if I could afford it I'd just have some fancy dressmaker make all my stuff for me. Somebody who knows how to make patterns, because you can't buy patterns in my size. And I would have to be very, very wealthy. I couldn't work as a secretary and afford that. What I do is that I try to dress as simply as possible. I have a couple of nice pairs of cotton pants and a couple of nice comfortable shirts that have been made for me by a fat woman who made clothes for herself and made some for me and sold me some of the ones she got tired of. Most fat women I know who have jobs either sew for themselves or get someone to sew for them because clothes are just not available in decent styles.

I can't even get shoes, which is another problem. Because I have a short, wide foot, I have to buy men's shoes to get them wide enough, but they don't come short enough.

*Cynthia: So what do you do?*

Judy: Well, recently I went to a large-size shoestore in the men's department, and they had one pair that fit me.

*Cynthia: So you ended up with the one pair?*

Judy: I bought the pair that fit. And I felt lucky that there was one pair.

*Cynthia: How would you like to see it different?*

Judy: Well, I would like to be able to buy clothes the same way everybody else does. I'd like for there to be as much availability and choices of colors and styles and sizes and within the same price range. It really makes me angry when they change the price at a certain size.

*Cynthia: For the exact same thing?*

Judy: For the same exact thing. And then they say, "Well, it takes more material." That's bullshit. If they're selling 100 of this item in sizes under a certain size and five or ten over that size, they could divide the extra cost of material between the 110 people and it would be only a few more cents for everybody. Instead, I have to spend five dollars more. It feels punitive.

*Cynthia: You're being punished.*

Judy: I'm being punished for being fat. Some people would even say that charging more is *incentive* for me to lose weight. It's just bullshit. But the attitude often is, "Well, you could always lose weight and then you could be like the rest of us. It's your fault."

*Cynthia: Is that true? Can you always lose weight?*
Judy: No! Of course not!

---

Editors' Note: Cynthia Riggs is in the process of starting a mail order business that will be geared toward high-quality clothing made from "healthy" fibers that will fit a wide range of fat women, and that will also be affordable to a large group of women. She says:

"The end product will be a mail order catalogue of natural fiber clothing for fat women. This will include hand-dyed 100% cotton T-shirts, V-necks, three-button long-sleeve shirts, long underwear, tank tops from size large to xxxx. Also, there will be a line of international clothing from South America, Mexico, India, etc., that will fit very large women. There will be 100% cotton parachute pants (drawstring pants that tie at the ankle) which fit up to size 48 waist. There will be 100% cotton drawstring pants which will be made to specifications.

"I am looking for women who make, design, or decorate clothing and who are interested in having me distribute for them. I am interested in any requests that women have regarding what they would like to see available in a catalogue such as this. At present the parachute pants and cotton shirts are available, and anyone who wants information about these items, or the catalogue, or who would like to be on the mailing list can write me at P.O. Box 203, Cotati, CA 94928."

# Traveling Fat

## Elana Dykewomon

*Some notes from 1982 on fat and: public spaces, community, friend-ship, politics, class, sex, and ethnic identity.*

I was hanging out in america and there are lots of ways to do it.
I was a fat womon traveling around alone with a dog.
I was a lesbian who had made her contacts ahead and the homes
spread out in welcome like a net.
I was a Jew who hungered for other Jews in the wide spaces
of the midwest.
I was a poet who put on a shiny tie & a silk vest twenty times.
The vest was made special, by a friend, to fit.
And I said what I thought was good to be said, and mostly
it was good, but sometimes I was wrong.
I was strong and tough enough and charming.

How else is a fat Jew lesbian poet gonna get by?
Listening to the radio, staying home, staying alone, like
they mean us to.

Who means you to be left out?
Who don't?

Who doesn't mean for fat womyn to be left out?    Don't answer
too quick now.  A womon gathers a lot of scenes as she goes.  Here
she records a bunch of them, to show something about what it
means, fat womyn trying to be a part of community, fat travels in
the country.

For the sake of definition, we'll say here that a fat woman is a
womon who weights over 200 pounds at an "average" height, or is
a womon who endures one or more of these things:  access problems
in public places, job discrimination, random & frequent attempts
at humiliation from strangers (or family & friends), having to go

to special stores or catalogs to find clothes that might fit. Who endures these things in the present. You might not expect that there would be womyn who aren't fat womyn, really fat womyn, who would want to join this group; who would, themselves, feel left out if asked to leave, but there are. That's what I mean about not answering too quick. It's a complex group of scenes.

Scene: The first Fat Womyn Only performance anyone remembers. Fat Lip, May 1982, in Berkeley. Let's say there are at least 20,000 fat womyn in the S.F. Bay area. Thirty or forty come, some from out of state. A thin womon gets turned away, much to her surprise. Some not very big womyn get in, making it a little uncomfortable for some of the others. It's a good night. This is not to reproduce their script, which covers too much of the body and spirit to paraphrase. But to let you know it happened. Afterwards womyn talk, coming from many different feelings about their bodies and the bodies of other fat womyn. There are a lot of challenges and different, important, recognitions. It was not a safe place for every fat womon there, but it was an important place.

The next night, Fat Lip gave a performance in S.F. open to all womyn. There was a big difference in the "feel" of it. There were fewer fat womyn among the 150 who were there. The laughter of thin womyn was suspect, but not questioned. Sitting among thin womyn, you could feel them go blank when a huge womon shook her booty in their faces. You could feel them thinking they understood, now, what it's about, the lifetime humiliation, the daily figuring it out, how to fit, how not to be left out without being noticed, how to live. You could hear some of the thin womyn thinking they had done their political duty, and they were glad it was going to be over soon. And you could hear decades of silences breaking in the faces of fat womyn, you could hear that too. These are first times. If they didn't give every fat womon all she needed, or gave thin womyn too much, they were still wonderful, rare gifts.

Scene: The Jewish Feminist Conference, S.F., late May 1982. Some of the Fat Lip womyn were advisors to the coordinators. The coordinators provided for fat womyn in ways that I never experienced at a conference. At the beginning, statements were read on behalf of womyn whose needs and presences are most often ignored — older womyn, mothers, working class womyn, Sephardic Jews, disabled womyn, lesbians, fat womyn. Of course some statements were carried out better than others. But even the statements made a tremendous difference. There were no diet drinks or foods, there was accessible seating provided for fat and disabled womyn and their friends. There was a fat affinity group, fat workshops, and theatre by the Jewish womyn in Fat Lip. There was, among others, a printed statement on Fat Liberation, written by Judith Stein. So thin womyn attending the conference got told. We didn't have to tell them, or to figure they didn't know.

It's hard to convey exactly what this meant. Meant to me. And of course part of it was being among so many Jews, so many Jewish Lesbians. But at the dance Saturday night, I danced with a fat womon whom I love, and I felt safer, prouder of my body, than I have any other time in any other public place, certainly in any other group of mixed thin and fat womyn. I felt like it had been said, "if you out there who normally own the dance floor are having a problem, tough shit." I felt that the thin womyn there had heard it, and although their hearing it didn't necessarily change how they felt, they were keeping their vibes to themselves. That joy, that ability to move, to finally move, that moment of feeling like we, together, were a proof, proof positive of everything that had been said and done, that was a gift.

But you never really know the value of a gift until you come to expect it as part of life, as part of the awareness of the womyn's community, and it isn't.

The scenes changed. I've been living in the americas for over thirty years, I shouldn't have been surprised, but I was. The surprises taught me.

Scene: The National Women's Studies Conference, in Arcata, California, June 1982. The organizers of this conference had not seen fit to waive the registration fee for two womyn who were coming only to lead a fat liberation workshop—so they couldn't come. The organizers did, however, leave the workshop on the schedule. That was more like the conferences I remembered. The group of womyn who met to discuss fat liberation without facilitators spent an hour or so struggling with the old myths about fat womyn, especially that fat womyn aren't healthy, and couldn't expect to have enjoyable sexual relationships with anyone. I mean, that's what the fat womyn said. The fat womyn who said different (me and one other) were the clear minority. The thin womyn were either insulting or quiet. I wasn't ready, then, to do what had been done for me. Expecting someone else there to articulate what I believe, I suddenly found that I had to speak about it for myself. Which made me pissed and scared. For the first time in years, in a room full of womyn, I said something about my lovers, and heard—you know how you can hear, sometimes, exactly what's going through women's minds, even if they don't say it? — heard half the womyn in the room, fat and thin, think: who does she think she's kidding? She doesn't have lovers, probably doesn't have even one. She's just trying to make up for being fat, poor thing. Boasting to feel better. Hmph.

Well, hmph. Later at this same conference, a womon, Max Dashu, was giving a slide presentation about the suppressed womyn's histories in the Sahara and Sudan, and China. She was talking about foot-binding—now this may seem out of place here, but it got to me, it seemed like the link and the key. She was talking about the transition times, when men were taking power from womyn, and how one of the things they did in taking power was to invent class, subject and divide women along class lines. And one of the ways they helped class work was to impose the most hideous restrictions on the bodies of upper-class women. So that if women wanted class mobility, which meant some access to power, or sometimes simple survival (if not for themselves, for their children), they could prove themselves desirable only by being successful at self-mutilation. They had to reach for the very things that crippled them, in order to maintain or better their class positions, and pass that crippling on to their daughters.

Hmm, I thought, that's just like dieting.

There in that classroom I got a flash of how it's all set up—set up one generation after another—what it means, now, "you can't be too rich or too thin." How well it works, will keep on working, because the vast majority of women will never be thin. Thin enough. How well the hope of class mobility keeps every mother dieting, and handing the diets down to her daughter, hoping the daughter may do even better. When you combine this with the fact that many non-white peoples tend to be heavier than white folks, dieting becomes a tool not only in enforcing class but in encouraging assimilation. The more you are successful in looking like the ruling class, the more your mother thinks you may succeed, even if you have to leave your mother behind to do it. This has been working well a long time.

Later, in the discussion, some white womon was trying to bring up clitorectomies, in a patronizing, "isn't it horrible what they do" way. Max pointed out that it's easy for us in this culture to focus on a custom in another, thinking it's so grim—and that that's one of the ways racism works, thinking that a particular practice is the province of a "lesser" people, never your own. The same womon would never have brought up stomach-stapling. Or even thought of it in the same way.

I was talking about this, months later, with Judy Freespirit, and about the flash I had had about dieting having the same class function as foot-binding. She asked if that had been said in the discussion. No, I said. I didn't think so, she said.

All of that at a conference I just went to to sell books.

So I should have known a little better about what it was going to be like, when I was on the road, a fat woman traveling alone. But I didn't get it.

Until: I went out to dinner in Eugene with my lover Dolphin, who's small, and two friends. Real good friends, long-time friends. One of them is skinny, and one a little zaftig, but a very medium size. The friend who's zaftig was talking about going to see her family. We were eating Greek food outside, under the trees. She was talking about how she and her sisters had been comparing themselves in the mirror recently, how they had done that as kids, as teenagers, competing in that dangerous country, mirror-land. But this time, she said, she looked at them, now they were straight and married, they didn't look so happy, so gorgeous. She found herself surprised to like how she looked. My friend said she thought she looked good, looked better than any of them, even if she was fat.

Even if. I lay down my fork and stared at the cold fish. Right there it broke, I felt wrong to be eating in front of these thin womyn, ashamed and angry. Dolphin kept trying to get my eye. When she finally did, I shook my head — No, I was trying to say to her, don't say anything. I feel bad enough, this is humiliating, and so far only I know how it is that I'm humiliated, even if you can see it; even if you can see it, even if you can understand it, you don't know how it feels, keep your mouth shut. — But she didn't.

My zaftig friend saw something going on, but she didn't see my face, because she was sitting next to me, only Dolphin's. Dolphin said something like: "If you sit here and say you thought you looked good 'even if' you were fat, imagine how Elana must feel. Not even in the discussion. A creature from another planet." Words to that effect.

It was how I felt then. Transformed from one of the gang into a creature from outer space whose body is beyond all normal sense of proportion so simply isn't included in the spectrum of relationships. It was different from something I could be either angry about or repress, the way I had felt at that Women's Studies Conference. I was ashamed, and isolated, among womyn I love, and it was a shock. A Big Deal. My friend, she got it quick, said, "O shit, it's like when someone said I'm pretty even though I'm Jewish." "Yes, something like that," I said. She apologized and was sincerely sorry. And that's life. I mean, we all walk around not looking at what's in front of us, since we don't have any way to recognize it, even when we've been told we should be able to. We learn stuff from each other's pain at our mistakes. Later, in another city, she "made it up to me," and that's more than most of us get, even from our intimates, let alone our friends.

But that's when I figured it out. Traveling around the country as a fat womon was not going to be a bed of roses. Being in other womyn's houses. I had thought I had prepared myself for being sociable, for being likable enough to get through the rough spots, to meet the womyn who thought what I was about was neat as well as those who thought I was full of shit. But I had forgotten to prepare myself for what they were gonna think when they looked at me.

That night after dinner, we went to a lesbian video show. For the first hour, all I could think about was how I was the fattest womon in the room, something that I couldn't remember worrying about in the last two years, having been in rooms where size had changed, where the proportions of womyn had begun to feel different. And besides, having a "rep" clears space ahead of you, it tends to give a legitimacy — or notoriety — before you speak, so you don't have to worry that no one's paying attention to the fat girl.

But there I was, a "fat girl" again — the one nobody knows, the one whose clothes don't fit right, who keeps tugging at herself hoping that this or that roll of fat will be less noticeable, maybe she won't be noticed at all, maybe no one will know she was even there (but why does she keep overhearing conversations about dieting during intermission?), she just wants to see the picture show like the rest of the girls, maybe if she tries hard, no one will mind her being there, or worse, make fun of her for being there, when obviously fat girls don't go to those things, don't go to anything, they don't belong, they don't even fit in the seats, they're wrong to try.

I had this figured out before. But each time you get it, it stuns you more. At each level, it's hard to separate the reasons for the way you've learned to present yourself in the world. You try to follow yourself in the best of conscience, not because you're trying to prove stuff to your mother or somebody, not because you're trying to get even, not because you're trying to make up for what other people might find wrong about you, but because you're try-ing, simply, to be honest. But there are moments when you're bound to have very extreme doubts about your own motives, and quite some suffering and rage. Even simple confusion, doubting what you know you know.

Out there on the road, womyn were not going to necessarily be my allies. They wouldn't have seen Fat Lip or been to the Jewish Feminist Conference, they could pass over the articles about fat liberation in the feminist and lesbian papers—or not believe them. They could think stomach-stapling, like psychosurgery, doesn't happen anymore. Certainly not to lesbians, not their friends, or peers. Womyn who might say in a discussion of dieting: Is this the new thing we have to be p.c.* about? What has dieting got to do with anything? —

What does it.

But even then, I held onto this fantasy. I thought that out there in america there were groups of fat dykes everywhere who, if not always together, were at least giving each other support, encourage-ment to love their own and each other's bodies, who were doing the work they could in the womyn's communities, and who were being met by an at least accepting, if not always responsive, com-munity. I'd heard about a couple of fat womyn's conferences (was it only two in five years, and I just thought there were more?), seen a centerfold of fat dyke photos in the *Inciter* and had been spoiled by the handful of fat womyn doing this work in the Bay Area and Seattle. It was just a fantasy.

In some of the cities I went to I did meet fat dykes. One or two. Who felt isolated, and in pain. Who felt that no one took them seriously when they talked about fat politics, that it still doesn't qualify as real political thought, it's viewed as a leisure pursuit of the bourgeoise who want to be left alone to be self-indulgent in peace; or that it's "cashing in" on the political groundwork done by other groups (even if fat womyn are members of the "other groups"). Mostly it's just too hard. To be one woman, going against the grain.

---

\* politically correct

I was in a lot of thin womyn's houses. I can't begin to tell you how many refrigerators were full of diet soda, light beer, lo-cal salad dressing. Among womyn who were quick to eat brownies, or go out for pizza. Among womyn who otherwise ate "health food" and womyn who ate "junk food," vegetarians and omnivores. (The need of diabetic womyn to have access to sweet-tasting things without using sugar is not in question here — I'm talking about the ways womyn buy into the institution of dieting, not the need some womyn have to keep careful watch over their blood sugar levels in order to stay alive.)

When I left Oregon alone, the first city I went to was Minneapolis. I expected Minneapolis to be a place with a high consciousness about fat politics. I was there for a week before I met another fat woman, who had come to the coffeehouse on Friday night on the rumor that she might meet another fat dyke and separatist there, who was me.

The Minneapolis coffeehouse is well known for being a good, chemically free alternative to the bar scene. I had old friends who thought it was a wonderful place. When I went there, I was still in the middle of my fantasy. I walked out of my fantasy, down unramped steps, through a corridor of posters offering this or that therapy, into a room of young, thin, predominantly able-bodied, white and light-skinned womyn drinking a lot of diet soda, with a big display of T-shirts that only went up to x-large. I hadn't been in a mostly lesbian-run space that didn't have T-shirts going up to 4x for some time. I felt like somebody had dumped a glass of water on my head. OK, kid, you're back in the world again.

The woman who had been waiting for me introduced herself — she and a friend of hers were the only other fat womyn in a large crowd, and her friend was the only fat womon dancing. It's another story, the things we said, or how the three of us ended up dancing together, what that meant to us, how long it took. I'm just describing a scene, where fat womyn recognize each other with a raw and pulsing nerve exposed, and no one around them notices.

Later, I had to tell my friends, the womyn I was with, what I felt, why I was so upset. I also had to read in the coffeehouse in two days. It was hard telling my friends. Asking them what message they thought a thin womon gives, going around with a diet soda in her hand. What a fat womon swallows, drinking it too. They got the point, though. They did good, and that was its own kind of gift. They negotiated with the coffeehouse womyn, who were responsive and said they would not sell diet drinks at the reading, provided I have a statement about it.

So there I was, I had to do what had been done for me. This was the statement I came up with:

"The coffeehouse has agreed not to sell diet drinks at this performance, at the request of myself and other concerned lesbians. Usually I just start reading, but they asked me to make a statement about that request. There's lots of good written material about Fat Oppression, and I encourage you all to read, or reread, what's been published, so I'm not going over that ground now.

"I assume that this community intends for its spaces to be safe and accessible for all the lesbians in them. When you sell or buy diet drinks, you make it unsafe for fat womyn to be with you. When you sell t-shirts that only go up to x-large, you are defining that as the size limit for womyn who come here. Dieting, not unlike foot-binding, is a male-created institution which obsesses, weakens, sickens and kills womyn; enforces class oppression and the assimilation of ethnic peoples. It's easy for us in this country to condemn cultures which practice clitorectomies—and not so easy for us to look at how we participate with our 'own' patriarchy in defining a natural condition among womyn as a disgusting sickness. I hope next time I read in Minneapolis there'll be no need to make this statement. All our bodies should be all our joy."

It seemed like at least some of the womyn that night appreciated the statement—I never really got feedback about it stirring anything up. Like I did when I made a similar statement in the Chicago coffeehouse—there, having no close friends in the city and arriving only a couple hours before I was supposed to work, the coffeehouse womyn did not agree to stop selling diet drinks for the duration of the reading. That's where the complaint "is this the new thing we're going to have to be p.c. about?" came back to me.

This isn't to trash the coffeehouses in those cities—a lot of work is being done by a lot of womyn trying to make space for womyn as best as they can figure out, starting from their first identifiable needs. And as usual, the womyn who do the most get criticized the most. But the almost universal physical inaccessibility of most womyn's spaces, for instance, came as a tremendous shock to me, traveling. I may not be able to tolerate the arguments about dieting, but I know where they come from, how pervasively they're "socially sanctioned." I can't imagine a case for inaccessibility, although I've heard lots of excuses. Which is to say, we have done a very little bit, we need to do a lot more, there's work we need to get down to.

But I felt like I couldn't just write down the statement that I read in the coffeehouse, because it's incomplete without the contexts from which it comes. Without your knowing how I stayed up all night that first Friday in Minneapolis, writing in my journal, calling back to Oakland to talk with an intimate, how hurt I felt, and how unexpected that hurt was.

Later I was used to it. I wasn't surprised anymore when I found the diet shit in womyn's houses, and I had the ability then to choose what, and when, to say about that. The second half of the trip I ended up staying in fat womyn's houses, or the houses of friends, more often than not, and that helped. Because for the first three weeks I found I could barely eat in front of anyone, which is an old problem, something I had forgotten, a self-consciousness and discomfort, a sense that other womyn are watching. I waited it out; it wasn't, you know, a terrible hardship. I just remembered who wasn't there, saw who didn't come to the readings, who did not feel safe to leave their homes, who would not assume that I would try to make the spaces safe for them, who couldn't believe that the womyn in their communities would make the spaces safe for them.

A womon in one city where I read wrote to another, in a city in which I was going to read, that I didn't look like what she had expected. I didn't look like a star. Susanjill said, "She meant you were fat." I said, "I'm glad you said that, that's what I thought too." But it was a correspondence between thin womyn, I was in a thin womon's house, I wasn't about to risk telling her that that's what I thought her friend meant.

There were a lot of other scenes. In Lincoln, there was a brunch of fat lesbians, five of us, we talked, but we never talked about being fat. We acknowledged that. It was good to be together though.

Not quite as good as it was the last reading I did, in San Francisco, for the last "Fat Friday" event at the Women's Building. Zoe Mosko had put up an exhibit of photographs of fat lesbians, for the month of October. I was on the road, nervous in midwest cities, while the first three "Fat Fridays" went on — Fridays where fat womyn shared their arts in the photo gallery, surrounded by pictures of fat lesbians, with full houses of all-sized womyn. I got reports on how great the events were, Fat Lip doing theatre, Judy

Freespirit showing a videotape, "Freespirit in the Flesh," Ruth Jovel, Ronda Slater, Sylvia Kohan doing a night of theatre, comedy, and music.

For my turn, I had intended to read a story I had written, "Speaking of Fat Out Loud At Last," among other things. But I had never read the story out loud. In Denver, on my way west, I spent a day preparing for Fat Friday. As I started to reread the story (for the first time in six months), I realized I was terrified. There, toward the end of the journey, with the diet vibes of the womyn's community deep in me. I couldn't believe how many times I had written the word "fat" in eight pages, I couldn't picture standing in front of a group of lesbians anywhere and saying "fat" that many times.

I called up Susanjill in Oakland, I said, "I can't do this." She said, "I've been trying to tell you that for months. You hadn't reread the story when you told me you were going to perform it, had you?" "No," I said, "and I don't think I can do this." "But you're going to, aren't you?" "Yes," I said.

And I did.

I did something else, too. I told about a dream I'd had, the night before that first reading in Minneapolis. I drempt that I got up in the womyn's coffeehouse and said: I've put away the reading I was going to do. Instead, I'm going to spend the next two hours telling you in graphic detail every food I ever used while making love, how I used it, where it was put, how it tasted on her, how it felt on me, how we ate in bed. . . . In Minneapolis I had seen it as a kind of revenge, making an audience of mostly thin womyn squirm in their seats.

But on Fat Friday, in a room of eighty lesbians, half of whom were fat, I wished that I had it to tell.

But that's another story, isn't it?

After all, this was just to record the basic statement and its contexts, to try to talk about an understanding of how the fear of fat works. It works because it's being manipulated in us to enforce class divisions, racisms, womyn-hatred. And we give it the room to work because it's so close to us, it's our own bodies, that we don't see it as coming from outside ourselves, we don't name it for the weapon it is.

And it works because so many of us are so often afraid of how we might please each other, of how beautiful the body is, in every moment of her size and age.

## 5. They're Trying to Kill Us for Our Own Good: Medical crimes and the dieting war against women . . .

# Intestinal Bypass

Betty Shermer

I'd like to tell about the intestinal bypass operation. As a fat woman I saw no alternative but to submit.

I had an intestinal bypass operation on September 18, 1973, at a hospital in Los Angeles. This is surgery for weight loss. Some doctors also do this surgery on fat people who need other surgery, so that they will be thin enough to have the other surgery. In this operation the small intestine is cut and sewn back together so that, instead of the food you eat going through the full twenty-three feet of intestine, it goes through only three feet or so. As a result, your body only absorbs a little bit of the nourishment you eat. You lose a lot of weight. In one year I lost about one hundred pounds, which is average for three feet of intestine. The doctors didn't put me on any kind of diet. They told me that if I could have restricted my eating, I wouldn't have needed the operation in the first place.

They told me that, after I'd lost one hundred pounds, if I were going to lose any more I would have to diet. They told me I would probably not gain anything back. The most I might gain back would be fifteen to twenty pounds, and that's because by the end of the year that three feet of intestine would have changed so as to absorb enough food to keep me from losing any more weight. But if I ever had to have my intestines reconnected with the piece they bypassed, I'd gain everything back.

The biggest danger with this operation is damage to the liver. I got yellow jaundice from it, and my liver is damaged as a result. I have to have blood tests every three months for the rest of my life. If I should have trouble with my liver now, the best thing would be for me to have the intestine reconnected. I'd never do that unless it was a matter of life or death, and even then I don't know if I'd do it.

When I went in for the operation, the doctors warned me about every possible thing that could go wrong. They told me that one person out of every ten who have the bypass dies. The week that I had the operation, I heard about three people who had died from it; one of them was a thirteen-year-old girl in a city near where I lived. They explained how my liver could become permanently damaged. They told me I'd have to take mineral supplements and go for blood tests for the rest of my life, and that I'd have diarrhea for a year or more afterwards, especially intense and painful in the first six months.

You had to pass certain criteria before they'd give you the operation. You had to have had psychotherapy. Luckily I'd had that for two years. You had to weigh over three hundred pounds. Luckily I did. You had to have tried every other known method to lose weight and failed at them all. Luckily I had done it all. My age was in my favor—I was thirty-two. You had to be healthy. The hospital gave me every conceivable test—heart, blood, chemistry, X-rays, everything. I was in perfect health. After two months they scheduled me for surgery.

After the surgery I was all right for the first three days. Then I started having a high fever, and the doctors couldn't get it down. From there on my troubles started. I had a 105-degree temperature on and off for two weeks. At first the doctors could not find the infection. They gave me antibiotics to fight the fever, but they gave me an overdose, and I had a bad reaction to it. They finally found the infection in the left side of the incision. They opened the incision all the way to the stomach, to let it heal up from the stomach naturally. My side drained for two years. During that time they opened my side again, about an inch deep, looking for the source of the infection—but couldn't find it. I finally went to another hospital, where they operated on my side—four inches across and three inches deep. They found twelve inches of wire that had been left in my side. So after two years my side healed.

Meanwhile, right after the operation I got yellow jaundice and a collapsed lung. I lost half of my hair. I lost the skin on my hands, feet, and legs. I think that was from the fever. The doctor told me that the lining of my stomach had rotted; this was also from the fever. I was nauseous, throwing up constantly. I couldn't even keep water down. I could not brush my teeth because it would make me throw up. My mouth was always dirty. I couldn't get anything clean. I'd wake up with my side draining over everything. I didn't want to get near anyone because I knew I must have a terrible odor. I didn't want my friends to hug me. I didn't want anyone near me. I was so deathly ill I didn't care if I lived or died. They told me they would not know for six months whether my liver would heal. I became very, very depressed.

The doctors sent me to group therapy because of my depression. I walked into the group and found out that everyone in the group was a terminal patient, with cancer, tuberculosis, etc. It freaked me out. I thought I deserved this because I was fat. When I realized that they had classified me with the terminal patients, I just thought, "Dear God, what have I done? What have I done? I've done something in my life I can't reverse," because I was too weak to reverse the operation. I took complete blame, complete responsibility, because I had asked for the operation.

By that time I had lost a good sixty or seventy pounds, and death then wasn't as acceptable to me as it had been before. When I had first asked for the operation, I was so depressed and so oppressed about my weight that I felt maybe it was best that I did die, if I couldn't do something about it. I had tried every possible way to lose weight. At that time I didn't know any of the medical information liberated from medical journals by Fat Liberation groups like the Fat Underground—especially the information that fat people don't eat more than thin people. I could see no other way out. I could no longer tolerate the way I felt about myself, the way I was treated about being fat—afraid to go to a public place because some child would say something and embarrass me; taking a class at a college and not being able to fit into the chair; terrified of eating in a restaurant with friends, because until the moment I sat in that booth I'd be wondering, would I fit or not?

I was terrified and embarrassed in front of my friends. I felt there was no personal happiness for me. I had no chance of any kind of relationship. I had many, many friends, but they would go home to their families, their lovers, their boy friends, their children, or whatever, and I would be alone. Therefore I very often felt I would die from loneliness.

I just had no choice in this society. My life had been nothing but problems, sorrow, worry, loneliness, rejection, and unhappiness. I couldn't see any future of anything getting better. I could see no hope for me.

I look back with great sorrow that I felt such a need to have the bypass. I was in perfect health before, now I'm not. But I feel 100% better being 100 pounds thinner in this society. For each twenty pounds of fat there's 20% more oppression. Now I almost never have children calling me names. I can go into any restaurant and feel confident that I'll fit in the booths, and I feel a little better accepted socially, but not a whole lot. I'm still a fat person, but I'm not what doctors call "morbidly obese" so I'm not pointed out as much.

My crime was being a fat woman in this culture. For this hideous crime, I was punished with years of painful diarrhea, and I almost paid with my life. My health may be wrecked forever, and who knows what my life expectancy is *now*.

I think it's amazing that fat people hold up as well as we do. I think fat people are the strongest survivors of any people because we've had to be. All our lives we've known nothing but oppression — no equality whatsoever in getting a job; having relatives jokingly embarrass you in front of a whole roomful of other relatives, thinking they're witty or cute. It's a life of loneliness and sorrow and feeling that you somehow deserve it.

I've always felt that I must be a lazy, worthless, useless person that I could not do a simple thing like staying on a diet. I never talked about this feeling, but I have always felt so, quietly. So having an intestinal bypass operation felt like taking the easy way out.

Some facts about this operation: One to ten percent die, depending on whom you talk to. Twenty thousand of these unnecessary operations are performed yearly now. That means about two thousand people will die rather than be ridiculed, shown contempt, and persecuted for being fat.

Five percent of all who go through this don't lose any weight at all.

The average weight loss is one hundred pounds. But since you have to be at least three hundred pounds to qualify for the operation, you still end up fat anyway. A little less oppressed — but still fat.

*Now I see what I went through as a medical crime against women:* $10,000 worth of what amounts to cosmetic surgery just to help me fit into a society that punishes women for being fat. I know now that being fat is not a choice. A 99% failure rate for all reducing diets is not a choice. And I'm not alone with the oppression anymore. I work in the Fat Liberation Movement and have the support of a collective of fat women, the Los Angeles Fat Underground.

Are doctors the healers or the mutilators? When doctors imply that almost any risk is preferable to being fat, they are perpetrating the cultural myths that fat people "overeat," have no will power, etc. I know now that these are lies.

# Weight Loss Surgery: Miracle Cure or Mutilation?

Louise Wolfe

TYPES OF OPERATIONS: The two major types of weight loss surgery are intestinal bypass (jejunoileal bypass) and various gastric procedures generally known as "stomach stapling" (gastric bypass, gastroplasty, and gastric partitioning). Intestinal bypass involves disconnecting most of the small intestine. This operation has been done since the 1950s, but due to numerous side-effects, it has generally been replaced by the newer gastric procedures.

Gastric bypass (first performed for weight loss in 1966) involves separating a two-ounce (50 ml.) portion of stomach. The intestines are then reconnected to the small section, totally bypassing the rest of the stomach. The intestines may be attached by two different methods—"loop" and "Roux-en-Y." In the mid-1970s, a stapling device was developed which simplifies the gastric weight loss operations. During gastroplasty, a 12 mm. hole (stoma) is left at the end of a row of staples near the greater curvature of the stomach. With gastric partitioning, the stoma is located in the middle of the row. Both types of stomach stapling (without bypass) allow the food to pass through the entire stomach but at a much slower rate. Because none of the procedures have been standardized, the advantages and hazards of specific procedures for stomach stapling have not been clearly established.

EXPERIMENTAL PROCEDURES: All of these operations are still experimental. No long-term (20-30 years) and few short-term studies are yet available. In 1978 the National Institute of Health received follow-up reports of five to seven years for intestinal bypass, two to three years for gastric bypass, and none for stomach stapling (without bypass). The stapling procedure itself is only about five years old. Very few animal experiments preceded human experimentation in any of these procedures. Thousands of "obese" patients are having gastric operations performed, and no one is even sure that permanent weight loss is achieved. Doctors

Susan and O. W. Wooley have stated: "If a totally effective anti-obesity drug were discovered today it would be many years before it would be available to the public and if its mortality and morbidity risks were comparable to those of gastric and intestinal bypass it seems doubtful that its use would ever be approved" (*American Journal of Clinical Nutrition,* Feb. 1980).

PATIENT SELECTION: The four most widely used criteria for surgical intervention are:
- patient must be "morbidly obese" (usually for at least two to five years),
- patient must have dieted (unsuccessfully) for at least one year,
- patient must be eighteen to forty-nine years old, and
- patient must have a concomitant disease which would presumably be alleviated by weight loss.

"Morbid obesity" is defined as either 100 pounds "overweight" or, more commonly, at least double the "standard" or "ideal" weight (as defined by Metropolital Life Insurance charts). Several operations have been done on women who weigh less than the required amount. Some doctors have advised patients to intentionally gain weight in order to qualify for the operation. (This cannot be done if the five-year minimum is always required).

The dieting requirement is apparently used to test a patient's motivation and to prove to the public that surgery is used only as a last resort. Since dieting works only one to five percent of the time and most fat people have spent a lifetime dieting, this clause seems meaningless.

The requirement of a serious medical problem is often ignored or interpreted lightly. In cases involving uncontrollable hypertension, heart ailments, or diabetes, the health benefits may sometimes outweigh the risks of the operation. Also, severe mobility problems may make the operation seem a reasonable alternative to some. However, these cases are rare, and the operation is frequently performed for primarily cosmetic reasons.

Cosmetic operations are justified under the category of "psychosocial handicap," and surgeons report "striking psychosocial rehabilitation" as a result of the surgery. This simply means that the patient is now receiving compliments instead of insults and rejection.

163

LONGEVITY AND MORTALITY: Doctors justify radical intervention by claiming that "morbidly obese" patients have a mortality rate ten times that of a "non-obese" individual. Even if one accepts their statistics, they then make an unproven assumption that losing weight will bring the "obese" person's longevity odds back to "normal." Doctors Wooley discuss surgical treatments: "There is no evidence that their use increases longevity; in fact, the reverse may be true" (*Women's Studies International Quarterly*, 1979). As they do with deaths caused by dieting, statisticians will undoubtedly take all deaths caused by weight loss surgery and include them in the evidence to prove that fat people die at an early age!

*The American Surgeon* (Aug. 1978) summarized mortality rates for intestinal bypasses as ranging from 1 to 15%, with an average of 4%. Gastric procedures may be slightly better, but most reports range from 1 to 5% with a 3 or 4% average mortality rate — one considered acceptable by many surgeons.

HEALTH HAZARDS (MORBIDITY): Doctors are also making an unproven assumption about health. Dr. Labhart states that "too often the operation [intestinal bypass] converts a healthy fat person into a sick thin person" (*SA Medical Journal*, July 23, 1977). Since these operations are ostensibly performed to improve health, it is amazing how many side effects are considered a normal part of the procedure — malnutrition, diarrhea, liver damage, and kidney failure (intestinal bypass); nausea, vomiting, hernias, stomach perforation, and spleen injury (gastric operations).

These side-effects frequently lead to rehospitalization and additional surgery, including revisions and reversals of the original procedures. (As many as 25% of original intestinal bypass patients have had their operation reversed.) To my knowledge, no U.S. studies have compared the health and longevity of surgical weight loss patients with fat people who chose traditional treatment (or no treatment at all). This information is greatly needed in order to adequately evaluate weight loss surgery.

One irony of the rush toward weight loss surgery is that generally most surgical procedures are considered more hazardous when performed on "obese" patients. Many surgeons even refuse to operate until patients lose weight. Hopefully, one side benefit for all fat people will be the application of knowledge gained from these operations toward other more traditional operations.

164   LOUISE WOLFE

INFORMED CONSENT: Informed consent is virtually impossible because both patient and doctor are so influenced by anti-fat prejudice. In 95% of intestinal bypass cases, patients "purposely deny the truth about past medical and social problems" (*Obesity/Bariatric Medicine 10*, #1). A patient also "may not hear the explanation of risks, because he wants the operation and perceives only the facts that support his decision" (*American Journal of Nursing*, June 1974). One Chicagoan advised others "not to listen to other people. If you have any questions, talk to your doctor." (Are doctors not people? Imagine telling someone buying a house, "Listen only to the realtor selling the property.")

Doctors are far from impartial. Not only is about $6,000 worth of revenue for the hospital at stake, but numerous studies show how biased most doctors are against fat people. They are thoroughly convinced not only that all fat people have one foot in the grave, but that all are also unhappy and self-destructive. The NIH Conference on Surgical Treatment of Morbid Obesity (1978) said, "Patients should receive a thorough explanation about the risks, benefits, and uncertainties of each bypass procedure and be permitted to choose between them." The option of choosing no procedure is not even mentioned. People considering the operation are visited by "Staples, Inc." but no one is asked to express the opposing view. One local woman, angry about her operation, was no longer invited to speak once doctors heard she was warning people against the operation.

CONCLUSIONS AND RECOMMENDATIONS: I have done my best to present accurate up-to-date information on surgical weight loss. I am not, however, pretending to have presented an objective report — my personal bias is clear. I am very angry and concerned about the light-hearted widespread acceptance of such dangerous, unproven experimental techniques. Doctors are again offering a personal solution to political and social problems: "If the seats are too small; change your body, not the laws. If people find you ugly, change your body, not their attitudes." Sadly, fat people are practically breaking down the surgeons' doors insisting on the operations, regardless of the hazards involved.

The premises involved in weight loss surgery are the antithesis of the fat liberation movement: that all fat people are extreme health risks, that all are gluttons who overeat constantly, and that fat people can improve their self-esteem and social life only by losing weight. Fat activists must unite to make the concepts of fat pride and fat power reality, not just a theory. We must organize more self-esteem and consciousness-raising groups so that unhappy fat people will have an alternative to diets, surgery, and the traditional propaganda.

Above all, fat people must demand strict, scientific controls of all medical experimentation, especially surgical. We must stop volunteering to be human guinea pigs.

Dr. John Jesseph, president of the Central Surgical Association, has the best idea yet*:

"This isn't a good operation. Why don't we just quit?"

---

* In response to a paper by Freeman & Burchett, *Surgery,* Sept. 1980, which compared gastric bypass and gastroplasty.

# *untitled*

## Sue McCabe

You always said you had the "Boatfield Family Hips." Your mother had them, her mother, and on and on. You told me you were overweight as a teenager, and I never asked you, Mom, what was it like for you?

Years ago I remember watching a baby being stuffed with licorice at a baseball game. I asked you if I was that fat when I was a baby? Your reply: "Yes, we had to sew two diapers together to fit around your waist." I wanted to cry, "Why, why did you let that happen to me? Why do you say 'I love you' and hand me something to eat?" I need you to love me, Mother, love me, but without the food.

Nights you couldn't sleep. Vacuuming the rug at midnight. We pledged to each other — Mother and Daughter — with tears on our faces and hands grasping each other's that we would get thin. We would make it. In the morning your body against the kitchen floor, hands and head pounding the tile. Such anger and pain I have never seen. The police with compassionless faces slipped handcuffs over your wrists. My mother, barefoot in your nightgown, taken away from me. When you came home from the mental hospital, you always took a quaalude with your diet pop.

# One More Time

## Kathleen Hagen

I had determined that when I returned from my vacation in San Francisco, where I expected to eat everything that I could ever possibly want to eat, when I had, figuratively speaking, had my "last supper," I would go on yet another diet. This one was a new one which I had not yet tried. I have tried most of the weight loss programs over the years. It usually involves: calling the center, being greeted by an enthusiastic receptionist, being set up for a "free consultation," and being whisked into a program so quickly that I don't know what hit me. It then involves living on a starvation diet, being constantly hungry, being weighed in each week by bone-thin, hyper, over-enthusiastic womyn who have never been fat and who, you get the feeling, believe that your weight problem is caused by laziness and carelessness if you're a womon, and by overfeeding by your wife or mother if you're a man.

Pretty soon, I usually begin to rebel against the straight and narrow strictures of any of these diets, and I have yet to make it through a maintenance program to lose all the weight I set out to lose. This only adds to the cycle of failure; I eat even more than I did before, and put on even more weight than before I began the diet.

It has been four years since I have been through this cycle, and I swore the last time that I would never do it again. Yet, here I am dieting again. This weight loss program is well researched, and I have learned some things about myself and my eating habits over the years, so I have some reason to believe that I will be more successful this time. Even so, this diet has had its share of horrors.

It began with trying to find a center that was accessible by public transportation. All of the local centers for this particular program are in suburbia, which says something about who has the money to spend on expensive diet programs. Then came the initial interview, when the staff learned for the first time that I am blind.

168

That's always a great moment, whether it be in a diet program, a psychotherapy group, a social situation, or an employment interview. One of the great truths I have learned during my various bouts of receiving therapy, a truth which definitely correlates with my experiences in weight loss programs, is that if you're disabled, you have to take care of the therapist or nurse and help them dispel their myths and fears about disability before you can get help from them. Thus, a disabled person has to be well enough to give therapy before she can get any.

At my initial visit, we set up an appointment for me to see the doctor of the program for medical clearance to go on the diet. A few days after my initial visit and before my doctor's appointment, I received a call from the program nurse. She explained that the diet was complicated and that I might have trouble with the instructions. She said that it was clear from my questionnaire that I had a roommate, and could I bring her along so that they could explain the diet to her to insure my success. I explained that I was unwilling to do that, even had it been logistically possible for us both to come. I said that I was the person solely responsible for what I ate, and they would have to find a way to explain the program to me. Once again I was extremely angry that my lover would be mistaken for my keeper or caretaker, but this is also a part of being in society if you are disabled.

Then I underwent the ordeal of the doctor's visit. I was put in an examination room to wait for the doctor. The nurse asked me if I would need help undressing. I told her, flushing with humiliation, that I could manage this myself. I heard the nurse whisper to the doctor outside the door that the patient was blind, and that he should be careful not to trip over her cane and break it or hurt himself in the process. The doctor, thus armed with knowledge about my blindness, entered the room and said to me: "Hi, I'm Dr. J——, I know you can't see me, but I'm over six feet tall, 185 pounds, and very good-looking." Here is another of those tired truths about being blind and female. It is a strange phenomenon that many males seem to share. They are disconcerted with the fact that a blind womon cannot see them. Over the years, it has become fairly simple for me to determine whether males are good-looking or not by societal standards just by the way they approach me. A "handsome" man will say: "I know you can't see me, but I'm very good-looking," and will then proceed to describe himself. A man who is considered ugly will either say: "Gee, in some ways it would be nice not to see. Then you don't make judgments on a person just by how he looks. You give the person a chance to get to know you first." Or the "ugly" man will say: "Gee, you can't see me," laughing uneasily. "I can tell you I'm good-looking and you'll believe me."

The doctor, having established by implication that he was good-looking, had used his sexuality deliberately to put me in my place and to make me uncomfortable. The implicit message was: "If you lose weight and stop looking so sloppy, you might even be desirable to a good-looking man like me." During the examination he said: "I usually prescribe exercises to go along with the diet, but I suppose most kinds of exercise you wouldn't be able to do." I told him that was a large assumption on his part, since he hadn't even outlined to me what exercises he usually prescribed. "All right," he said belligerently, "what kind of exercises can you do?" I told him that I had mostly been too undisciplined throughout my life to follow any rigorous exercise program, but that I took brisk walks on weekends. He finally suggested that I incorporate stair-climbing into my day, since my office is on the fifth floor. He added that probably the other girls in the office would join me on the stairs when they saw how much weight I was losing and how good-looking I was becoming. He took the stethoscope and listened to my heart. He then said expectantly: "Now, do five sit-ups." I knew that he expected to have my heartbeat speed up considerably and that it would be standard for him at that point to give the lecture on the value of exercises. I deliberately did yoga deep-breathing while I did the five sit-ups. Afterward, he listened to my heart again. "Hmph," he said grudgingly, "maybe those weekend walks are doing you some good after all."

When the examination was nearly completed, the doctor suddenly said: "Do me a favor, spread your arms apart, put your hands together and touch your middle fingers." I thought at first that it was a part of the examination process and did as asked. He said: "Oops, your fingers didn't meet right in the middle. Try it again, you'll disappoint me if you don't succeed." I did it once more. He said: "Well, that's a little better. You know, most blind people I have examined can put their fingers right squarely together, and most sighted people can't without looking first. It's because you people rely on touch, and you have to know exactly where your fingers are." I realized that this had been an experiment for him to prove something about blindness and had had nothing to do with my physical examination at all. He said: "Okay, the examination is over, you can get dressed now." He turned his back and started writing on my chart, presumably. I realized that he did not plan to leave the room while I dressed. I realized that he did not think it mattered since I was blind. I thought about demanding that he leave, and then decided that the door was within immediate reach. If he so much as physically moved a finger toward me, I could open the door, and the nurse's office was immediately outside. I realized that I really did not care if he did see me dress. I already felt bruised and raped by the examination. I dressed as quickly as possible and left.

The rest of the program hasn't been so bad. At least it has been predictable in its frustrations. For the first few times that I came to weigh in, the nurses clucked around, afraid that I wouldn't be able to find the scale, afraid that I would fall off the scale once I had stepped on it, amazed that I could walk quickly through a room, amazed that I could type my own food lists and not make mistakes. They keep asking me if I recognize their voices. Actually, I don't recognize one from another. Most nurses sound alike to me. I think that nurses and flight attendants must learn a certain kind of voice as part of their training. The other predictable thing about this program is that the books and lesson plans are written by men, pronouns used are usually feminine, and the style of the book is patronizing. This is, of course, because most persons on weight loss programs are womyn. Thus, as usual, we have men setting up the standards for how we should look, how we should feel about ourselves, and how we can best change our appearance in order to please men.

I am in the process, for one last time, of losing weight. I do not contend that all womyn should lose weight just because they are considered fat. I just advocate that we each sort out the myths from the realities for each of us about how we use food. I suggest that we recognize the kind of oppression we suffer concerning our bodies just because we are womyn. I recommend that we find the best way for each of us to live with oppression and to retain self-respect. I hope that we as womyn who are societally considered to have a weight problem will seek each other out and share our knowledge, caring and love with each other. Most of all, I hope that we can learn to respect our own bodies in whatever shape they are, and I hope that we can learn to maintain ourselves in a way that will please *us* instead of trying to fit our bodies' shapes into the ideals of *others*.

# Conversation with Nancy

*A conversation between Lisa Schoenfielder and Nancy. Nancy has* buli-
mirexia, *an eating disorder characterized by binging and purging.* Buli-
mirexia *is the combination of the terms* bulimia *(binging) and* anorexia
*(self-starvation).*

*Lisa: Well, I think we should talk about when you were growing up and
how you felt about yourself. Were you fat then? Was anyone in your family
fat? In general, what were the attitudes in your family about looks and that
kind of thing?*
Nancy: I don't remember anything particular about food or being
fat. No one in my family was fat. I guess I was kind of chubby,
but I never really thought about it too much.
*Lisa: Do you remember the first time you became aware of attitudes about
fat at school?*
Nancy: The first thing that I remember was in fifth or sixth grade —
that was when stretch pants with the loop over the bottom were in
and they were skin-tight. And I had this friend who must have
been really skinny, because I'd look at her in stretch pants and
then look at me, and we both looked so different, and I couldn't
figure it out for a long time what the difference was, and then I
figured out that her legs were a lot skinnier than mine.
*Lisa: And you thought she looked better?*
Nancy: Yeah, I thought she looked better.
*Lisa: Did you go on diets?*
Nancy: Yes. The first diet I went on must have been when I was
maybe a sophomore or junior in high school. And my mother
thought I needed to go on Weight Watchers so she put me on that.
She cooked all my meals for me and everything. And I really didn't
take it too seriously. But then after a while I started getting crazy
about it. I went to my friend's house one day and I remember
eating a Ding Dong and then I started eating all this stuff. I'd go
in the freezer and eat the frozen candy. And the freezer was locked.
I had to figure out how to get it unlocked.

*Lisa: So what you're saying is that your mother froze the candy and she also locked the freezer? Why?*

Nancy: 'Cause she didn't like us to eat sugar and she didn't want us to have pop, candy, or gum or anything like that.

*Lisa: It sounds like she definitely had some attitudes about size and eating and stuff.*

Nancy: Yeah, she definitely did. She was really concerned about weight herself and would not eat very much and she thought that we should be that way too. That it was real important to be thin.

*Lisa: When you went on diets — like when you went on Weight Watchers — were you successful?*

Nancy: I lost some weight, but I gained more weight back.

*Lisa: How does your mother eat?*

Nancy: Now all she eats is cheese and crackers. That's about it.

*Lisa: And she stays pretty thin?*

Nancy: She's really thin. I think she's like a size 4 or 6. And when I was young she was just normal-size — 12 or something like that. She just says she doesn't want food. For special occasions like Christmas, she has these special things she'll make — red cake and cookies and stuff. And she'll give them to everybody else, but she won't have any. Or she'll just have a little tiny bit. She says she doesn't want them.

She always comments about my weight when I go see her. If I've dropped a few pounds, she thinks I'm doing really well and she's nice to me and she thinks that my life is going good when I'm thin.

*Lisa: What does she say if she thinks you're looking a little heavier?*

Nancy: Then she just doesn't say anything — well, she used to say stuff. She said if I didn't quit eating and gaining weight, then they were going to have to roll me away to school. Stuff like that.

*Lisa: Want to talk a little about that poster she has in the house?*

Nancy: You mean the one that says, "You can never be too rich or too thin?" My mother's really concerned with social class and appearances, like money and clothes and what the kids are doing — just how everything looks on the outside.

*Lisa: And you've always thought of yourself as not buying into that?*

Nancy: I always sort of thought that I didn't, and I've really gone pretty much the other direction by the lifestyle I've chosen and the things I've chosen to do. I am in direct opposition to what she wanted me to be.

*Lisa: After you got out of high school, what kind of issues came up for you around eating and food?*

Nancy: After I got out of high school, I went away to college. The first year I got really sick, and I was prescribed valium, and they said it was anxiety. I couldn't eat and I lost a lot of weight. Like, food would look real good and I'd go into the cafeteria and pile all this food on my plate and then I'd take it back to the table and I'd take a bite and I'd be nauseated and I couldn't eat it. That went on for quite a while. Eventually, as time went on, I was drinking and so my eating pattern was real erratic. I would just eat maybe one meal a day — usually dinner — and I wasn't too concerned with whatever it was. I can't remember caring about my weight or what I was eating or how many calories it had in it.

*Lisa: Seems like since I've known you, you've been someone who's fluctuated quite a bit in weight — more than most people do. Ranging from being pretty thin to getting just a little chunky.*

Nancy: I guess that's true, I just haven't really paid too much attention to it. Until recently. Till the past few years.

*Lisa: Since you've become sober.*

Nancy: Yeah.

*Lisa: Like when you became sober, you sort of maybe opened up a whole area where you had to think about it more. And somewhere along the line you started getting freaked out about eating and food and weight?*

Nancy: Yeah. After I'd been sober just a real short time, I learned about macrobiotics. Before, I thought people were really dumb who ate natural foods and stuff like that. I just didn't think it made that much difference. When I was eating macrobiotically, I had all these rules — you can't eat after 10 PM, you can't eat dairy products, you can't eat meat, you can't eat sugar, you can only eat until you're not quite full, just — you know — until you're 80% full. That one really worried me. I started eating macrobiotically and really paying attention to what I was eating and how much I was eating and whether I was eating the right things in the right combination and all that kind of stuff. And that was after I'd been sober just not too long. After I'd been sober about a year was when I really started having problems with being concerned about gaining weight and how I looked and all the time being concerned about what I was eating and whether it was good for me or not.

*Lisa: And you were afraid also about being fat?*

Nancy: I started being real afraid because I started gaining weight.

I started getting real afraid that I was going to be fat. At first I didn't really think that I was afraid of that. I would think, well, I'm just concerned because I'm eating too much. I really didn't see for a long time that I was scared of being fat.

*Lisa: At some point, was the behavior that you were doing what would be considered bulimic?*

Nancy: Maybe a little. I didn't really know anything about being bulimic. But I guess it would be considered that, 'cause I would eat vast quantities of food and then throw it up. I would eat a lot of food, drink a lot of water, and then throw up. But I would eat all macrobiotic food.

*Lisa: At some point when you were eating a lot and throwing up, did you feel like, "Hey, I can do this — I can eat as much as I want now, because I'm going to throw it up later"?*

Nancy: Yeah. It wasn't a pleasant experience to throw up. It was kind of like, whenever I started on a binge, I thought I might as well just really do it up good.

*Lisa: So you sort of knew ahead of time you were gonna throw up when you were done eating all this stuff?*

Nancy: Yeah.

*Lisa: Did you do some fasting then too?*

Nancy: Sometimes I couldn't really throw up, so then I would maybe go on a fast for a few days or just eat rice for a few days and then I started getting into exercise and I would worry about it all the time, whether I was going to go exercise and if I didn't, I was really going to put on weight and I'd just better go do it. I was all the time worrying about food and what I was eating and how fattening it was and in my head trying to figure out how much I was exercising and whether I was going to work all that off. Living with that all the time.

*Lisa: Did you feel like you did the exercise excessively too?*

Nancy: Well, I know that I worried about it excessively. I don't know if I exercised excessively, but I probably did. One time I hurt myself jumping over a hurdle, and normally I would think that it would be good for my health if I would not run for a while, and let my body heal. And I did take a little time off, but not enough time 'cause I was too scared to. Sometimes I'd work out and go lift weights for 45 minutes or so and then I would go swim for an hour. And sometimes for a while I was working out for 2½ hours a day. That's quite a bit.

*Lisa: Did you start using laxatives?*

Nancy: Just after I tried to give up vomiting, I started using laxatives on a sporadic basis. I started using laxatives more when I was just eating regular. Then I started thinking, it's almost like any amount that I eat is too much. And so then I started using laxatives all the time.

*Lisa: How did you feel during that time? Did you feel good at certain times or did you feel weak or sick?*

Nancy: I stayed in bed a lot. I was depressed a lot. And when I was fasting and exercising and doing what I thought I should be doing, I knew it wouldn't last. I can't remember feeling very good during that whole time. I remember a lot of days when I just couldn't get out of bed all day. Eventually, I started going to a group for bulimics.

*Lisa: How did you come across that?*

Nancy: I saw an article in the paper about it.

*Lisa: What was the group like?*

Nancy: Well, the group met during lunch, so everybody brought their lunch and we ate together. I think that was kind of a good thing, 'cause it was getting to the point where I didn't want to eat with other people at all. The group really didn't talk very much about being fat or fear of being fat. But I think most women who are bulimic really are scared of that. All this time I'd thought that I hadn't been concerned about it and that it's not really important. All the things that my mother talked about that were important— I just thought that I had really forgotten about it or never listened to it in the first place and that it didn't have too much to do with me or my life. And I think that it really did.

*Lisa: I have a hard time finding stuff that connects fat oppression and hatred of fat in society with bulimia and anorexia. They connect it to a lot of stuff, but very few places connect it right to a real fear of fat and to the fact that as long as fat is hated in this society, those eating disorders are going to come up. What do you think about that?*

Nancy: I know that I have had and still do have a lot of fears about being fat, about the way I look, and thinking that that's real important. That's the way I've gotten a lot of power in my life. And not wanting to give that up and being scared that it's going to be taken from me.

*Lisa: Power— by looking good then you have a certain amount of power?*

Nancy: Yeah. You get away with a lot more and have a lot more privilege.

Another thing that was happening when I was going through

that real bad time was that I felt like I couldn't talk to people, and I was real scared, particularly in the women's community, because of fat politics. I thought, there's really something wrong with me, or I'm really a terrible person, because I put so much value on how I look, and I questioned how can I be sincere in liking and loving other women who are fat, if I have a fear of that myself. So I felt really isolated. I couldn't talk to anyone about it.

*Lisa: I see you suffering from the same force that I'm suffering from. Somehow I feel that there's a force that's made me miserable as a fat woman and that same force has come into your life and has affected how you feel about yourself to the point that it would start occupying your mind as much as it did on a day-to-day basis.*

*I feel like fat women have definitely borne the brunt of the whole thing for a long time by having it come out in such clear ways how much we're hated, by being totally ostracized by society. I feel like feminists have taken a real interest in eating disorders — a much more heavy-duty interest in that than in fat politics as a serious issue. They haven't connected with them. And I would like to see them connected. And I think if they were connected then there would be stronger movement against that kind of thing.*

Nancy: You think the feminist movement is dealing more with the emotional issues of why a woman may be anorexic or bulimic?

*Lisa: Yes.*

Nancy: Instead of political and social reasons?

*Lisa: Yeah. I think it hasn't been dealt with, and I think that it's particularly threatening to women who have eating disorders like bulimia or anorexia to think they share an issue with fat women when that's the thing that they're frightened to death of — I mean, literally. I saw Kim Chernin, who wrote* Tyranny of Slenderness, *on the Phil Donahue Show, and at one point Donahue said, "We're not talking about letting ourselves turn into fat slobs or anything like that." She just sat there while he said that and sort of shook her head, like, "No, we're not talking about that." And to me, that is what we're talking about. What we're talking about is existing whatever size we may end up being and not feeling that there's something to fear. That we don't have to fear not being loved, not being accepted, and just not having anything left if we become fat.*

Nancy: The women's movement has really created a lot of confusion in roles for women. It's like the only sure thing that's left for women is how you look, because pretty much we've been told through the women's movement that we can't depend on men anymore for this power, and we haven't come far enough to depend on our careers or our own self that much, so it seems like the looks thing has really gotten big, but small at the same time.

*Lisa: Yeah, it seems like it's the last thing that they have a hold of us on. It's like there's one way that they can keep us under control.*

Nancy: They're doing a damn good job.

*Lisa: Yeah. I'd say they are, when they can keep women minute-by-minute concerned with what they look like or what they're putting in their mouth.*

Nancy: I can definitely see the connection that you're talking about. But the thing that really confused me a lot was that I thought that I didn't buy into any of the looks stuff and that I didn't need it. I thought that doesn't concern me, I don't relate to those kind of people, I'm not in that environment. So I was really baffled as to why I would be so concerned with my weight, because, with fat politics coming out more and more in the women's community, it's been sort of okay to *not* be concerned about this stuff.

*Lisa: What you're saying is that you felt there was enough support around for you not to have to feel that way. Because you definitely aren't running around with this country club set of people like your mother, and it wasn't like you were gonna lose friends over gaining a few pounds or something like that. But there must have been something that was working against you.*

Nancy: Yeah. That's what I'm saying—there was still that obsession to be thin.

*Lisa: You think you're not the first woman in the community that is maybe a little worried about it?*

Nancy: I would definitely say I'm not the first woman in the community to be concerned about her weight. And I definitely think that no one wants to talk about it.

*Lisa: Why do you think that no one wants to talk about it?*

Nancy: Well, I can only say why I don't want to talk about it. I think it's a stupid thing to be concerned about in the first place and if I don't accept my own self—whether I'm fat or thin or whatever—then it makes me scared that fat women will think that I don't like them because they're fat. Which is probably true—I mean, if I can't accept myself being fat, then it would be hard for me to believe that I could accept someone else.

*Lisa: Do you think the looks thing really does function in our community, the lesbian community? That being thin is still where it's at?*

Nancy: I think it is. I know that by my own self and by my outward appearance and by the way that I would normally talk to women in the community, I would appear to have no concern about how I look or about being fat. But I know that I do. And I can see that same concern in other women.

*Lisa: You can see it in the ways that they choose to live?*

Nancy: Who they choose to relate to and how they dress.

*Lisa: It's a pretty subtle force.*

Nancy: Yeah, real subtle. Especially when everybody is trying not to have it be there.

*Lisa: You're saying that you don't know if there's a hidden obsession for thinness that's in the community and has come from the same place that society's getting it, or if there's a hidden obsession because fat politics came in and it's pretty threatening to have somebody say, "I don't want you to buy into this." That's why I see it as so important to make the connections between eating disorders and fat oppression — because it's an issue that affects us all in different ways, and fat women are getting the worst of it. And I agree with you that it's been a problem, because a situation has been set up where women are afraid to talk about where they're at personally.*

*I think fat politics has not been taken real seriously by the feminist movement. There always have been fat women and there will always be fat women. Diets have this really big failure rate, and the feminist movement has just ignored the fact that dieting isn't successful. I've even read articles that will go through a whole thing of saying that dieting isn't successful and they'll end up saying, "But, if you want to lose weight. . . ." I would just like the feminist movement to take a general stand that these issues are related. I think the reason that they don't is because then it means that everyone is going to have to start putting a damper on dieting and on diet products. The issues around fat politics have been ignored. The information from the medical studies and tests that have been done has been ignored. I can understand why the medical industry and the people that have a lot to lose by letting this information out would try to ignore it, but I can't understand why a feminist movement that has dealt with so many different issues like this hasn't dealt with this one.*

Nancy: Historically, the women's movement has looked at political and social causes of oppression. When eating disorders come up, they look at emotional, individual causes. You know, "what's wrong with this woman?"

*Lisa: Blaming the victim.*

Nancy: Right. The fear of fat is very pervasive.

*Lisa: What kind of fears do you have around getting fat?*

Nancy: I never get scared about health problems connected with being fat. I mean, I would sacrifice my health to be thin, so why would I be concerned about my health if I were fat?

*Lisa: What women are talking about when they talk about being afraid of getting fat is not health. They're talking about a privilege that has to do with looks.*

Nancy: And I think part of it, too, is a wanting to be better than other people. Sometimes I have in my mind that, if I'm thinner, I'm better. Last night when everyone was going out for ice cream, I kind of wanted ice cream and I kind of didn't want it. After they were gone, I thought, now why didn't I go? I really think it had to do with, it would look good if I just said, "No, thank you, I don't care for any." You know, like, I'm above that kind of thing. Or, I don't eat food like that. I think it has to do with control over myself plus proving something to other people.

*Lisa: There's a lot of things connected up about discipline, something about thinness and looking good has a lot to do with being disciplined, and that's something we seem to really value a lot. When someone's fat, people think they're out of control and how could they let themselves go like that.*

Nancy: I think that has a lot to do with it. Being thin is one way I can prove to myself and prove to other people that I'm in control. That's always been a big thing with me, control.

*Lisa: And that was a big thing with your mother, too.*

Nancy: Yeah, a big thing with my mother. Any kind of emotion or anything like that was a sign of weakness. And I think it has something to do with denying myself something I want. Sometimes I get a good feeling from that. I mean, it's not a good feeling, I don't feel like happy/joyous about it, but . . .

*Lisa: It's a powerful feeling.*

Nancy: Yeah. But not really. I think it just shows how shitty I feel about myself—why don't I give myself permission to feel good, to enjoy some ice cream? Why punish myself by not letting myself have it? But most of the time, I don't think about that stuff consciously until later.

*Lisa: Men have always tried to find ways to keep women occupied with something to keep them out of the way, and when women started trying to get out and about more and live more their own lives, the only way to keep them down was to keep them obsessed with something that would take a lot of their energy; and this definitely takes a lot of energy.*

Nancy: It would be amazing to think of the power that women would have and the things that women could do with their lives if they weren't concerned with what they were putting in their mouths and how many pounds they'd gained or lost.

*Lisa: You mentioned that you were at a woman's house the other night and you saw some drawings that were of bigger women, and that you liked that.*
Nancy: I was thinking of different books that I've read on diets that tell you to put a picture of yourself that you don't like on the refrigerator or somewhere, and then look at it and tell yourself how disgusting you are. Well, I mean, even just thinking about that makes me want to cry. That somebody would actually think, well, let's tell these women to put these pictures up of themselves and tell themselves how disgusting they are. I mean, that is just terrible. And you know, after you tell yourself you're disgusting for a good number of years, it's really hard to believe that you're not disgusting. And that's why I liked the drawings — because I thought that they're really nice drawings of beautiful women, and to have some of those to look at would kind of maybe reverse that conditioning that I have experienced and continue to live with today.
*Lisa: Yeah, there's not much out there to reverse that.*
Nancy: There sure isn't.
*Lisa: I think that's one of the next big steps in fat politics. It's this big thing that I've definitely avoided — the self-esteem part for me as a fat woman. I have this voice in my head that sort of says, "Well, if women want to sit around and try to feel better about themselves, that's fine. I'm dealing with these issues of being fucked over, and the real political end of it." But what I realize is that I'm not dealing with myself, and I think that, in some ways, the only way we'll ever really be able, any of us, to deal with the political part of it is to start dealing with ourselves about it.*

# *Fat. Not fat.*

## Robin Goldner

How does she do it?

Easy. She throws up.

Easy?

Well, she never learned to accept her body. She still stares at
the Coppertone suntan ads.

That's disgusting. I thought she's a feminist.

She is. She's a lesbian.

She's thin . . .

Yes, but she throws up her food.

But why?

I told you. She never learned to accept her body.

I thought you said she's a feminist.

I did, but it's her outlet. Whenever she gets nervous or anxious,
angry or depressed — she just eats more than you or I could
ever imagine, and throws it up! Just like that! No
consequences.

No consequences?

Well, sometimes she gets tired, and has something like hangovers.
Her eyes look tired and red. She's not beautiful. She farts
a lot. Her mouth and tongue burn. Throat hurts. But
nothing, really.

Oh, really? When did this all start?

In high school. She had no one she felt she could talk to.
half of her was a happy cheerleader having sex with boys when
they wanted her to, and the other half was miserable, knowing
how shallow she was and how lacking in self-definition.

Definition?

Yeah, but by the time she began to develop a sense of herself,
her desires and talents, it was too late. Her pattern
for dealing with negative emotions worked too well. She
never learned to process them or expose them to anyone.

Instead, she bloats her belly until there's no room inside to feel the real pain. Then finally, she takes her power, pulls the plug, and empties it all into the toilet.

So she isn't fat.

No, she isn't fat, but can't you understand? She's throwing her brains out. She can't enjoy a meal without wondering if she will empty it into the toilet. She can't enjoy her friends because she's afraid they'll find out. She can't focus on her work because whenever she comes to a hard part, she diverts herself for hours, inflating, then purging herself.

So, she isn't fat.

No, she isn't fat. She isn't honest. She isn't happy. She isn't successful. Sometimes she can hardly function. Sometimes she feels more alone and depressed than before she started. She feels trapped, misunderstood, isolated.

Ah, isolated, but not fat.

No, not fat.

# Medical Crimes, or, Since When Have Men Cared About Our Health?

Kelly

Depressingly enough, it seems to those of us who work within the fat liberation movement that every month we discover a new thing that doctors are doing to us. There's no question that taking amphetamines is dangerous, and that wearing girdles in order to appear thin does harm to internal organs, especially in growing girls. And most of us have heard of women who have had their jaws wired shut to prevent them from eating solid foods, and of some kind of surgery that they do to fat people that makes food literally slide through you. But as we got more and more into paying attention to what we heard and read, the list of things they do to mutilate and kill us kept growing.

Up until recently, the most common form of experimental surgery being performed on fat women was the so-called intestinal bypass. This is an operation which links the stomach almost directly to the anus. Food passes so quickly through the system that it is hardly digested. The women who have had this done have suffered from such side effects as loss of hair, permanent diarrhea, severe vitamin and mineral deficiency, arthritis, and, for ten out of every one hundred women, death on the operating table. Others died afterwards, from the other side effects.

Intestinal bypass surgery had such devastating consequences that doctors searched for something else to do to us. The most common kind of experimental surgery being done now is gastric stapling. This involves opening the woman's abdomen and implanting a surgical "staple" through her stomach to block off most of the stomach's capacity to hold food. Her new smaller stomach capacity is now anywhere between three and ten ounces depending on how zealous the surgeon is feeling. (Newborn infants are fed more than three ounces of food per meal.) Any attempt to eat more than a tiny amount of food results in vomiting and in pain. Eleven out of one hundred women are currently dying on the operating table. And several major medical centers are abandoning

185

this "technique" because of severe after-effects. The data is still coming in as to exactly what health problems are being caused. The horrible irony of both intestinal bypass and gastric stapling is that women end up losing very little weight, compared to what they are told by their doctors. A 250-pound woman might lose 50 pounds this way, if she's lucky. It's generally around a third of what she is told she needs to lose, more often less than a third.

But past failures have never stopped those innovative guys in medicine. They are working on a dazzling number of new procedures to make you "healthy." There's stomach binding, where they put your stomach into a fabric sheath. By limiting how far the stomach can stretch, the "treatment" reduces the amount of food a person can ingest. Most can't eat more than three ounces before they feel pain. The doctors are very excited about this because only 10% of their victims are having any ill effects. (The idea that having pain while eating is an ill effect is beyond them.) They are also working on "balloon gastroplasty," which means that they put a balloon into your stomach. The pressurized balloon supposedly creates a constant pressure giving the sensation of being full, and it also compresses the stomach, reducing its capacity. Only two of the five dogs involved in the initial experiments died—doctors are optimistic.

Creative weight loss "experts" have big dreams for our future, too. They dream of food that contains absolutely no nutritional value, so that all those "out of control" fat people can eat all they want and yet never really have eaten at all. They are working on thick liquids that coat your stomach and intestines to prevent your body from absorbing nutrients. Or how about an ultra-sound device pointed at your body tissues that will dissolve your fat into a warm gunky fluid to be drawn out by big needles? They're doing this in France right now and are trying to get it approved for use here.

So, why is all of this news to you? Because the victims don't exactly send out announcements about the fact that they are feeling like such utter failures that they have resorted to surgery. Tens of thousands of women are having one or another of these experimental operations every year. Gastric stapling costs anywhere from $3000 to $10,000. Doctors are getting very very rich.

---

The information cited in this article comes from the work of Susan Wooley and Vivian Mayer (Aldebaran). See the Bibliography at the end of the book for specific references.

# *Bypass*

## Mona Hudson

I did it again. The bathroom scales read 270. I had regained most of the weight I'd lost the past few months and was on my way back up to over 300 pounds — again. Seemed like every time, regardless of the method I used, I regained all of my previously lost pounds — plus a few extra. My highest weight was 333 pounds, ten months ago. My only hope lay in surgery. After all, my sister had the bypass just eight months ago and had lost over a hundred pounds, not to mention 90% of her stomach, her stamina, and most of her hair. She still believed, and I agreed, that the risks were worth it; so I decided to have the gastric bypass and stapling as soon as possible.

Before being accepted for the operation, I was required to undergo several blood tests, X-rays, physical and mental exams. While waiting for the test results, which took several weeks, I was torn between fear that I wouldn't be accepted and fear that I would. I considered myself a devout coward and avoided pain at all cost. So, to voluntarily go under the knife seemed crazy to me. But more painful and crazier still would be to continue hating being fat. Twenty years of shame and lost or avoided opportunities were enough.

At last I received notice I was accepted for the surgery for "morbid obesity," and the surgery was scheduled for October. I spent the time traveling and eating at a furious pace, to fill the time and to avoid focusing on the coming pain.

Lying in the hospital bed, wearing two striped hospital gowns (two, because they did not have one in my size), I was partially numb, trying not to think about tomorrow. The embarrassing abdominal shave and enema were over. The respiratory therapist had explained to me the importance and techniques of using the "birdy" to keep my lungs clear the next few days. That was to avoid pneumonia and complications. I had a TV in my private room to fill the time but was never able to concentrate on it and just kept it on for company. I finally slept after asking for a sleeping pill.

Morning surgery was repeatedly delayed, due to an emergency. As I passed the hours, playing pinochle with my sister, my apprehension grew. Eight hours late, I was finally wheeled down to pre-op, where someone took my glasses and left me with blurred vision and a pounding heart. After a few long minutes, which felt like an eternity, the surgeon himself wheeled me into the operating room. They had neglected to give me a pre-op injection to relax me, so I was alert, tense, and blurrily aware of my cold, metallic, white surroundings. For whatever reason, no nurses were there, just the two silent male doctors, disguised in green, who injected me with something and finally put a rubber mask over my nose and mouth.

I woke up, groggily, in post-op ICU. The pain was indescribable. I tried not to breathe, as each breath was a stab through me. Vaguely, I remember nurses touching my shoulders, telling me to take deep breaths. I overheard them tell a doctor that my blood pressure was too high. I was so weak, all I could do was to repeatedly whisper, "Pain," to the nurses. My eyes remained closed that evening and most of the next day. I remember being wheeled back to my room and repeatedly saying, "Pain." They told me I had to wait two hours for the anesthesia to wear off before they could give me a pain shot.

Finally they started giving me morphine at regular intervals, without my having to ask for it, for the first few days. After that they gave it to me every four hours, when I asked for it. I slept uneasily most of the next few days, having dreadful nightmares. The nightmares continued through the next couple of months at home. I was always in pain, despite the pain-killers, and every move was a draining effort. Exercise was crucial to prevent blood clots, so on the first day following surgery I had to sit up in bed; the second day I sat in a chair a few steps from my bed. The third day I walked to the door with support from two male orderlies. The fourth day I walked across the hall to the nurses station. Thereafter I walked through the hallway at least once a day, each step taking unbelievable effort and leaving me shaky, sweaty, and exhausted.

Besides the weakness and pain, I was further hampered in my movements by the many tubes attached to my bladder, arms, and nose. I cursed the catheter but came to appreciate it after it was removed and I had to drag myself out of bed to the bathroom. My arms and hands were bruised and sore from the IV which supplied me with nourishment. I didn't eat anything but root beer popsicles, juice, and ice during my stay in the hospital. "Solid" foods such as jello and broth I promptly upchucked, while holding a pillow against my stomach to ease the tearing muscle spasms.

The most uncomfortable tube was the one which led from a machine through my left nostril on into my stomach. It was to keep my stomach clear of mucus and blood, and also to provide an entrance for nausea medicine. My throat was raw from the airway during surgery, and the tube aggravated that to the point that I was hoarse and choked on it.

All of these had to be carefully moved as I walked, so as not to be torn out. The catheter and nasal tubes were removed after the first days, but the IV remained. That was because of the dehydration from my refusal to drink, since I promptly threw up, and it tore at my stitches.

The average hospital stay for the bypass was five to nine days. I was there twelve days, as I was dehydrated from my refusal to drink the required amount of liquids, and from diarrhea. The only liquids I could keep down were ice and root beer popsicles. The doctor refused to release me until I kept down a certain amount of liquids and was able to pass gas to show my intestines were functioning. The gas extended my abdomen until it was rock-hard, and caused cramps. When I had the energy, I walked the hallways and rocked on my bed to try to get the gas moving. It took five days. To top everything off, I got diarrhea which the doctors couldn't stop. Having to get out of bed once or twice an hour, dragging an IV stand, to go to the bathroom exhausted me. Cleaning off afterwards was even more frustrating and embarrassing. I couldn't lean over because of pulling the incision, which ran from the left side beneath my armpit to my navel.

I didn't think I'd ever get out of the hospital. I was depressed and feeling sorry for myself. Finally I passed gas, lied about the amount of water I was drinking, and the doctor released me in spite of the diarrhea. I felt foolish having tears in my eyes, but I could go home to my sister, who, having had the bypass herself, would help care for me.

The first two weeks after arriving at my sister's were miserable. I couldn't raise or lower myself, to sit or sleep, without assistance.

Once in bed, I could only sleep on my back, propped up, for two hours a night. I had to be propped up or I would gag, cough, or vomit from the stomach acid. Consequently, most of the time I slept in the front room recliner, covered with a blanket. I couldn't get warm enough, and was immobile until my sister or nephew helped me up.

Nourishment, the first two weeks home, consisted of liquid vitamins, liquid Tylenol, ice, root beer popsicles, and broth. Food revolted me, and I consumed the liquids only because of my sister's patient prompting and dire threats about becoming dehydrated, as she had. I could take water only in frozen form, to allow it to melt slowly and not gag me or cause severe suffocating chest pains and vomiting. Coughing and sneezing were agony when food went the wrong way.

After two weeks, my diet expanded to include jello, split pea soup, cottage cheese and apple sauce. My thirst returned with a vengeance, and I was frustrated with it. I had to swallow water a teaspoon at a time to avoid pain. Soup had to be reheated several times a cup, as it chilled before I could get most of it down.

Five weeks after homecoming, I could eat soft-boiled eggs, yogurt, canned fruit and vegetables, vegetable soup, bread and crackers, all eaten in small, frequent portions. I was delighted to discover I could now drink Coke, a nice change from popsicles. Ice continued to be the most comfortable way to consume liquids. I became slightly dehydrated and was forced to drink more.

After two months my diet included raw salad vegetables, raw fruit (a few bites only), boiled chicken (a few bites only), and fish. Meat from any source, but especially beef, felt like lead and caused stomach spasms until I vomited.

By Christmas, nearly ten weeks after surgery, I was free to explore which foods I could tolerate. Friends and family patiently gave me spoonfuls of their meals to see what I could eat. Meats, starches, sweets, milk products, and vegetables such as corn, potatoes, beans, carrots, and peas were definitely undigestible. Peanut butter was my chief source of protein. I was always in pain, especially in my back. It was ten months before I could swallow fluids without immediate discomfort.

While I was gratified that for the first time in twenty years I felt full, I also felt resentment. I was often hungry, and I longed for a taco, hamburger, French fries, and ice cream. "Healthy" foods such as jello and salads bored me silly and soured my disposition.

I got to be a real pain in the butt. I would jealously say to my sister and nephew, "Are you eating again? You can't really be hungry," while glaring at them.

As the months went by, I was still weak and tired. Any physical exertion, such as a walk, left me near exhaustion and shaking with fatigue. This continuing weakness discouraged me immensely. Even though the doctor warned that it would take a year to recover from major surgery, I didn't believe it. I figured that, being only thirty, I would bounce back quickly. Now, doubts assailed me about the wisdom of having had the surgery. Pounds dropped off, but they had before, only to be regained. Would this time really be an exception? And at what long-term cost to my health?

Emotionally, I was in turmoil. I, who had always prided myself on being "in control," was alternately teary, hostile, fearful, and cheerful, all within a short time span. My family role as the "jolly, helpful, fat girl" was changing with a lot of effort on my part, and my relatives were resentful and perplexed. Family and friend relationships which had been highly food-centered were knocked off balance. And I, with great trepidation, was trying to enjoy the social benefits of parties, holidays, restaurants, and movies, instead of the food "goodies." I was used to being a "loner," and attempting to skillfully socialize (such as chit-chats and visits) nearly drove me up the wall.

Now, it's the end of September, nearly a year since I had the gastric bypass and stapling. Health-wise, I'm well and mostly adjusted to my new eating requirements. My bladder surgery seems to have torn loose, and I will have it repaired later in the year. I still have the pain when I overeat or eat the wrong things, but I expect that. I seldom vomit if I'm careful. My last physical showed that I was nutritionally well-balanced and healthy.

My present weight has stabilized at 191 to 196. As I can eat more now, it's much harder to lose. Unfortunately, I have rediscovered sweets, my downfall in the past. Now I must count calories to lose weight, and exercise more. As soon as I resolve some emotional conflicts, I'm confident I'll lose the rest.

I wished I could like myself fat, but I couldn't. There were too many childhood years of "fatty" insults and threats of violence for being "different" for me to forget. Most hands raised to me were physically/emotionally clenched, and my fear and distrust run deep. This surgery was an act of faith in myself, that my courage and intelligence will be greater than my childish anxiety and fear.

By March I finally felt well enough to work again. I would have started earlier but had to care for my sister, who had had two more surgeries, bypass-related. And, unfortunately, I developed another bladder infection. This was a problem I never had until the bypass. This one required medication as well as increasing my water intake. I also had "urinary frequency" and "dribbling" which I couldn't control even with medication and muscle exercises. I was unable to work or sleep because of frequent trips to the bathroom. Consequently, I entered the hospital in April to have my urinary tubes tacked up.

Emotionally, I'm much healthier and happier since the bypass. At 31, my life looks promising and exciting. I like myself more and have the confidence to tackle most areas. Sexually, I still avoid most intimate relationships. Despite my weight loss, I'm unsure of my sensuality and unhappy with my naked appearance. I wish my emotions could agree with the intellectual, liberal, feminist sides of me. Then I would tell the world, "Fuck all of you! I'll eat, wear, and be what I want, and love myself for it!" But I'm not there yet.

# A Poem About My Sister Caroline

### Sue McCabe

Though we were both fat
you wore a bikini at the beach
while I rarely went
you went to parties to get drunk
while I stayed home alone
you always talked in a big loud voice
while I talked softly with my own
you rarely smiled
while I prided myself in making you laugh
now you are thin
while I am not
each morning you take a kaleidoscope of pills
a yellow appetite suppressant
a white thyroid pill
a blue vitamin pill
a red water pill
two, three, four brown ex-lax
and now when you look great on a tennis court
you are too weak to play

# 6. A Spoiled Identity: Fat women as survivors . . .

# *learning to breathe*

## Elana Dykewomon

you pull me up the slope
"you're lazy," you laugh and
the laugh travels
through our common fat
"if i can do it you can, c'mon!"
still i want to use the stairs
want to get away, don't look
i can't do this & breathe,
& we're too close for me to hold my breath—
we get to the top
i turn my head to suck up air
you are breathing as hard
and i know for a certainty
you don't expect me to keep going thru this
so don't notice

whales take each breath consciously
they choose when & how to breathe
every whale shares that ability

but it's not the same with us, we judge
i could swim across the lake
if i didn't hold my breath underwater
three strokes    four    always breathing
on one side    the side away from shore
don't watch me breathe

my body betrays me when i believe
breathing hard is weakness, proof
that i shouldn't try to do
what i just did
hiding to breathe as if air
were liquor or sugar,
an addict of necessity,
every act so damn stoic, over-thought
starving out the hungry sacks
at lung bottom
for fear of being caught
for fear that i can't, am not
as good, as strong, as fast as you
or that you won't wait
when i need to do it differently
that you won't wait when i need you

i imagine us old womyn climbing up
laughing & gasping at the top
of any hill      comfortable
glad to move & breathe
able to be out of breath with you

>     but we are both out of breath now
>     i don't have thirty years
>     to learn the companionship
>     you offer me
>
>     & i don't have thirty years
>     to learn how to breathe

# A Spoiled Identity

## Martha Courtot

I wish that you could see me as I truly am. Instead, when you look at me what you see instead of the me that I am is a catalog of assumptions about fat women which manages to erase me from the situation. This is the experience of living with a spoiled identity.

Have I let myself go? Am I lazy and stupid? Do I sit at home all day eating chocolates and hating myself? Am I not smart enough to understand what good nutrition is? Am I a compulsive eater, out of control, not able to stop myself from gorging on food? All of these assumptions come directly from your head to surround the real person I am. And because I know these assumptions are there, or think that I know, I surround you with my own assumptions.

You will never be trustworthy! You are stupid for believing a cultural propaganda about fat women which is full of such obvious lies. You cannot allow yourself to be sexually attracted to fat women and so I will not risk my own vulnerability and open myself to you in this way. There is something cruel about you; you will always be something less than human to me, since to be human implies a consciousness of other people's pain — some understanding of the oppressions other people suffer from.

Thus you and I are both confronted by false personas as we look at each other. And all of this happens very quickly in the first few moments we see each other. It may be what we have to give each other could be important: but we will never know this.

It is not possible to unspoil this identity. If our sense of self could come only from within, then those among us who are strong could possibly work on affirming our beauty and strength and this would be enough. But human beings are social animals and from infancy on our identities are formed and grow from an interplay between the kernel of consciousness which is ourselves and the cacophony of contradictions which is the outer social world. So that by the time we are adults who we are is so layered by who the world says we are that we cannot escape from their judgments which now live inside us.

And these judgments are perilous to our integrity. It would be so much easier if I could direct my anger only at you — at your insensitivies and cruelties, which are many. But these cruelties now in adulthood have taken their place within me and when they speak to me it sounds like my own voice speaking, telling me how unworthy I am. It tells me not to risk when risk is the only thing I can do to survive. It tells me over and over again that I am fat and ugly, fat and ugly, fat and ugly — lazy, stupid, greedy, devouring: that I eat too much, take up too much space, that I do not deserve love.

At the end of this chain of hatred lies a monster in wait, ready to kill all that is self-loving in me. And the enemy within has so much material from the outside to batter me with! (Fat women in this culture *are* battered women.) And somewhere always in me is the kernel of pure self, which is loving to myself, which appreciates the strength and joy in my body, which tells me I do indeed deserve my presence on this earth, which reminds me this chain of hatred is forged with vicious lies, enemy lies, life-destroying . . . And so there is a constant war within.

While the outside war rages. And it is a war in which I am almost alone against the world. Experiment. Pretend you are a fat woman and watch television for a day. Count how many messages there are which tell you that you are ugly and must change. Listen to how many remarks your friends make about "being too fat" and diets they are on and having to lose weight when they are already thinner than you will ever be. Look through magazines for a positive image of a fat woman. Then imagine what it is like to be a fat woman walking down the street, at the mercy of everyone who has been given permission from this society to hate and despise her. What would you do when they called you names? Are you surprised then that fat women often do stay at home, do not get the exercise they need, do sometimes eat for comfort? Are you surprised? How would you feel if you saw a bumper sticker which said, "Save the whales — Harpoon fat chicks"?

Every day radical fat women are exposed to "radical" literature which pictures the fat capitalist devouring the thin "peasants." A very romantic image, but false. My mothers as many generations back as I have photographs of them have been fat, and we have all of us been poor. Not one banker among us hillbilly women. This myopic stereotyping is another example of the racist and classist bias which continues to dominate, whether it is the country clubs of the rich or the coffeehouses of the lesbian community.

If I let myself accept what the world, what you, say about me, I at least am able to reduce the conflict in my life. If I can act stupid and lazy, eat compulsively, disbelieve there is any sexuality in me, then I can conform to the world's view and I can live a life that is not contradictory to your view of me. I can be the jolly fat woman that you expect. I will make a great friend to you, because I will have no expectatons of any return. You can take and take from me and I will never show you my anger. Instead I will turn my anger against myself: in the darkest parts of the night my rage and your ignorance will join to destroy me.

A different strategy in this war is to face the rage that is in me: rage at you for making me something I'm not, rage at myself for being a fat woman and thus vulnerable to all the cruelties this society has to offer "the other." I can give you my anger over and over again — I can refuse to accept what you say and think about me. I can explore my own insides and learn the truth about myself. Although this is a more satisfying and enriching life than self-abnegation, it is a life of constant conflict, anger, and dis-ease.

A third solution is to patiently devote my life to changing your attitudes. Giving lectures to classes of young women where perhaps all but one will walk away thinking, "I will never let myself go like that" . . . doing performances in which all the risks are taken by me, the performer, while the audience sits in the dark hoarding its secret prejudices . . . writing essays and letters to editors of offending newspapers, trying to correct your assumptions . . . and all of this could take a lifetime of work and only my own life will have been used up — the work will still be there, to be done by other strong, surviving fat women. Meanwhile I am a poet who needs to be doing my own work of poetry which I insist is important, and I am a mother who needs to be mothering my daughters, and I am a lesbian who needs to be loving women and doing other political work. This "fat work" is exhausting to me, draining of some of my best energies, devouring parts of my life that are important to me. I can't escape from the resenting thought that I shouldn't have to be doing it, especially when you are a lesbian. I can't understand why you haven't made the crucial connections in regards to the oppression of fat women. My thought is that this is your work as much as it is mine. And I am needing for you to begin to do your share.

There is no doubt in my mind that this culture wants me, as a fat woman, dead. Whether this early death comes from the stress of oppression, economic exile, the steady harassment from a crazed culture, the toll of learning from an early age a terminal self-hatred, or whether it comes through the physical toll that diets, operations, and other abusive treatments that fat women are expected and encouraged to undergo (often by their best friends), the results remain as deadly.

Every day as a fat woman the hard core of self-respect and love which I have had to make for myself, insist on for myself, against the grain of the culture, against what almost all other women were saying to me, comes under assault. I really am fine as a fat woman. I am often beautiful. Unless I develop a wasting disease (as my grandmother did) I will never be thin. It has taken me many years to accept this about myself. I will not postpone my life any longer, not for anyone's standard of beauty. There are so many of us, it profits none of us to have to battle our own communities for the right to exist.

All of my life I have had the opportunity to acquire the skills of the oppressed, as a working-class fat woman. Learning how to listen, keen intuition, paranoia, becoming conscous: I have not been able to live as so many have, sleepwalking through others' lives. I learned early what damage words could do, and what an intensely powerful tool exclusion is. I learned this from the outside, and this knowledge informs every act of my life. I ask you now to learn this, to listen to my experience, and to change.

Women are bombarded with lies about ourselves from birth onward. It is not surprising that so many of us believe the lies. But for lesbians whose lives are already on the edge of fugitive, we cannot afford to encourage these lies in ourselves or in other women. Only the truth will save us. Not one of us can afford to feel good about ourselves because we are white, or thin, or middle-class, or young, or "able-bodied," or any of the other "safe" categories which are supposed to make women acceptable. Because when we build our acceptance of self on such flimsy accidents of time and place, we are building cages for our sisters and hammering shut the locks. And we have sealed our own doom in a patriarchal consciousness which is deadening.

Those of us with "spoiled identities" are gifted with the role of the outsider. So I come here today as the outsider to tell you this:

listen, pay attention, your mirrors are lying to you, and you, acting as a mirror to myself and other fat women, are lying to us; your fear of the "other," your fear of me, the fat woman, the Medusa, is turning your own life and future possibilities to stone. And you are doing real damage to lives without number.

Fight anti-fat propaganda. Fight it for your fat friends and for yourself. Learn the truth about women's lives. Learn how to recognize dangerous propaganda, even when it comes from women you trust. Break through the lies in yourself now, for all of our sakes. And take this work with you, to make a world that will be possible for all of us to live in, as self-affirming and beautiful women.

Finally, see me as I truly am.

The main body of this speech was delivered at Sonoma State University, Sonoma County, California, at a lecture sponsored by Ruth Mahaney of the Women's Studies Department.

I would like to give credit to Judith Freespirit and Vivian Mayer (Aldebaran) for their early courage and work on the subject of fat oppression.

My own work on the subject has also benefited from the work I've done with Cynthia Riggs and Hannah Banahn. The many supportive conversations we have had have become an integral part of my work. They will always have my gratitude for their spirit and courage in the face of so much opposing us all.

"A Spoiled Identity" was first published in *Sinister Wisdom 20,* Spring 1982.

# Fat Politics

## Laurie Ann Lepoff

*This paper was written for Lesbians; and if non-Lesbian people read it, I have a concern that it not be taken as a put-down of the Lesbian community. I wrote it with the belief and trust that it will be heard, for if I had never come out, I doubt that I would have grown to a place in myself where I could have made such a statement.*

In my first two years of high school I was smart and I was petite. I kept a safe distance from my peers by being a "brain." No one knew quite what to make of me, but they left me alone. Their response was one of respect and even fear. When I got fat, the difference was unbelievable. It was as if everything I had to say was invalidated by my fat. Nobody took me seriously anymore. I was ridiculed and scorned. Nobody is more aware than I of the privilege and power that comes with acceptable appearance, because the power I lost when I lost access to that appearance was enormous. And I was kept powerless by a system which is insidious. Everywhere I looked I saw media impressing upon me the power of being thin in the world — and the degradation of being fat. The message is internalized by *everyone*.

Even those closest to me, who loved me and thought they were doing so for my own good, tried to shame me into losing weight. It is as if fat women are under an obligation to be ashamed and disgusted with ourselves, to be constantly at war with food, to be always on a diet or promising to start one next week. We are made to feel that we don't have the *right* to nurture ourselves, we are embarrassed to be caught eating! Who does she think she is anyway, eating? She's fat. She should be eating cottage cheese and celery. It is not our right to eat? Who the hell are you to be even thinking that you know what I should be doing for my own body and mind's health, that self-deprivation is for my own good?

A friend once told me that her mother, who was fat, stopped

going outside after a while and my friend never understood why. My friend was neither blind nor stupid, yet she really meant it — she never understood why. We are made to feel that we don't have the right to walk around on the streets, so repulsive are we. There have been times in my life when I refused to go outside for months except when absolutely necessary because I could not take the jeers and public ridicule that I endure today nearly every time I have the audacity to walk around in broad daylight.

A few years ago I spent three months going out every day to look for a job, and it was easily the most degrading and humiliating experience of my life. There is no prejudice quite so blatant as that which exists on the job market against fat women. I couldn't get a job as a dishwasher and no secret was made as to why. The only employers who hire people like me are those few who are smart enough to know that once they get me, I'll most likely be so grateful that I'll never complain, never quit, and never ask for a raise because we both know what my chances are for ever getting hired anywhere else.

There is little validation anywhere for our struggle. We are rarely encouraged to love ourselves (even by our "liberated" feminist sisters), to consider ourselves beautiful, to nurture ourselves. We are expected to hate ourselves, deprive ourselves, and consider ourselves ugly. We maintain a shred of dignity by convincing ourselves that we are working on getting thin and that eventually we will be OK (thin). We desperately need each other's support to feel strong, powerful, beautiful, and — most importantly — angry. Yet we are so accustomed to despising our own bodies that we despise the fat bodies of our sisters. We oppress each other outrageously. We get together and talk about diets. We don't take our pain seriously. We don't validate each other's experience in this bitter bigoted world. We skim over the agony of our lives under the assumption that everything that happens to us is really our own fault and we deserve it for being fat. We don't stand up against outrageous bigotry because we accept that it is somehow justified. I feel more solidarity with a fat/suburban housewife than I do with my slender Lesbian sisters, although I can expect as much support from that housewife as I could from a closet dyke who believes herself to be sick and perverted. I don't need to hear from women who are not fat and who "just happen" to be in relationships with other women who are not fat that I need to learn to accept and think of myself as beautiful. My negative self-image does not exist in a political vacuum.

When I lost a lot of weight and was thin, I could talk to anyone about the terror of getting fat again because I knew that as an attractive woman I would be listened to. When I got fat again, I didn't dare speak to the oppression of actually being fat, because who would take me seriously? Fat people, particularly women, are not respected. It is assumed that our problem would be solved if we would just lose weight. When I was seeing a shrink who was (of course) not fat, I would talk circles around what was really bothering me before I would admit to a thin person that I felt oppressed around being fat, for fear she would say (or think), "Well, why don't you just go on a diet?"

When, in fact, I mustered up the courage to speak of my oppression to a friend, someone I love very very much, she responded just so: "But isn't there some choice?" she said. "Choice" is not the issue. The "problem" is not my being fat. The problem is how I am treated because of it. You don't solve racism by bleaching everyone's skin the same color (white, of course). Remove the offending characteristic and everything will be peachy. Make us all the same and we'll stop oppressing each other.

I responded to my friend's question with considerable antagonism. "Why don't you just go straight if you feel so fucking oppressed as a Lesbian?" I spat into the phone. "I'm sure you could pass if you really tried. All it would take is a little will power."

More than anything I wanted, I want, to be understood, but I resent like hell having to explain myself, as if to excuse myself for being fat. If I tell a sad enough story, maybe she'll understand and give me a little support. Just how bad do things have to be before I get to just go ahead and be fat? Why the fuck do I have to explain myself to you, you slender, privileged bitch? You live in this world, you have eyes, you see what abuse I have to take! How much pain must I suffer before you accept my oppression as valid? Who the hell are you to sit in judgment on me?

I cried for an hour after that confrontation, feeling incredibly alienated and alone. I had jeopardized that feeling in our relationship, our basic shared struggle as Lesbians facing a straight world, by exposing another oppression which we don't share, and which is so great that by comparison I hardly feel my oppression as a Lesbian. And she seemed to respond with total lack of understanding. She didn't know what I was talking about. I thought, hell, if this is how it feels to expose myself to someone who loves me, how can I confront someone who doesn't even like me? I thought maybe I should sit on these angry feelings and accept the support I can get for what I can get it for. If I lose my Lesbian support, I'll have nothing.

But as it happened my friend really took in the words I spat at her in my rage, and now I have her support where I really need it. It is clear to me that I will never get the support I need unless I stand up for myself and *demand* to be taken seriously.

In the straight world, the excuse for oppressing fat women is simply that fat is considered ugly, and women are expected to be attractive for men. In the Lesbian culture, the excuse is health. You're fat because you don't take care of yourself—it's unhealthy. Besides which it doesn't fit the popular image of your healthy athletic dyke. What utter crap. People do all kinds of horrible things to their bodies for a variety of reasons and are not expected to be asexual because of it. Smokers screw up not only their own health but everyone else's who has to breathe the same air, and they are not degraded by their peers and each other for "letting themselves go" and ruining their health. Is it because they are less offensive or could it be that they are encouraged and promoted by the media and we are not? "Health" is used as an excuse to degrade us, just as the medical establishment would have it that everything that ails us from influenza to clap is due in its entirety to our "unhealthy" condition — our fat. I know a woman who has scars in her throat from sticking a toothbrush in it to force herself to throw up every day, along with eating two boxes of Ex-Lax in order to lose weight and I wonder how many of you would consider her actions healthier than mine? Is it really my health that worries you, or is it that somewhere in your mind you still think I'm obligated to be beautiful in some male-defined way?

Everyone who has been on the diet cycle is familiar with a range of food mind-fucks that go with the dieting expectation. We use food as a drug — to numb ourselves from the pain of our lives — and hate ourselves for it afterwards when the numbness wears off. We go on strict diets and when we slip up a little we stuff ourselves the rest of the day because that day is ruined anyway. We become immersed in hopeless despair — we can't stand to be consumed by the struggle with food every second of the day — we give in — we hate ourselves. We eat until we are so sick we can't move. We feel so much shame we refuse to leave our rooms or the house we live in. I have done all of these things for long periods in my life, and I am not unusual: all fat women know them, they are the result of our oppression.

When I lost sixty pounds, very fast, once in my life, I had to get my head into a mind-set of self-hatred, non-nurturance, complete self-denial to do it. When I tried to get out of that headset, I felt like I would have to spend every second of my life fighting the urge to eat. I felt I had no control. I tried to fill up my life with so much activity that I wouldn't have time to eat. I knew I could never relax. I felt like the effort would drive me crazy. The thought of getting fat again and everybody seeing it and losing respect for me, the thought of losing the *power* I had gained by acquiring a "normal" appearance, was so terrifying that I was in a state of panic. No one who knew me then had any idea how close I came to killing myself at that time. They all equated my new attractive shape with a state of physical and mental health. My mother still carries pictures around of me when I was on the verge of suicide, to show people how beautiful and healthy I once was.

My point, in case anyone has missed it, is that I am infinitely more healthy now than I have ever been. I rarely eat compulsively, numb myself with food, I never feel obligated to eat ten candy bars if I "blow it" by eating one. I made a decision never to diet again. I don't spend any of my precious energy on self-destructive battles with food. And for this decision, I lose the power to command respect in the straight world, to find employment, to engage in physical exercise in public without incurring public ridicule, and many other basic human rights.

Do I have to fucking beg to be respected in my own community, to get validation for my struggle to love and respect myself in the face of enormous pressure to feel ashamed instead? I think I deserve a pat on the back for just having survived my life. Fuck you all for your damned righteousness and your insensitivity and your screwed-up male values of acceptable standards of sexual attractiveness. You don't just "happen" to not be attracted to fat women (as lovers, that is — I'm sure such a thing would never prejudice you against your friends), like straight women just "happen" to prefer men to fulfill their sexual and emotional needs. Did you ever come out (as a Lesbian) to a straight friend and learn that the thought of making love with a woman is so repulsive to her that she thinks she would vomit on the spot? Where do you think she learned that response? A facilitator at a drop-in rap group once told me that the reality of the situation which I just had to deal with was that fat simply is not attractive. I didn't question it at the time, but now I ask, who says so? The media? The *men?* Could it be that you all just swallowed the package that's been crammed down our throats since infancy and you never thought to look beyond it to consider something else?

This article originally appeared in *Plexus,* May 1975, and in *Issues in Radical Therapy,* Summer 1975.

# coming out: notes on fat lesbian pride

thunder

i've been out as a lesbian for about four years. i am also a radical feminist, which in part means that i seek out the root causes of oppression in all its forms, using an analysis and understanding of my own experience as a starting point. since coming out as a lesbian, i have called myself a radical dyke with pride — taking joy and inspiration from the depth of the implications of the first word and the strength of the second.

coming out as a fat woman — acknowledging my size, accepting it, feeling proud and gaining strength — has been a longer journey, and in many ways a lonelier one.

i have been fat, to a greater or lesser degree, since birth. at least, that is my feeling. i have pictures of myself as a girl which show a not-thin-but-certainly-not-fat child. but i have been aware of my size, and of disapproval for it, for as long as i can remember; regardless of my actual physical size, i have always felt, and have been treated, like i was fat. my brothers and sister had a nickname for me early: "ali baba and the forty chins."

i began to gain really noticeable weight when i reached puberty. my mother's reaction was a blend of disavowal and acknowledgment; she would not accommodate my weight gain by allowing me to get larger-sized clothes when/as i needed them, but she encouraged/pressured me to join weight watchers. she hoped that my weight gain was temporary, and tried to insure that it would be. she sincerely believed that she was working in my best interests. i disagreed (then as now), but i felt unable to combat her authority. my stint with weight watchers might be called a failure — i lost weight in the beginning, but began regaining it while still on the program (an experience which i have since learned is not uncommon). i eventually stopped going altogether.

when i was 15, my mother encouraged/pressured me to go to a diet doctor. the regimen this time consisted of a 500-calories-a-day diet supplemented by daily shots of some chemical/vitamin compound, which my mother administered. again, i lost weight in the beginning, but began regaining it, and more, fairly quickly.

these battles with my weight became, in many ways, battles with my mother. it was she who instigated and enforced these diets. she watched my weight more closely than i ever did (or have). she controlled my clothing purchases, which played a large part in determining my self-image. and so on. she was acting in the best tradition of "policing" — a woman trying to make another woman conform to male standards. the inevitable consequences of policing are threefold: men avoid having to take responsibility for the creation and perpetuation of their standards, giving the illusion that women choose to do certain things when in reality they have no choice; some women appear to have power over other women, when actually they are being used as agents of their own, and others', oppression; and all women spend time and energy fighting each other instead of working together against their oppression.

i know why my mother did the things that she did; she really believed that she was helping me become more acceptable to society's standards by losing weight. i can intellectually understand *why* she did these things, but i have always hated *that* she did them. i know now that she was acting out of love and caring for me, but i felt then that she must not have *really* loved me, since she was so intent on changing me, and since it was apparently so easy for her to subject me to what i considered gross indignities (and still do). it angers and saddens that this is the twisted nature of mother-love and mother-daughter relationships in patriarchy: the policing ethic demands that strange and horrible things be done in the name of love.

fat was always an issue in my family; if it wasn't me, it was my father, who was often on a diet or planning one, or my sister, who virtually starved herself for over a year. there was always an emphasis on losing weight, even when, as in my sister's case, there wasn't a lot for the person to lose. she started not-eating about the time she reached puberty — a direct parallel with my own experience. in both our cases, the push to reduce us began just at the time when we were becoming women, beginning to develop physically and sexually. in my case, there was more outside pressure than whatever internal "desire" my sister might have had. however it came about, each of us was somehow motivated to lose weight at precisely the time in our lives when we should have been gaining it, in the hips and breasts—weight that would and does identify us particularly as women. both of us, to some degree, felt comfortable and/or ashamed enough of our impending woman-hood to want to make it as invisible, as unnoticeable, as possible.

in recounting some of my experiences about my weight, i've used words like "ashamed" and "indignities." i used these words at the time—when i was 12 and 15—because that's how it felt. *being* fat didn't feel humiliating, but what i went through as a conse-quence of being fat was often humiliating. pride and shame have always interacted—an innate pride in and acceptance of myself on the one hand, and a superimposed sense of shame on the other. shame kept me from actively resisting attempts to make me lose weight, but pride "decreased" my chances for "success" in these ventures, and ultimately led to my coming out as a fat woman.

the pride/shame dynamic, the struggle between my "self" and my "training," has manifested itself in a variety of ways, often un-noticed at the time. shame kept me in weight watchers, but pride found no cause for celebration in my "10-lb. lost" pin—there was no sense of accomplishment, only of loss. shame allowed my mother to take me to lane bryant* for clothes, but pride found nothing there that i liked or would buy. pride once motivated me to buy a button which says "how *dare* you presume i'd rather be thin," but shame kept me from wearing it until just recently. now pride makes me want to write for this anthology, but still shame keeps me from sharing many of my thoughts with the women i know and love. i am encouraged, however; pride has gradually grown stronger, until it no longer makes feeble efforts to assert it-self, but instead has become a positive, moving force in my life.

going from *being* a fat woman to *coming out* as a fat woman is not an easy journey to plot; like any process, it's more gradual evolu-tion than sudden change. but there are a few specific instances which jolted the process along. they parallel the feminist move-ment's infamous "clicks"—moments of awareness, or articulation, when something that seemed inconsequential suddenly gains new and enlightening importance.

the first "click" came this summer when i read a *time* cover story on "the new ideal of beauty." the cover model was not only thin, but she had no bustline and virgually no hips; the little "shape" she had was caused by the contortion of her pose. but for her long hair, she was almost unidentifiable as a woman. i thought, "is

* a chain of clothing stores for the "full-figured" girl and woman.

this the new ideal of female beauty? to look like a little boy?"

the next "click" came early this fall when i was talking to a friend who was (and still is) dieting. i asked her how she was feeling about it, and she said, "i feel better—being thinner is so much better for me, you know—and besides, my lover is really happy."

then i began thinking about "that word"—fat. i had never liked using it—i preferred "big," "large," or, best yet, "zaftig." i started thinking about the power of the word "fat." it's very much like the power of the word "dyke"—a strong word, so easily and so often used to injure or intimidate the person it's used about/against. i've reclaimed "dyke" and use it to describe myself—and have a lot of support for using it that way. reclaiming the word "fat" is more difficult, partially because of a lack of "fat community," but also because it's so big a part of my past—a word used against me more often than "dyke" was/is, a concept/fact that i've been wrestling with and often suffering from for so much longer. my whole life. so there's more to reclaim, more to redefine, more to work through.

the latest "click," and the loudest so far, occurred about a month ago. i was in the midst of my annual clean-the-closet-and-re-organize-my-life ritual (you know, trying on old clothes, throwing out what's too far gone to keep, etc.). i wound up being confronted by a pile of clothes that didn't fit—pants that wouldn't fit up over my hips, tops that wouldn't button. i realized that i had been holding onto these clothes in the hope/anticipation of the day i'd be able to wear them again. though i thought i had long since accepted my weight, and knew i didn't feel like losing any, i had kept the idea in the back of my mind that someday i'd "get my act together" and lose weight. the pile of clothes in front of me confirmed that. so i decided to give away what i could, and throw the rest away. that decision was the most liberating one i've made in *years*. i smiled. i laughed. i did a little boogie in the middle of my clutter. i couldn't contain my pleasure and pride. i got rid of more than old clothes—i rid myself of over 5 years of old false hopes and false desires, and the useless, nagging guilt that i hadn't lived up to those hopes and desires.

riding this wave of elation, i tried to tell a few of my friends of my triumph. their reaction was cool and confused: they couldn't understand the importance of the event and my reaction. they could see that i was happy, and they were happy *for* me, but there was a real lack of communication/connection—they simply could not fathom my pride.

in my community (as in the lesbian feminist community in general), lesbian pride is taken for granted; indeed, pride is the *sine qua non* of feminism — pride in ourselves, individually and collectively, and the strength to act and resist which grows out of that pride. but in this same community, fat pride is virtually nonexistent. i see radical feminists who believe in themselves and their strength as women trying to reduce their size — which is to me the ultimate contradiction. but they are, in their quest for smaller bodies, acting out the culture's dislike and fear of women's bodies, with all the mystery and power they represent. kim chernin described this phenomenon this way:

> We have strong, ambivalent feelings about the relationship between a woman's power and her size, and they are reflected in our dislike for large, fleshy women.
>
> Thus the male-dominated culture calls for slender women, unconsciously seeking to limit the symbolic physical expression of their power. And the women themselves accept this tyranny of slenderness not only in the submision to the male but because of their own ambivalence about their own bodies. ("How Women's Diets Reflect Fear of Power," *New York Times Magazine,* October 11, 1981)

in the feminist community, a woman's spiritual, mental, and emotional growth are seen as essential to her strength. but if her body undergoes parallel growth, this is seen as a sign of weakness, not strength.

there is a lot of support among feminists for the woman on a diet. a woman looks better when there's less of her to look at — this patriarchal value is accepted and perpetuated unquestioningly. dieting women receive support; for a fat woman, the "support," at best, takes the form of a lack of harassment — not real, positive acceptance and support for the way she is. fat women are tolerated, as a rule, but i get the feeling that thin women would prefer it if we would just disappear (euphemistically referred to as "slimming down"). fat women accept and perpetuate a lot of these ideas, too; it usually takes the form of self-hate.

when fat is a feminist issue, it usually means that someone has come up with a "correct," feminist reason to diet, and usually a feminist way to diet. the idea behind this is that being fat is oppressive to women, and that being thin is therefore liberating. being fat is *not* oppressive, any more than having breasts is oppressive — to be fat is to be oppressed. the idea that some women may not want to diet, or may not want to be thin, or may actually *like* themselves as fat is never seriously considered, by either mainstream or feminist theorists. there has not been a rigorous, thorough analysis of fat and how it affects all women by the feminist community, because everyone, most fat women included, sees the issue as marginal. fat women's oppression is seen as minimal. or nonexistent, or overexaggerated, or inconsequential in the light of the struggles against race/class/sex oppression.

this attitude keeps fat women from talking about ourselves, because no one can or will relate to what we say. this leaves us without community, without context, without a framework within which to examine and understand our experiences, without a method for our own liberation, without support.

we must first overcome our own self-hate, and then develop an analysis of fat that takes into consideration women's power and societal attitudes about that power. we have to define what it means to be fat — not in an abstract psychological or behavioral context, but within the reality of our own experience as women. we must reclaim, redefine, and, most of all, E-X-P-A-N-D.

# Attraction and/or Intimidation: Fat Women's Sexual Dilemmas

Karen W. Scott-Jones

I was a virgin until I was twenty-six. Amid the sexual revolution sweeping my generation through the late sixties and early seventies, I remained on the sidelines — permitted to cheer the participants on but never to join in. At seventeen, I'd been told by my best friend in high school (who'd had enough experience with boys, or said she had, that I considered her an expert on such matters) that people "your size" couldn't have sex — it was a physical near-impossibility. Looking back now, it seems crazy to me that I believed her, but for the next several years I figured that every man who looked at me was feeling either total disgust or pity because of my terrible secret shame: I couldn't fuck. Such feelings are a testament to the depth of our brainwashing as fat women in a fatophobic culture.

My predicament was compounded by the fact that I had already decided dieting didn't work — for me, anyway. In attempting to lose weight during my high school years, I ended up even fatter and was convinced I'd never be able to approach a "normal" size. So, at some 300-plus pounds, I was (the fattest person I'd ever seen) fat-liberated by default. It was a tacit agreement with my friends, all relatively slim, that my weight was NOT to be a subject for conversation, and it was a point of pride with me to ignore the daily ridicule and street hassles I was subjected to. But I was also totally isolated, both from other fat women and from access to any information that might enlighten the prejudice of "authorities" like my high school friend. In 1969 I happened across an article in *Avant-Garde* magazine by a man who loved fat women. Reading about his sexual experiences with them felt like the force of a bombshell exploding inside me. The women he wrote about making love with were my size and even bigger! The sudden revelation (not only *could* I fuck, but there were actually men out there who might find my body attractive!) had profound implications — if not, immediately, for my sex life, then certainly for my politics. Within a year of reading that article, I was a fat activist, firmly ensconsed as a charter member of NAAFA (the National Association to Aid Fat Americans), the then-recently founded New York-based organization I was to be associated with for a number of years. I began commuting regularly to NAAFA meetings and social events from Connecticut, where I'd taken up residence with my parents after graduating from college and not being able to find a job. The realization that my weight was keeping me from being hired was another impetus for my activism.

When I first began to translate my experiences into politics, I realized how my anger and frustration (like much of the anger and frustration all fat women in our society feel, whether we acknowledge and use it or turn it against ourselves through dieting and other forms of self-abuse) was directly related to fat women's status as sexual pariahs. This "status," in turn, is (directly or indirectly) responsible for our oppression. Certainly most, if not all, of the discrimination we face is based on our failure to measure up to looksist standards of acceptability for women today. The issue of health is no exception to the rule — for women, "health" is just another parameter for judging our attractiveness, as a perusal of the front covers of any cross section of magazines on any newsstand in the country will make abundantly clear. (It is the *appearance* of health, according to current notions, which is really important, not health itself, or women wouldn't be killing themselves, literally, trying to get and stay thin.) All this intensely negative conditioning toward fat female bodies programmed into just about everyone, fat or thin, male or female, is at the root of our feelings about ourselves as women as well as a basic cause for our mistreatment; dealing with our sexuality, then, is fundamental not only to becoming "sexually liberated" but to confronting the socially enforced taboos we encounter in other areas of our lives as well.

As for sex itself, coming to terms with our bodies — developing a positive self-image, freeing ourselves to explore and express ourselves sexually — depends not only on us, on what we do and feel and think, but on the images that others hold of us, consciously or unconsciously. These images often work to place severe restrictions on our self-expression and limit our options, no matter how free we may *feel* free to be. Once I'd realized that I did have sexual options after all, that there were, for example, "fat admirers," men (and women) who found me desirable, I had to begin dealing with the preconceptions these people had about my sexual nature

217

as a fat woman. As a result, despite the fact that my social life had done an abrupt about-face and my status had shifted from wall flower to sex object almost overnight, for several years after joining NAAFA I still hesitated to take a lover.

To a girl who hadn't had a single date all through high school and college, this newfound attention was, to say the least, flattering. But the rampant sexism among the men I encountered offended me, as did the options they seemed to be offering: a series of one-night stands; an affair with a man married to or living with a thin woman, who snuck off to NAAFA dances to find the fat woman he secretly desired; "conquest" by one of the self-appointed studs out to "score" with as many fat women as possible; or a relationship with a guy who couldn't get thin women to go to bed with him for one reason or another and who figured that a fat woman would be grateful for any attention from a man. For another thing, while I wasn't about to diet to please any man, I also wasn't going to try to *gain* weight for one, something some fat admirers wanted from a prospective lover. And finally, none of these men's apparent notions about fat women's sexual identity seemed to fit mine: I was neither so perpetually horny I'd go to bed with any man, anytime, nor a great Earth-mother type, nor a totally "feminine" woman bent solely on pleasing a man; I was simply a young fat woman looking for a male person with whom I could develop a relationship.

What amazed me at the time about the goings-on I witnessed was how often the men found exactly what they were looking for: fat women who embodied their (to my mind) stereotyped fantasies with apparent relish. I couldn't understand why there was such intense competition among the women for the men, who, for the most part, I felt, weren't even worth a second glance. My naivete in underestimating the pressures on fat women, in social and/or sexual opportunities "offered" them, to attempt to satisfy not only their physical needs but their need to be validated as a woman by being chosen by a man—(as one woman in NAAFA told me, "I don't feel self-conscoius about my weight if I'm with a man because I'm advertising to the world that somebody finds me desirable")—has, I think, been corrected through firsthand experience since then. My first affair, a painful three months with a man who quoted poetry while we made love but who didn't "believe" in foreplay—nor, as I found out only after I'd fallen madly in love with him, in any other rights for women—taught me volumes about the compromises all women, and fat women in particular, make with our integrity to fill our physical and emotional needs.

In the eight years since then I have become increasingly aware of the double bind facing any sexually active fat woman: the more options we create and/or take advantage of, the more we realize what the conditions attached to these options are — what we must, in effect, give up to get laid (or have a relationship, or get married, or whatever) *this time.*

I first began to really count costs after a near miss with a man I became acquainted with via a radio interview on Fat Liberation. For three years he made increasingly obvious passes at me whenever we met, from double entendres and innuendos to staring down my blouse. When I finally got the courage to confront him about what he'd been doing and tell him I was attracted to him, too, he absolutely insisted that I'd completely misread his intentions toward me; that, while he admitted to finding me attractive, he had never had the slightest thought of an affair with me because he considered me a friend, not a potential lover. Looking back at the frustrating night I spent sitting with him in my car till 3 AM listening to his rationale, I realize that he probably wanted me to seduce him — "overpower" his resistance — so he could have what he wanted without having to take responsibility for wanting (or doing anything about wanting) it. Because I believed his bullshit (and was so humiliated by having acted on my "misinterpretation" of his actions that I quit my volunteer work at his radio station shortly after the incident), I *didn't* seduce him. A few weeks later, when I asked him to give back some cassette tapes, my only copies of a fat activist workshop, that he had offered to copy onto reel-to-reel tapes so that I could edit them into a radio documentary and into two tapes for Fat Liberator Publications to distribute, he told me he'd "lost" them — the only time in his ten years or more of radio work that he'd *ever* lost a tape of anyone's.

Such passive aggression is only one of the manipulative games I've been on the receiving end of from lovers and would-be lovers as they attempt to deny their emotional conflicts in responding to me sexually — the push/pull of their desires vs. their fears about my body and their reactions to it. I have learned that a fat woman's body, because of its abundant femaleness, is perceived as powerfully erotic by many men (whether consciously or unconsciously); the sexual images associated with them are so pervasive that I know fat women who are routinely approached on the street by strangers offering them money for sexual favors. At the same time, a fat female body is also powerfully intimidating, partly because men are afraid of their desires toward it and partly because of their fear (and/or suppressed desire) of being physically over-powered by a woman. The bigger the body, the more blatant the sexual imagery associated with it and the more conflicted the re-sponse (in terms of behavior) is likely to be). Many of the prob-lems fat women experience with our partners can be traced to this approach/avoidance syndrome — it accounts for the lovers who "come and go," for example, who can't deal with having had sex with a fat woman (and enjoyed it); it also explains the ones who never show up in the first place, after making a date, then call days or weeks — sometimes even months — later, wanting to repeat the same pattern all over again. These two phenomena, in particular, are similar to what lesbians and gay men sometimes encounter from closet gays — people who harbor a suppressed de-sire for a particular sexual experience but hate themselves for doing so and often try to project their self-hatred onto their partner. In the case of fat women's "deviant" sexuality (as defined by our so-ciety), because he cannot control or dominate her physically as well as he can a smaller woman, a man may be more likely to use other means of gaining power over her and thereby hope to con-tain his own out-of-control impulses which are causing him such conflict.

The difficulty in dealing with partners who have such emotional conflicts about us is that often we are the ones who end up taking on ourselves the blame, shame, and guilt for their problems. When I was told by a man with whom I'd been experiencing an intensity of sexual pleasure I'd never believed possible, after four days of sexual and emotional intimacy, that we couldn't be lovers because my fat "repulsed" him — it hadn't bothered him all the hours we'd made love — I was angry at first but soon lapsed into depression and eventually tried to slash my wrists. I understood, intellectually, the game he was playing: he'd been fat as a child, was a chronic dieter, and both envied and resented me for being comfortable with my weight. By rejecting me after first giving me a taste of what pleasures I'd be missing, he was punishing me, in effect, for being so free. Yet despite the fact that I understood his hidden motives, still it nearly destroyed me physically and did devastate me emotionally.

Shortly after this experience I fell into a relationship with a graduate student who I wasn't really attracted to (I probably wouldn't have been able to respond sexually to anyone at that point), but who seemed like a sweet guy and who, after knowing me for all of one week, confessed to having fallen in love with me. He wanted me to get a divorce (my husband and I had separated over a conflict over open vs. closed marriage — he wanted it open and I didn't) and move with him, when he finished his doctoral dissertation, to the Southwest. Meantime, however, he refused to live with me, and when he knew I had become emotionally dependent on him, or, as I think of it now, addicted (I can't call it love), he did a 180-degree turn on me and announced he was becoming a "swinger" and I could like it or leave. Because he paid my shattered self-esteem the supreme compliment of liking my body, I took the most incredible psychological abuse from him for ten masochistic months before finally dumping him.

In the year since then I've been alternating between short-term sexual involvements and periods of self-imposed celibacy. While I find neither a satisfactory arrangement, I have been unwilling to test my strength and endurance against another relationship yet. Though I know, given my propensity for passionate involvement, that I'm only putting off the inevitable, my current relationless-by-choice status allows me a certain rational perspective on my experiences — with help from my fat women's support group. Our meetings, in fact, often return to sex-related issues no matter what topic we may be discussing; and this again points to the vital nature of the subject to us as fat women, and how invaluable having such a forum is. Not only is it important for the exchange of information unavailable from the outside world (like the meeting at which one group member, who mentioned having problems with her lover because they'd been able to have sex only in one position, received not only specific instructions on other positions but emotional support to experiment further sexually), it is also important, because of the constant flux of self-definition and redefinition we go through in response to how we find ourselves being treated by the world in general and our closest associates in particular; we need a safe space to return to periodically — a place where we can be reminded that our identity as fat women is not dependent on the whims of whoever may be ruling our emotions and/or bodies at the moment. It is important, too, in validating our experiences, sexual and otherwise, so we know we're not the only fat woman who's been dumped on in a particular way; and in validating our individual and collective strengths which enable us to endure the hassles, pain, and psychological devastation we all face — and, like Phoenix rising, to come back ever stronger and more sure of ourselves with each rebuilding of our psyches, to come back with boundless energy to create meaningful lives and loves, despite the overwhelming forces which oppose and inhibit us.

For my own part, having in a sense come full circle since I began exercising my sexual options, I realize that, while I am still both angry and frustrated, I am also enlightened about why I feel this way. I know a lot more about the rules of the Relationship Game for fat women, and the risks I take in breaking them; but most important to me, I know that whatever choices I make in future concerning my options, and however they may turn out for me, I will always have another turn at finding what I am looking for — as long as I choose to take it.

# "There's nothing to compare with how you feel when you're cut cold by your own . . ." *

Nedhera Landers

About a week ago I read an essay in *Sinister Wisdom* by Martha Courtot, a white lesbian feminist and one of the first women I read who connected lesbianism and fat oppression. She knows pain. I could almost hear it as I read her article.

But, as much as she knows, as torn up as she's been, I wonder if she knows what it's like to be forced to walk down the street with your eyes straight ahead and not daring to look right or left, because you know what's coming. The feet move fast — faster than usual, the throat constricts and goes dry (you don't swallow — that would indicate emotion) or you taste the beginnings of vomit, laying bitter at the back of your tongue. You *know* what's coming. Sometimes nothing and sometimes an avalanche. It doesn't matter which. Your stomach gurgles, your muscles tense. By the time you've gotten through the two-block battle zone and to the bus stop, you're sore all over, out of breath, and there's a pain in your stomach acute enough to make you bend forward for relief. Does she know what it's like "to be cut cold my your own"?

To state briefly, historical events involving Black people have demanded that we either bond or die. We didn't have a choice. Those bonds are now centuries deep. Much of the culture we share is joyous and worth celebrating. But, as time has passed, other people's ways have intruded upon and influenced Black culture to the point that some now call us a *sub*-culture of the predominant white society. Still, the deep bonds remain.

All of this is not to say that the above doesn't happen to fat women of other races. However, what I am saying is that it hurts more because I don't have those deep bonds and ties with any other group

---

* Barbara Smith, in "Across the kitchen table, a sister-to-sister dialogue," by Barbara Smith and Beverly Smith, in Cheríe Moraga and Gloria Anzaldúa, eds., *This Bridge Called My Back* (Watertown, MA: Persephone, 1981), p. 124.

I belong to. I was raised to consider my Blackness before anything else I might be: a woman, a writer, a lesbian, etc. I was raised to know that, even if I didn't feel my Blackness as all-pervading, the predominant culture did.

White women don't have to "prove" themselves worthy of admission by way of being invited to join the "club" or being included in special editions of magazines that normally feature white culture.

The above can and does happen to almost all fat women but how much more hurtful to a woman of color who knows herself to be "nowhere at home" except in her own race?

In school I wanted to belong to the "in" crowd. They had the most coveted boys, clothes, and bodies. I, too, wanted to be thin, expensively dressed, and popular with boys. Instead, I was fat, dressed in "Chubbies" department clothing and was only popular as a "good listener." I didn't belong.

In college I volunteered to be on the committee to run the college's women's center. The committee consisted mostly of white women (including our teacher-sponsor) and one very cute, petite, fryed-haired, light-skinned, male-identified Black "pixie"-type woman and myself (ever the fat, Black lesbian). They all got to plan activities. I was one of the two or three fat (and/or outcast) women who was "allowed" to do the shitwork. We weren't attractive enough Amazons or movement beauties along the lines of a Gloria Steinem. We didn't belong.

When I found the lesbian movement I thought I'd really found a place for myself. I believed this even though most of the women were white and playing "dress down" (something I didn't have to play at since I didn't have the money to dress *up*). There were those few sisters I'd meet along the way who, when I talked to them about how alienated I felt in many bar and party situations with white women, would say they didn't understand what I meant but they really had to get back to their $300.00 a week jobs on the Gold Coast.

Much later I discovered the Black lesbian community. But, along with its outreach of warmth to other Black women (and some few Black gay men), much of the baggage of society in general is carried around. There is still an emphasis on straight hair and "smooth" (as opposed to coarse or kinky) curls and as thin a body as possible. Generally fashionable clothes are also much in demand.

I'm not criticizing my Black lesbian sisters for wanting to "dress decently." We've been without a long time. Many of us, in many ways, are still playing catch-up. But, there comes a point when we lose perspective and adopt the values that have contributed to our suffering and partial destruction. Adapting body types to fashion is not just vain and futile, it can also be life-threatening. Yet, we forget, or try to, every time we force ourselves to follow a ridiculous and restricting reducing diet. Do we have nine lives like a cat? Is that why we hold life so cheaply — seemingly willing, sometimes even eager, to waste and destroy our lives? Or is it that we've been so blinded by the hype that we really don't believe in the premise of "death by diet"?

Death by diet. Does that seem like a ridiculous premise? Well, consider those women who died trying to emulate Twiggy. Consider the women who died of malnutrition on the liquid protein diet. Now consider society's response to these "deaths by diet" and the everyday guilt and shame visited upon fat *women,* especially. In a Chicago *Sun-Times* column by Ann Landers a few years ago, a reader wrote in about a black box she'd heard of that could be attached to one's refrigerator and activated by opening the door. It made insulting remarks about the person's weight and had a derisive laugh. The reader wanted Ann Landers to tell people how abhorrent she thought it was that there was a device to run down the (presumably) already low self-esteem of the fat person trying to lose weight. Landers, with all the arrogance of the societally acceptable thin person, told the reader that she was ". . . for anything that gets those chowhounds off the groceries." In an interview in *Family Circle* magazine, Cloris Leachman was less witty but no less graphic about her distaste. "I just can't bear fat bodies. I think there should be fat catchers, like dog catchers, to go around and put big nets over fat people and take them all someplace and get them slimmed down. And then, show them what really good eating is. Because, what they're doing is advertising their unhappiness and their anger or frustration for everyone to see, and I don't want to see it."

The number of people with the above attitude is amazing. In her book *Such a Pretty Face,* Marcia Millman quotes a woman who seemed deeply resentful of a fat woman whom she saw in a bus station. She described her as neatly dressed and wearing a slightly unfashionable hat. She was wearing short white gloves and a skirt suit and was carrying a suitcase. She made a phone call and then waited for the bus with the other passengers. The woman doing the describing now departs from objective observation to convey her feelings of disgust — feelings she is very surprised she has. She tells about how she thinks the woman takes up too much room (even though she is sitting in one seat like everyone else) both on the bus and in life in general. She sweats too much, the woman thinks. Why doesn't she lose weight?

As I read this I kept wishing that "disgusted" woman was in the room with me. The anger I felt at her was mixed with pity because she seemed convinced that women weren't supposed to take up much space and, above all, not be noticed unless she's attractive to men or male-identified women. Her disgust is a natural result of the unnatural conditioning she received while growing up in a patriarchal society.

This society promotes stereotypes, myths, and outright lies about its members who aren't WASP males. According to current societal myths, fat women have only two choices about their roles in this society. They are either Madonna or whore. Being fat, whether the fat person intended it or not, is an act of defiance against an oppressive society and is the result of public humiliation, private pain, and solitary comforting. The myth of the super-sexy, exotic Black "chick" joins the perception of a young childless fat woman as whore to become doubly oppressive.

My mere existence shows up society's lies in great relief. Being Black (and a chick) would eliminate my being fat. But, since I am fat, young, and childless, that must mean I'm a whore out of desperation for a man. But, since I'm a lesbian and men aren't central to my life, that would eliminate my whore status. So, according to current myths, I don't exist. When I assert my presence and insist that I am indeed fully present, I become an object of ridicule. But, of course, I'm not supposed to fight back.

Fat liberation is an attempt at eliminating stereotypes, exploding myths, telling the truth, and fighting back. The days when I took being "cut cold by my own" are dwindling to a precious few. I'm going to fight back — for myself and *all* my sisters because, now, *women* are my people, my own.

# *Wandering Jew*

## Judith Masur

In and out.
Easier to be out of it    I thought
the different one
passing for whatever it is that makes *you* comfortable
willing to overlook how we're not from the same side
of the Pale.

I am the zero
through which many different colors pass.
Refracting their waves
I translate myself
into indigo
into rose    magenta
viridian
to harmonize with your dominant tone.

Careful to blur my edges
I project my image
as some throw the voice.
Mirage weaver,
I case my spell far from my center
and by the time you plunge your knife in me
I will be gone.

# Fat and Old:  Old and Fat

## Marjory Nelson

*I laugh at people who tell me I need my fat for protection, implying that if I understood that, I would lose the fat; implying that I no longer should need protection. As if I didn't need protection from all of the fat phobics who harangue me with tales of how I "just" need fat for protection.*

Feeling fat and old, old and fat.  The words fit together like they belong with each other, like they belong with me.  They roll off my tongue like a ball and bounce around my being sometimes for hours, sometimes for days.  "Old and fat."  It seems as though the words have lived deep in my consciousness forever.  Until recently, I believed that the consciousness was there because this was the worst that could ever happen:  that I would become a fat, old woman.  To me that was synonymous with being useless, depressed and poverty-stricken, dependent on my children or society for all my needs, helpless like an infant.  The fact of "fat" only compounded the problem to mean that those who cared for me would hate me even more.  I would be more burdensome.

I remember hearing my mother use these words to describe herself when she was depressed:  "I'm *just* a fat, old woman," she would say, "a fat, old woman."  My mother and most of her friends were large women.  As a child, it seemed to me the normal thing for middle-aged and older women to be fat.  They looked very powerful.  I liked them that way.  I wanted to believe I could grow up to be powerful too.  I would feel embarrassed for mother whenever she said, "I'm *just* a fat, old woman."  I could feel her pain, but I didn't understand where it was coming from.  I thought she could lick the world.  It wasn't until many years later that I could appreciate how much the world had beaten her.

I remember my mother coming home from a meeting or a shopping trip and rushing straight to her bedroom to pull off the stiff corset that bound her body so rigidly.  When I was a child, I would follow her and sit on the bed watching, fascinated by the sight of her soft flesh tumbling out of its captivity, flowing out of its casing into freedom. Mother would let out a sigh of ecstasy that you could hear all over the house. It seems strange now to write this, but when I was so young, mother's corset looked to me like armor that she put on to protect herself when she went out into the world. Because it was easy then to see her as a warrior, her corset became a symbol to me of greatness. I looked forward to wearing one myself.

My mother struggled with her fat sporadically after each visit to the doctor. She may have been in the first generation of women to do so. Doctors were always putting her on diets, nagging her, scaring her, telling her she would drop dead of a heart attack or a stroke if she didn't lose weight. That attack on my mother's being started when she was in her fifties. It was just after World War II, the time of the cold war and the dawning of the feminine mystique. But I never made any connections then.

Mother finally stopped going to doctors. It was cancer that killed her at the age of 74, intestinal cancer. Ironically, in that last battle, it was her fat that prolonged her life. She had enough flesh on her body to withstand a year and a half of disease, two operations, and massive chemotherapy. She was still fat when she died, but she certainly didn't die of her fat. I've sometimes wondered whether the cancer grew as a rebellion of her body against all those years of being squeezed into a corset.

I'm writing about my mother because she contributed so much to my own set of beliefs about being old and fat. By the time I was old enough, big enough, to pull on my first girdle, I understood that corsets and girdles were designed to diminish a woman's size and had nothing to do with being warriors. From this new perspective, I began to resent my mother's powerlessness and, with it, her fat, which now became a symbol of her weakness and mine. I would not be fat like her. And I would never be old. That's when I ran away from myself inside.

I ran away inside. I set my body on a course to move through all the expected rituals. I vacated my premises. I learned to smile, to be "nice," learned to be an Amerikan woman. I ran away from a body that was flesh, soft, vulnerable, fat and female, threatening pain and oppression, promising certain death. I diminished myself.

When I gave up my body, I gave up my mind and my spirit. I spun around an empty center, a woman with a hole inside. The men liked it. They want a woman who's a hole, who has one, who is one, who absorbs them, takes them in, gives them room and gives them back themselves. An empty woman. A container. A receptacle. I dieted and tried to keep my body thin to be a proper vessel for the man and for the woman who I thought I was. I trusted doctors who butchered me and ministers and shrinks who confused and mystified me. I thought I was doing right. I was living a lie and I didn't know it.

But that couldn't go on forever. My body rebelled in pain and in sickness. I started making changes. I became a feminist and a leftist. I took on all sorts of protests and causes, working out my anger at a system that had violated me in such a deep place. And finally, when I had lived a half century, I had to take on me. I had to come to terms with my body, with my mind, and with my spirit. I had to learn how much they are connected, how much I walked around internalizing all the violence of this system. I had to vomit out the violence. I had to learn to fight back from deep inside myself, to fill my void, my emptiness, with my own being; with a consciousness that goes beyond being a victim.

I had to learn to live with who I have become, to live and love a fat, old woman. It's been one of the greatest struggles of my life.

Some people tell me, "You don't look your age." They stopped saying, "You're not so fat," when I topped 200 pounds. It doesn't matter. The denial misses the point, for it only reaffirms the fact that fat and old are *not* good things to be in this society.

The hatred that our society shows fat women is similar to the hatred expressed for old women. I recall a day walking on the beach, passing a young, white couple, remembering how I flinched as the man twisted the woman's arm to force her to look at me, and with jeers said, "See, that's what you'll look like if you don't stay on your diet."

As though I couldn't hear.

As though he didn't care if I did.

As though she could not respond, "I hope I will look like her," and be a sister.

What kept her on his side? What kept her quiet? How did he use her fears to control her? To manipulate her?

He attacked me because he thought I wasn't supposed to be there on the sparkling sands of Carmel with all the "beautiful people." He didn't want me in his picture. It was clear to me that his message was for me and for the woman beside him.

On the streets of the city it is even worse. Older women become targets for purse snatchers, for mugging and, yes, rape, too. If anyone thinks that a fat *young* woman has trouble convincing police that she has been raped, try an old wwoman of *any* description. We are not allowed to be sexual. We are expected to be without sex organs, to be castrated.

Both fat women and old women are told that we are distortions of nature, that we are diseased. This opens the door for doctors, scientists, and the billion-dollar industries that survive on our flesh. Medical textbooks define aging in women as a clinical condition, so doctors prescribe estrogens which may make women fat and can cause cancer, too. Women spend fortunes on creams to smooth away wrinkles, in much the same way that we throw money away on new diets. The fancy creams don't work any better than the diets. We all grow old and older and some of us are fat and grow fatter. In both cases, it's a natural process.

As long as we believe that we can overcome nature, that we *shall* live forever, that we can be beautiful, that we will not go the way of our mothers, we are prey. Our bodies go on aging and getting fatter, while our minds struggle to deny these realities.

For me, the process kept me unsettled, always a potential victim. I wanted life to be different. Who doesn't?

Fear of fat, like the fear of aging, also has a lot to do with the fear of death and dying. As long as doctors go on telling us that fat will shorten our lives, as long as we go on believing them, we are vulnerable. When you get to be fifty, you think maybe you'll live another fifteen to twenty years. If you listen to the doctors preaching that fat will shorten your life by fifteen years, you realize that you're coming right up to the line. That can be very scary. It was for me. I never thought to question their statistics until I realized that they had said the same thing when I weighed only 125 pounds. Now, I can't even imagine weighing that little. But when I was 32 years old, my size mattered to me so much that I dieted to weigh 125 pounds. I am 5 feet 7 inches tall. I went to the doctor for some other reason, and he told me that I should watch my weight, that I was entering the "dangerous" zone.

Well, I'm here now. I'm so far into that "dangerous" zone that it's really hard to remember how I could have been so frightened by that doctor. Now I'm asking my own questions, like, "for whom would the danger exist if I got fat? For me? Or for the doctor and his lucrative practice?"

Now that I am finally both fat and old, I'm beginning to learn how much of my life has been controlled by this hatred and my own fear. It is *amazing* to me to discover how *deeply* these prejudices reach and how little they have been touched by all of my political work. How clear is the need for the fat liberation movement, for the older women's liberation movement; for both.

I sit at my kitchen table, gazing out the window, idly watching butterflies who dance above my garden, speculating on the giant roses made so fat and so magnificent from all the chicken shit I've fed them. I shift my weight around in my chair. I've been working here for hours, and my legs feel numb from sitting so long. I wish I had a decent chair to work in, and then draw a long, deep breath that ends in a yawn. I look down at my belly, noticing how it pushes against my jeans, swelling out under my breasts, pushing my T-shirt up in a bunch around my waist. I pull the shirt down over the zipper of my pants, hiding the place that's torn, knowing the shirt will ride up again quickly. Usually I can't see my waist. Usually I wear a smock or dashiki that falls down from my shoulders, hiding the contours of my body, the rolls of fat around my middle, the straining of my pants around my belly. Usually, I hide from this knowledge of myself.

Just like I did when I was pregnant. My belly bears the scars of three large babies. I hid myself then as I hide myself now. Of what am I ashamed? Of being a woman? Of being me? My body is the accumulation of all the battles I have fought and won. There have been *a lot*.

I sit here and contemplate my body, pondering the scope of a movement that could relate to all that I am and all that other women are. I begin to understand in a new way how control over our bodies is the bottom line of the women's movement, how this control must extend beyond reproductive rights into every aspect of our lives and health. Fat skin, wrinkled skin, brown skin, black skin, are all aspects of life that we have learned to judge and to hate. Each in a particular way. I think again of my "political" work and how it has seemed so far away from my struggles with my body, and other women's struggles with their bodies.

I think about my own conflict with the ideas of fat liberation four years ago when I joined my first fat liberation group. I was having a terrible time then with my body, with myself. Not only was I fatter than I had ever been, but I had a large tumor in my uterus which was causing excruciating pain and heavy bleeding and for which doctors advised surgery. And I was facing the problem of middle age, the sure recognition of the temporal nature of my life, wondering what I was worth, and trying to evaluate the meaning of my life's work.

I had recently moved to San Francisco and was working as an organizer for a center for women over forty. I'd gone through a lot of changes, sickness, and pain, and through it all, I clung to the women's movement as a way to make sense of my life. I'd begun organizing older women because I'd come to a period when I needed the support of women of my own generation, women who understood what it was to have raised a family, women who also were experiencing menopause, changes in their bodies; women who were facing death.

Since my mother had died of abdominal cancer, even though my tumor was not malignant I worried that I could be walking down her road. I still did not want that. I still wanted to have more control over my life than she had. I didn't really know what to do, but it seemed obvious that I *should* do something. I decided that I would learn to heal my tumor and develop a new and liberated set of attitudes about my fat. It was not so obvious to most of the women who were my age. They wanted to know why I didn't just go get my hysterectomy and get it over with, as though that were an appropriate ritual for passing through middle age.

I resisted.

Fortunately, the San Francisco Bay Area offers a lot of options. I found a healer who began teaching me holistic practice, and I joined a fat liberation group of young women. My healer was fat. She never once suggested that I ought to lose weight, although she did introduce me to juice fasting and yoga along with medication, visualization, and acupressure. The purpose of juice fasting, she assured me, was to cleanse the body of the toxins that cause tumors and disease. Yoga, a form of meditation, helped to quiet my mind. All of the meditation helped me to see the workings of my mind, my patterns of belief, my emotions, and my fears.

In the fat liberation group, I began to learn about the oppressiveness of fat phobia, that fat was a political issue. The women were wonderful. It was exciting to sit in a room where everyone was fat, to read the literature of the Fat Underground, and to hear fat women express genuine pleasure in food without the accompanying sound of guilt. Once more I thought of my mother, and how her love for good food — one of the main pleasures of her life — had been destroyed by doctors. I began to view my own life in a new way.

Unfortunately, it wasn't too long before I ran into a conflict between the ideas I was learning in the fat group and work I was doing with my healer. Fat Liberation, as I understood it, was saying that all diets are harmful. And here I was, on a juice fast. To the women, it was one more oppressive diet, and they didn't want to hear about it. To prove their point, I was losing weight. I think some of them suspected that I really was dieting to rid my body of fat but didn't want to admit it. That was true insofar as I believed that I needed to lose weight in order to get rid of the tumor. It was a complex situation, in which my fears about my health played a major role. It seemed as though there was a lot of denial on both sides. I felt that the young women did not understand me and my needs. They were healthy. But at my age, I had to deal "more realistically" with my body. I dropped out of the group and started my own group for older women through the organization where I worked. That made more sense anyway, I told myself. We called it *Fat, Female and Forty*. It lasted for several years and actually was a support group. Our perspective was liberal, not radical. We tried to accommodate the fat liberation views to our own needs. Since none of us had solved our own fears about our health, we remained skeptical, and tried to support every woman for what she needed. I was fasting, another was dieting, another wanted to learn to live with her fat, and so forth. I don't know now how we managed to fit all that together, but we did. Our finest activities were outings to beaches and hot springs where we learned to feel OK about being out in public in bathing suits. We started taking more pleasure in being *in* our bodies. Since we all showed signs of the ravage of years of living in this system, of operations, mastectomies, childbirth and nursing, that was quite an accomplishment.

My healing took several years and required some major changes. My tumor disappeared and I became pain-free. Now I'm trying to integrate new understandings into my life and work. I've gained back all the weight I lost, though I still use juice fasting as a health practice and I meditate daily. As my weight increased, I noticed that I no longer felt at home in the yoga class. I tried to "think myself thin" with my new spiritual tools but concluded that, if I were to remain anything less than very fat, I would have to devote all of my energy and a considerable amount of money to the endeavor. I was not willing to make this my priority as long as I felt healthy. Instead, I turned to examine the politics of the health and spirituality movements and sought out more information on the relation between health and fat.

Since then I have found extensive data which questions the insurance companies' and doctors' association between fat and illness. Where it exists, the key factor seems to be the oppression of fat people. Through observation and study, I've also concluded that it is simply not true that fat people are any more out of control than anybody else. We may be *more* out of *the* control of a political economy that feeds on our bodies and scapegoats us while starving much of the rest of the world. If so, that's just great.

The victim-blaming politics and the fat phobia of so much of the "new age" health and spirituality movements have deprived fat women of access to their benefits. But that's changing. Just recently I found a yoga class for fat women. Fat women are learning holistic healing. Fat activists in our area have organized conferences, photography shows, films, and even a readers' theater, thus creating a positive and exciting new image of fat women. We have weekly swims for fat women only. The women are all ages and all are very fat. We play together. And that seems like a miracle.

The fundamental question as I see it is whether *anybody* has the right to tell a fat woman that she should not want to be as she is, any more than anybody has the right to tell an old woman that she should look young. That human beings are measured and judged by size or color or any other aspect of their physical being is an abomination. None of us will be safe until we deal with and end this kind of oppression.

Basic to all of my healing was an understanding of how deeply my own fears about my body had controlled my life. I believe this is true for most of us; that's how we get caught. What I didn't know until I worked it out for myself was that if I met my fears, I would not necessarily be thin, or successful, or anything that anyone else prescribes for me. However, it is *not* my fear that causes the oppressoin. That still exists whether or not I fall under its control. Turnstiles and seats in movie theaters still refuse my body, and I'm no longer employable in a large range of occupations becaue of my fat, my age, and my politics. I don't know how I'm going to survive, but I know that I am a survivor.

I talk to my fat cells. They are part of me. They are a layer around me. They envelop me like a lover, giving me courage to go on working, to go on protesting, struggling with the MAN and with fat-phobic sisters. Who is to say that I should not have this being? Who is to say that I am deranged, out of control, or lazy because I have these cells? I look at my wrinkles. The map of my life.

Let it be so. I claim authenticity in every layer, every cell of me. I claim my integrity. I will no longer be a sacrifice to this culture, diminishing myself, my size. I draw my sustenance from the earth. She teaches me to store up her richness, to make a treasure of her abundance. I no longer fear the ripening which precedes death, the maturity which determines endings. They are mine.

I stand and stretch, and walk out to the street. It's midday, and most of the people I see are women. Some are fat. Particularly the older women, the poor women and women of color. That's who the fat women are. I see my reflection in a store window and see my mother. I laugh at myself and wonder why I ever thought I should *not* look like this, or like any of the other women on the street. I look at the thin women and wonder how many are on a diet right now. How many of them hate their bodies and think they are too fat? The struggle around fat now seems so obvious, I wonder why I never saw it before as a political issue. How could I separate my worries over my body, my dear, fat, old body, who is the source of my life, from all of the other struggles that have seemed so necessary, so vital to my life, and to the lives of other women?

I realize that the "worst" has happened to me. All that I've been warned about and worried about has occurred. The knowledge frees me. I know who I am. I'm fat and I'm old, and I'm home free.

# *Letter to Lisa*

## Sandra Tyler

Dear Lisa,

I have been trying to respond to your request for stories to be printed for some time now. Writing down any feelings or statements about being fat is very difficult. My feelings do not pour out in some long-sought release as I had hoped. I would rather take a nap than try one more time to recount any fat stories. It wearies me. That's the extent to which it has affected me to be oppressed for my size. Internally, I've taken on the job of policing myself to make sure I don't bother or upset anyone with any ideas or feelings counter to those most people have concerning fat. So— I'm really pushing away those feelings and have come up with a statement on fat from my perspective for your use.

I could recount a lot of unhappy incidents in my childhood which relate to fat or choosing to be fat. What seems really important is what incidents contributed to my awareness of my fatness? When did I know? I always felt different from others. I didn't always feel fat.

Did I know when I realized that I wasn't outrunning the girls in my gym class, I was outsmarting them? By planning my way carefully through the obstacle course, I could get there faster even though I couldn't run as fast. Did I already feel physically different by the time my mother taught me the women's commandments: Thou shall not show your underwear on the playground, take rides with strangers, sit with your feet uncrossed, walk alone at night? Or did I become aware the time I asked the most popular girl in class how she did it and she shared what I had asked with the class, to their delight and amusement? Was I different from the beginning or did being fat put a definite seal on my feelings of difference from others? I'm still not sure. Somewhere in my grade school experience it all blended together—the feelings of being different and when that difference became being fat.

Every fat woman has her own list of cuts and wounds as punishment for her size. I've got mine: Having my parents refuse to go places in public with me and deny the reasons; being the scapegoat for jokes throughout high school and college; boring, frustrating, fruitless searches for clothes; being the source of doctors' frustration or false patience; feeling loving toward children up to the age where they turn, observe my difference, and pronounce laughing sentence; being told I was incapable of doing jobs because of my size; and the astonishing assumptions of people passing in the street that they could or should let me know how they judged my body: "Hey lady, can two of us do it with you? It would take two," "My dear, I don't know you, but I have a wonderful weight loss program I know you'll be interested in"; therapists who go to great lengths to convince me they are on my side, to cover their assumption that what hurts me is not my environment but my stubborn refusal to change — you could if you but would.

Inside these dynamics, the loneliness grows and grows. Various attempts are tried to give those around us what they wish in hopes they will give love in return. And failing. And failing again.

Perhaps the hardest moments have been those when a new direction and hope of being heard appears and then proves to be more of the same. Enter the women's movement. Sisterhood. How wonderful the hope of developing your strength and purpose and the beauty of your life. How bitter the discovery that you and your sisters are spending a lot of time discussing their evolving sexuality, strength of purpose, job awareness — but not your own. You try to discuss your situation and watch your sisters' eyes shift and film over.

So, it becomes clear that a specific kind of women's consciousness, fat consciousness, is necessary. Which brings me to my own present. Struggling to learn about fat, develop a fat sisterhood, write it, practice it, demand it. And I'm hopeful.

That my fat sisters and I can find better health care, a safe place to exercise, jobs that we're qualified for, and understanding from thinner sisters that fat women embody the issue of looksism and have borne the brunt for years. Already I see it a little easier for fat sisters younger than I. Their pain is a little less, they're more aware of the oppression earlier than I was, and maybe they carry a bit less stress. And I'm hopeful that the film, the shadow, will drop from thinner sisters' eyes — their attempt to keep fat sisters invisible — and that I will see in their eyes an increasing awareness that our emergence depends on all of us emerging together.

Sandra

# Bibliography

## Books

Beller, Anne Scott. *Fat and thin — a natural history of obesity.* New York: Farrar, Straus & Giroux, 1977.

Bennett, William, and Gurin, Joel. *The dieters' dilemma.* New York: Basic Books, 1982.

Bruch, Hilde. *The importance of overweight.* New York: W. W. Norton, 1957.

Chernin, Kim. *The obsession: Reflections on the tyranny of slenderness.* New York: Harper & Row, 1981.

Grosswirth, Marvin. *Fat pride: A survival handbook.* New York: Jarrow Press 1971.

Louderback, Llewellyn. *Fat power.* New York: Hawthorne Books, 1970.

Mayer, Jean. *Overweight: Causes, cost and control.* Englewood Cliffs, NJ: Prentice-Hall, 1968.

Millman, Marcia. *Such a pretty face.* New York: W. W. Norton, 1980.

## Articles

Aldebaran (Vivian Mayer). "Compulsive eating myth." *Off Our Backs,* July 1979, p. 28.

Aldebaran. "Fat liberation." *Issues in Radical Therapy,* Summer 1973.

Aldebaran. "Fat liberation: A luxury?" *State and Mind,* June/July 1977, p. 34.

Aldebaran. "Fat woman." *Sister* (New Haven), December 1977, p. 8.

Aldebaran. "Health and fat awareness." *Issues in Radical Therapy,* Spring 1976, p. 13.

Aldebaran. "Liberal on fat." *Off Our Backs,* March 1980, p. 31.

Aldebaran. "Uptight and hungry, the contradiction in psychology of fat." *RT: A Journal of Radical Therapy,* November 1975, p. 5.

Bogen, Karen. "Too thin for Fat Lip?" *Plexus,* July 1982, p. 2.

Courtot, Martha. "You seen her everywhere." *Hagborn,* Summer/Fall 1980, p. 15.

Dudley, Betty. "Thank you, Fat Lip!" *Plexus,* July 1982, p. 2.

Fonfa, Gudrun. "'Looksism' as social control." *Lesbian Tide,* January 1975, p. 20.

Gordon, Rebecca. "When I was a fat woman." *Conditions 6,* Summer 1980, p. 56.

Griggins, Cynthia. "At what price slenderness?" *What She Wants,* January/ February 1983, p. 6.

Haditt, Marylou. "Waking up the silence." *Plexus,* September 1982, p. 4.

Hinds, Terry. "Fat is not a feminist issue." *State and Mind,* Spring 1979, p. 49.

Mabel-Lois, Lynn, *et al.* "More women are on diets than in jail." *Sister* (Los Angeles), November 1974, p. 4.

Marilyn, Gwyn. "Look again." *Commonwoman,* November 1980, p. 8.

Mayer, Vivian (Aldebaran). "Why liberated eating?" *Women: A Journal of Liberation,* 1981, *7,* p. 32.

Meyerding, Janey. Three-part series on fat oppression. I: "Who killed Cass Elliott?" II: "Self-hate as social control." III: "Free our spirits . . . feed our bodies." *Out and About,* May 1980, p. 25; June 1980, p. 12; July 1980, p. 20.

Mueller, Dian Kendrick. Interview with Euen Bear: "Fat liberation," parts I and II. *Commonwoman,* June/July 1981; August 1981.

Stein, Judith. "Fat oppression: Myths and facts." *Commonwoman,* February 1981, p. 5.

Interview with Judith Stein and Rae Rae Sears: "A political history of fat liberation." *The Second Wave,* Summer 1981, p. 32.

Taylor, Kate. "Mama, Mama, look at the fat woman." *Plexus,* January, 1981.

Wooley, Orland W., and Wooley, Susan C. "Obesity and women"— I: "A closer look at the facts" and II: "A neglected feminist topic. *Women's Studies International Quarterly,* 1979, *2,* p. 69; 1979, *2,* p. 81.

Wooley, Susan C., *et al.* "Theoretical, practical and social issues in behavioral treatments of obesity." *Journal of Applied Behavior Analysis,* 1979, *12,* p. 3.

---

EDITORS' NOTES:

1 Due to space limitations, we had to narrow down the original bibliography to few entries. This bibliography in no way constitutes a complete listing of the literature available on fat oppression.

2 Many of the articles originally published by Fat Liberator Publications are included in this anthology. The remaining articles are no longer available through Fat Liberator Publications, but some of them may be found in libraries or periodicals.

# ▦spinsters | *aunt lute*▦

Spinsters/Aunt Lute Book Company was founded in 1986 through the merger óf two successful feminist publishing businesses, Aunt Lute Book Company, formerly of Iowa City (founded 1982) and Spinsters Ink of San Francisco (founded 1978). This consolidation of skills and vision has strengthened our ability to produce vital books for diverse women's communities.

We are committed to publishing works outside the scope of mainstream commerial publishers: books that not only name crucial issues in women's lives, but more importantly encourage change and growth; books that help to make the best in our lives more possible.

Though Spinsters/Aunt Lute is a growing, energetic company, there is little margin in publishing to meet overhead and production expenses. We survive only through the generosity of our readers. So, we want to thank those of you who have further supported Spinsters/Aunt Lute—with donations, with subscriber monies, or with low interest loans. It is that additional economic support that helps us bring out exciting new books.

Please write to us for information about our unique investment and contribution opportunities.

If you would like to know about other books we produce, write or phone for a free catalogue. You can buy books directly from us. Our efficient fulfillment department welcomes your order and will turn it around quickly. We can also supply you with the name of the bookstore closest to you that stocks our books.

We accept phone orders with Visa or MasterCard.

Spinsters/Aunt Lute
P.O. Box 410687
San Francisco, CA 94141
415-558-9655